Now Dig This

Also by Terry Southern

Novels

The Magic Christian
Flash and Filigree
Candy
(WITH MASON HOFFENBERG)
Blue Movie
Texas Summer

Screenplays

The Magic Christian
Barbarella
Dr. Strangelove
(WITH STANLEY KUBRICK)
Easy Rider
(WITH PETER FONDA AND DENNIS HOPPER)
The Loved One
(WITH CHRISTOPHER ISHERWOOD)
The Cincinnati Kid
(WITH RING LARDNER, JR.)
End of the Road
(WITH ARAM AVAKIAN)

Collected Short Stories and Journalism

Red Dirt Marijuana and Other Tastes

Non-Fiction

Journal of the Loved One
Virgin: A History of Virgin Records
The Early Stones

Anthology

Writers in Revolt
(EDITED WITH RICHARD SEAVER AND ALEX TROCCHI)

Now Dig This
The Unspeakable Writings
of Terry Southern

1950–1995

Edited by

Nile Southern and Josh Alan Friedman

Grove Press
New York

Published simultaneously in Canada
Printed in the United States of America

Grateful acknowledgment is made for permission to reprint the following lyrics in this book: "Born in a Trunk" by Leonard Gershe, copyright © 1954 (Renewed) Warner Bros., Inc. All rights reserved. Used by permission. Warner Bros. Publications U.S., Inc., Miami, FL 33014.   "Fools Rush In" by Johnny Mercer and Rube Bloom, copyright © 1940 (Renewed) WB Music Corp. All rights reserved. Used by permission. Warner Bros. Publications U.S., Inc., Miami, FL 33014.   "Ivory Tower," words and music by Jack Fulton and Lois Steele, copyright © 1956 (Renewed) Edwin H. Morris & Company, A Division of MPL Communications, Inc. All rights reserved.   "I'll Be Your Baby Tonight" by Bob Dylan, copyright © 1968 Dwarf Music. All rights reserved. International copyright secured. Reprinted by permission. "Famous Blue Raincoat" by Leonard Cohen, copyright © 1971 Sony/ATV Songs LLC (Renewed). All rights administered by Sony/ATV Publishing, 8 Music Square West, Nashville, TN 97203. All rights reserved. Used by permission.   "Song of Bernadette" by Leonard Cohen, Jennifer Warnes, and William Elliot, copyright © 1980 Sony/ATV Songs LLC, Warnes Music, and William Elliot Music. All rights on behalf of Sony/ATV Songs LLC administered by Sony/ATV Music Publishing, 8 Music Square West, Nashville, TN 97203. All rights reserved. Used by permission.   "Lately," words and music by Stevie Wonder, copyright © 1980 Jobete Music Co., Inc., and Black Bull Music c/o EMI April Music, Inc. All rights reserved. International copyright secured. Used by permission.   "Respect," words and music by Otis Redding, copyright © 1965, 1993 by Irving Music, Inc. (BMI). All rights reserved.   "Up on the Roof," words and music by Gerry Goffin and Carole King, copyright © 1962 (Renewed 1990) Screen Gems-EMI Music, Inc. All rights reserved. International copyright secured. Used by permission.

FIRST EDITION

Library of Congress Cataloging-in-Publication Data
Southern, Terry.
    Now dig this : the unspeakable writings of Terry Southern, 1950–1995 / edited by Nile Southern and Josh Alan Friedman.
      p. cm.
    ISBN 0-8021-1689-2
    I. Southern, Nile   II. Friedman, Josh Alan.   III. Title.
PS3569.O8 A6 2001
813'.54—dc21   00-065472

Design by Laura Hammond Hough

Grove Press
841 Broadway
New York, NY 10003

01 02 03 04   10 9 8 7 6 5 4 3 2 1

FOR TERRY

Contents

New Journalism

The Quality Lit Game

Strolls Down Memory Lane

Introduction: An Interview with Terry Southern

BY LEE SERVER

LEE SERVER: *Terry, let's begin with that grandest and most admirable of your creations, a certain Candy Christian. Girodias and Hoffenberg have given their accounts of how she came to be; what's the real story?*

TERRY SOUTHERN: God only knows what's been said about the genesis of *Candy*, but the true account is as follows: There's a certain kind of uniquely American girl who comes from the Midwest to Greenwich Village—cute as a button, pert derriere, full wet lips, nips in eternal distention, etc., etc.—and so full of compassion that she'll cry at card tricks if you tell her they're sad. Anyway, I wrote a short story about such a girl—how she befriended a humpback weirdie to the extent of wanting him "*to hurt me the way they hurt you!*" Everybody who read the story, *loved* the girl—all the guys wanted to *fuck* her, and the girls wanted to *be* her—and they all said: "Yea Candy! Let her have more adventures!" So I put her in a few more sexually vulnerable situations—with her professor, with the gardener, with her uncle, with her spiritual guru, and so on. And this friend of mine, Mason Hoffenberg, read it and said, "Why don't you have her get involved with a Jewish shrink?" And I said, "Why don't *you* write that part?" So the great Doc Irving Krankeit (and his doting mum) were born.

Candy's escapades were the talk of the Quarter. "Gid" Girodias demanded to see the manuscript pronto; and, mistaking Quality Lit erotic-humor-allegory for porn trash, he agreed to publish it.

L.S.: *This was in Paris, the mid-'50s, when such books were taboo in the States, right? Can you fill us in on Girodias's set-up at that time?*

T.S.: Well sir, Mr. Maury Girodias had what you might call a "house o' porn operation *extraordinaire*." A man of infinite charm, *savoir-vivre*, and varying guises, he was able to entice impressionable young American expatriates, such as a certain yours truly, to churn out this muck by convincing us we were writing *Quality Lit*! Not only did the Hemingway types succumb to his wily persuasions, but (would you believe it?) *young American girl-authors* as well! Cute as buttons they were too! Darling blue saucer-eyes and fabulous knockers with nips in distention! Marvelous pert derrieres and full wet tremulous lips, the kind that quiver and then respond . . . but I digress.

L.S.: *Girodias and Olympia Press did root out quite a few great works, though.*

T.S.: Oh, his "operation" turned up some first-rate stuff—*Lolita, The Ginger Man*, things by Beckett, Ionesco, Henry Miller, and, of course, that veritable *crown jewel* of Contemp Lit, *Naked Lunch*.

L.S.: *The pay for writing* Candy *was pretty low, I believe. Five hundred dollars, for all rights?*

T.S.: I don't recall the fee involved, but it was hardly enough to get us laid.

L.S.: *Reading* Candy *as a kid, I'll confess to you, played a definite part in my growing into manhood—I don't intend to go into details. What would you read for "erotic purposes" as a youngster?*

T.S.: When I was young, they had what were called "*little fuck-books*"—which featured characters taken from the comics. Most of them were absurd and grotesque, but there were one or two of genuine erotic interest; "Blondie" comes to mind, as do "Dale" and "Flash Gordon" and darling "Ella Cinders."

For a while, convinced there was more than met the eye, I tried to "read between the lines" in the famous *Nancy Drew* books, searching for some deep secret insinuation of erotica so powerful and pervasive as to account for the extraordinary popularity of these books, but alas, was able to garner no mileage ("J.O." wise) from this innocuous, and seemingly endless, series.

L.S.: *You grew up in Texas. Can you talk a little about what sort of sex life a young man growing up in that region was likely to have in those days?*

T.S.: Texas is part of the car culture of the great American Southwest, where all social events revolve around the car. Every high school boy either has his own car or has the use of the family car for dates. In those days, the "dating scenario" was well established. It consisted of taking the girl to a movie, to the school dance, or to a roadhouse which had a band and a dance floor. Afterwards, there would be a stop for food, then the all-important period of "parking and necking." This was an accepted part of the ritual, and the guy was given about fifteen minutes in which to "make out."

There were several degrees of "making out." The first was "tongue." "*Did you get tongue?*" was a question frequently heard after a first date with an extremely nice, honor-student-type girl. Next was "knocker." "*Did you get knocker?*" they would ask. There was a big difference, of course, between "getting knocker" and "getting *bare* knocker." Getting "bare knocker" implied "getting *nip*" as well, but there was also the distinction of "*kissing* nip," which was considered to be quite a score—especially on the first date. Next in order of significant intimacy was "getting silk," which meant touching panty-crotch, and then for the more successful, "getting pube." The ultimate achievement— aside, of course, from puss itself—was to "get wet-finger," also referred to (by the more knowledgeable) as "getting clit." It was almost axiomatic that, under "normal" circumstances, to "get wet-finger" meant that the girl's defenses would crumble as she was swept away on a tide of sheer physical excitement— and vaginal penetration would be unresisted and imminent.

But this was the era, alas, of the damnable "panty girdle," especially for semi-formal occasions, where stockings were worn. It was well nigh impossible to achieve "full-vage-pen" by breeching aside the crotch panel of this snug-fitting garment. There was, however, a "technique"—one would take a pair of *kindergarten paper-scissors*, the harmless kind with *rounded* ends. These scissors are ordinarily *so dull* they will cut only the softest of paper, *but they may be given an edge—and a keen one!* so that during the height of the necking session, the precious girl, feeling quite secure in her sturdy garment, might permit certain fondling liberties—such as "vage under silk"—except this time the caressing hand would also carry the keen-edged paper scissors . . . and *snip*, the outrageous barrier was undone!

This was also the era of "forcible seduction," which is perhaps only different from actual *rape* in that the girl, despite a frenzied resistance, would invariably end up "*oohing*" and "*aahing*" ecstatically, and in the immortal words of the Bard, "begging for more."

Since all is fair in love and/or forcible seduction, another keystone element in the dating scenario was to try to "get her drunk." The potion of choice in this regard was vodka and grapefruit juice—presumably because the darling girl would not be able to taste the copious amount of vod in the astringent mixture—and so, in the (false) security of her panty girdle, and slightly whacko on vod, she might just relax her defenses long enough for the absorbent panty-panel (by now, of course, sopping with the nectar of her passion!) to know the keenness of your *scisseaux d'enfant!*

Golden days, now that I think back on them—and I do think back on them quite often.

L.S.: *We mentioned in regard to* Candy *that you were living in Paris in the '50s, making the expatriate, starving artist scene. What are your memories of the period?*

T.S.: That (late '40s, early '50s) was a golden era for Americans in Paris. All the great black musicians—Bird, Diz, Thelonius, Bud Powell, Miles, Kenny Clarke, etc., etc.—were first appreciated there, so it was a very swinging scene musically. Also, there is a large Arab quarter in Paris, and *hashish* was an acceptable (to the French authorities) part of the Arab culture—so the thing to do was to get stoned and listen to this fantastic music. That was the most important aspect of life in Paris in those days.

This was also a period of intensive research into the mind-expanding qualities of Pernod and cognac.

L.S.: *There were quite a few future literary heavyweights hanging about at that time, weren't there?*

T.S.: Yes, there were some interesting Quality-Lit types on hand. Henry Miller was still there, of course. And so was Samuel Beckett; William Burroughs, Allen Ginsberg, William Gaddis, and Bill Styron come to mind as well. Also there, off and on, were Capote, Vidal, and tip-top Tenn Williams. The *Paris Review* crowd was headed up by G. Ames Plimpton and Peter Matthiessen—the latter known as "Bush Master Math" because of his many hair-raising adventures on the Dark Continent and elsewhere.

L.S.: *Wasn't the town also known at that time for an abundance of, you know, wide-eyed American coed types, eager to lose their innocence?*

T.S.: Yes indeed. As for picking up those fabulous, full, wet-mouth, pertknocker American college girls in Paris, there were three standard ways: 1) pay a French person to annoy her at a cafe, then go to her "rescue," dispatching him with rapier thrusts of Parisian argot; 2) hang around the American Express mail line until the girl with perfect American derriere and nips arrives, then get behind her in the mail line, concealing your appearance with a newspaper; and in that way learn her name (when she asks for her mail); then follow her to a hotel or to a cafe—and when opportune, approach her with: "Say, aren't you Candy Christian?" or whatever. It can help if you are able to see where the letter she gets is from, then you can get some regional rapport and I.D. going ("Say, didn't you used to be a cheerleader in Racine, Wisconsin?"). The third surefire way is to go to the Louvre and sit on a bench in front of a large El Greco, studying it (between fab "*d*"s and "*k*"s, natch). Then, when the time is right (d and k wise), you make your move ("I know this is going to sound, well, sort of *forward* or *silly* even—but I couldn't help noticing how much *your hands* are like those of the women in El Greco's paintings.") This has *never* failed. Poon City! You are there!

L.S.: *Back in the States in the early '6os, you were doing a lot of magazine work. It seems to me, going over those articles, that you were anticipating or, really, inventing the whole "subjective journalism" style. I mean, Hunter Thompson's whole "gonzo" oeuvre is right there in something like your "Twirling at Ole Miss" and a few others. Can you discuss how you formulated this "revolutionary" approach to your journalism?*

T.S.: There are some Edgar Allan Poe stories—particularly one called *The Narrative of A. Gordon Pym*—where he uses a narrative style which has a strangely authentic documentary quality; I mean, in the light of its times, natch. Anyway, I think I first picked up on it there, from the great E. Poe. Then, of course, there was Henry Miller; he used the first-person narrative *so* convincingly—in the *Tropics*, and his other sex-adventure stuff—that most people *still* don't realize it was 95 percent fiction. So that is—roughly, to be sure—the genesis of it. The idea is to describe something in such a way that you truthfully convey the essence of it, without being boring.

L.S.: *What about* "Blood of a Wig," *one of your all-time greats. How much truth was there to that one? Did you work on a "skin" mag for a time?*

T.S.: I worked at *Esquire* for a two-month period, when Rust Hills was on vacation. My duties were to read the fiction submitted and try to come up with some good stories. The manuscripts were in two categories—the ones submitted by agents, which were referred to as "the manuscripts," and a second and larger selection, the unsolicited stories, and that category was called "the shit-pile." Ordinarily, the shit-pile would be read, or scanned, by some kid who had majored in English, or who had been promoted from the mail room, while the editors would read the manuscripts from agents—when they weren't humping their secs, that is.

My own policy, however, was to read the unsolicited manuscripts myself. I had a theory which involved the existence of a rarefied kind of 'quality folk-lit'—like Grandma Moses in painting—so I dreamed of finding something pure and primitive, and at the same time, weird and haunting. Maybe a story entitled *A Strange Event*, by Mrs. E. Johnson, would prove to be so extraordinary, so oblique and ambiguous as to defy classification. No such luck. And before my tenure was done I had so refined my critical faculties that I could reject a story after reading the first paragraph. Then it got to be the first sentence. Finally, I felt I could safely reject on the basis of *title*, and at last on the basis of the author's name—if it had a middle initial or a junior in it. Under this system I lost a few things by Vonnegut and Selby . . . but I never claimed it was perfect.

L.S.: *The title* "Blood of a Wig" *refers to what you described as your most "outlandish" drug experience. Could you recount for us said experience?*

T.S.: The word "wig" is street/drug parlance for "head." A "wig" is a person's *head*. To "tighten one's wig" is to get high. It also means *insane*. To say that a person is "a wig," or "is wiggy," is to say that they are insane—even though it could be in an interesting or even desirable manner. In the incident I refer to, the "wig" in question is Chin Lee, the Chinese symbolist poet who is incarcerated on the fifth floor of Bellevue. The term "red-split" refers to the blood of a schizophrenic, which has been found to produce radical changes of mood, etc. when injected into a normal person's bloodstream. The story is about a moment in history when this "red-split"—or "blood of a wig," as it were—was the drug-of-choice. One must be selective, however, and not ingest the blood (it has to be fresh and still warm) of just any run-of-the-mill lunatic, but someone *interestingly* insane, like, say, Chin Lee, or Ezra Pound.

L.S.: *Can we talk about your first screenplay,* Dr. Strangelove? *How did Kubrick come to hire you? The picture, as I understand it, had originally been planned as a straight drama.*

T.S.: The first draft of *Dr. Strangelove* was a more or less faithful adaptation of a novel called *Red Alert*, by Peter George. He and Kubrick had done the adaptation, and the result was a straightforward melodrama of the *Fail-Safe* variety. In fact, certain technical details in *Fail-Safe* were so similar to those of *Red Alert*—which had also been used in *Strangelove*—that Kubrick was able to get a court order forcing the producers of *Fail-Safe* to postpone the opening of their picture, because of the rather obvious plagiarism which had occurred.

Anyway, my own involvement came about when Kubrick realized that the hydrogen bomb and the-end-of-the-world-as-we-know-it were just too unusual to be treated in any conventionally dramatic fashion, and had decided to go the "black comedy" route. This was a decision not without certain immediate adverse ramifications; his partner, James Harris, who had acted as producer for most of his previous films, was so much against it that he withdrew from the production. However, back to the circumstances of my participation. It seems that not long before that, Peter Sellers had discovered my book, *The Magic Christian*, and had actually bought one hundred copies of it—which he then gave to his friends, on their birthdays, at Christmas, and so on; and he had given one to Stanley.

So Stanley phoned me from England, and I went over and went to work. We worked together on the script before and throughout the filming.

L.S.: *Wasn't Peter Sellers supposed to play a fourth part in the picture, but he had to drop it due to illness or something?*

T.S.: Peter was scheduled to play the role of Captain "King" Kong, along with the three other roles. When we had to replace him, Stanley said, "Well, Peter Sellers can't be replaced by another *actor*, it will have to be an *authentic gung-ho Texas cracker!*" I suggested big Dan Blocker, of *Bonanza* fame. A script was rushed to him—or rather, his agent, who rejected it in summary fashion as being "thoroughly pinko." Then Stanley remembered Slim Pickens, called him, and he was on the next plane.

L.S.: *He's great in the film; Sellers certainly couldn't have matched him for authenticity.*

T.S.: He wasn't an actor, he was a rodeo man. At the time of his discovery by Marlon Brando, for *One-Eyed Jacks*, he was working as a rodeo clown, perhaps the most demanding and dangerous job in rodeo, having to distract the bulls when a rider is down.

L.S.: *He must have been a little out of his element in London.*

T.S.: Before he came to England, Slim Pickens had not merely never been out of the United States, he had never been out of that area which makes up the western rodeo circuit—Texas, Oklahoma, New Mexico, Arizona and California. When he got to the studio, Stanley, who was in the middle of directing a scene, broke off, and called me over. "Listen," he said, "Slim Pickens is here, and nobody can understand him. *You're* from Texas, you go and talk to him. Ask him if his hotel room is okay, and all that."

I went to the production office, where Slim had just arrived, and was talking to the associate producer, a very la-dee-dah young British chap—who looked extremely relieved to see me. He jumped to his feet, "Ah, there you are, Terry! May I present Mr. Slim Pickens! Terry Southern!" Slim was wearing his boots and his Stetson hat. He grinned and lumbered towards me. "Mighty glad to know ya!" We shook hands and I fished out a bottle of Wild Turkey I had stashed for the occasion. "Wal, Slim," I said, reverting to the drawl of my youth, "you don't reckon it's too early for a drink, do you?" It was about ten A.M. "Why, hell no," he said with conviction, "ah can't recall it *ever* being too early for a drink of Turkey!" So I poured us out a few fingers each in two water glasses, and then I asked him about his room. "Did you get settled in all right, Slim? Is your hotel room comfortable?" He had a big swig of Turkey, swishing it around like mouthwash. "Aw, hell yeah," he said, wiping his mouth on the back of his sleeve, "it's like this Okie friend of mine says, 'Ah don't need much—jest a pair of loose-fittin' shoes, some tight pussy, an' a warm place to shit, an' ah'll be all right'! Hee-hee-hee."

L.S.: *Working with Kubrick had to be a high point in your film writing. Were there low points, run-ins with moronic producers, egomaniacal actors, that sort of thing?*

T.S.: On the movie *Cincinnati Kid*, I was with the two producers once when they were talking about casting the role of "Slade," the decadent, wealthy cracker who bribes "Shooter" (Karl Malden) to deal off the bottom to "Lancy" (Edward G. Robinson) so that "the Kid" (Steve McQueen) "can gut him." One of the producers said, "We gotta get a Rip Torn type to play Slade," and the other one agreed—so they started talking about Bruce Dern, Brad Dillman, etc., everybody *but* Rip Torn. Finally, I said, "That's a great idea, but why not get *Rip Torn* for the role—I don't think he's working right now." "No, no," they both said, practically in unison, "A 'Rip Torn *type*,' not Rip Torn himself!" "Why not?" I wanted to know. "Well, he's a shit-kicker," they said, "he's a troublemaker. We get a Rip Torn *type*, and save ourselves some grief." "I'll bet Sam would like to get him," I said, referring to Sam Peckinpah, who was at the time the film's director. "Sam Peckinpah is a shit-kicker too," one of them said. "Nothing but trouble," the other one said. "He wants to use a *spade hooker* for Slade's mistress—can you believe that?"

"That was my idea," I protested, "don't you see? It's the ultimate hypocrisy—Slade, the cracker family man and pillar of his community, has a spade hooker as his mistress." "It's *crazy*," said one of them, shaking his head. "It's *suicide*," said the other one, "*lose* it." So we lost it—and we lost Peckinpah, who was replaced by Norman Jewison. But we *did* get Rip Torn, instead of a Rip Torn type. And he proved to be the best thing in the film.

L.S.: *In general would you say that screenwriting is a less than artistically satisfying occupation?*

T.S.: Screenwriting should be avoided except in the *auteur* context, where the writer is also the director. Otherwise, his power, regarding the *protection* of his work—unlike that of the *playwright*—is only the power of *persuasion* . . . and trying to persuade the ordinary director or studio producer in matters involving taste, aesthetics, common sense, and/or even the most obvious commercialism, is like trying to persuade an untrained donkey. I have been fairly fortunate, working with people Like Kubrick and Tony Richardson, but those are rare exceptions indeed. About 99.99 percent of the time you are working with studio people—i.e., shoe-clerk, garment-industry morons who should simply be forced to wear earphones *permanently*, and kicked the fuck off the set, and on no account be allowed physically near a script, as they will invariably contaminate it by sheer osmosis. Like one of William Burroughs's characters—a narcotics agent called "Bradley, the Buyer"—they just sort of *ooze* a slime of putrefaction which will engulf everything within their considerable stench. I have a proverbial *trunkful* of award-winning box-office-smash screenplays which were reduced to garbage by the idiocy of producers and secondrate directors. And what is possibly even worse about screenwriting is that there is probably *no challenge* to it, except the challenge of the *deadline*—and that, of course, is hardly sufficient motivation . . . unless, natch, "the flour be low in yoah barrel," hee-hee-hee.

L.S.: *How did you happen to get involved in the infamous "Chicago Seven" trial? You were called in as a witness, right?*

T.S.: I testified regarding the action of an *agent provocateur*—reputedly working for the FBI—which helped to start the rioting, the *police* rioting, of May 16th. On the afternoon of that day, I was in a march from Lincoln Park to the amphitheatre. We were six abreast, and I was in a line with Burroughs and Jean Genet—the three of us were there for *Esquire* magazine. They were on my left and on my right was a lady about sixty-five—a very hip and knowledgeable elderly lady from New York, whom I knew vaguely through other protest marches and demonstrations. Anyway, about three lines ahead of us were these two strangely obnoxious guys, college football types, wearing T-shirts, khaki trousers, and sporting the latest in pig-bristle haircuts. They were loud, crude, slightly drunk, and seemed grotesquely out of place. The elderly lady had also noticed them, and after a couple of minutes she signaled one of the arm-band marshals who accompany the marches, and he came over. The marshal then recognized them himself, and gestured them out of the formation. They took off, and as they did I got a good look at them—enough to see that one of the T-shirts had "University of Notre Dame" emblazoned on the front of it.

Well, that evening about seven, we were in Lincoln Park, just sitting around, smoking dope and talking. I was watching Allen Ginsberg teach a group of young people how to do the *"Umm-mum"* when these police prowl cars started pulling into the park, moving very slowly across it, and officers with bullhorns saying, "This park is closed. You will leave the park at once." This went on for about twenty minutes, with no one leaving, but with no one causing any trouble either. And then, just as one of the prowl cars eased into our immediate vicinity, less than 20 feet away, a guy stepped out from behind a tree and threw a brick against its windshield. The car stopped, its searchlight went on, two cops jumped out, putting on their gas masks as they came, and unhooking the riot sticks from their belts. They had obviously radioed the rest of the cars, because now, all over the park, they started laying down tear gas, and beating the shit out of everybody in sight. Throwing the brick had been the cue—and as luck would have it, several people saw the guy do it . . . but I may have been the only one who saw that he had a pig-bristle haircut and wore a Notre Dame T-shirt. So that was my testimony at the Chicago Trial: that the police riots at the Democratic Convention were prearranged, by Mayor Daley, and were triggered by an FBI *provocateur*. Hot stuff, huh?

L.S.: *In the mid-'70s you joined the Rolling Stones on what, if I recall rightly, was dubbed the "Cocksucker Blues Tour." Any sordid details you care to tell us about?*

T.S.: Mick is currently writing his autobiography, and an astute interviewer recently asked him, "Mr. Jagger, are you going to reveal the details of your many and well-known sexual indiscretions?" To which he replied, "Well, I don't mind *revealing* them, but I was so out of my gourd most of the time that I don't think I can *remember* them." That's sort of how I recall the Stones tour. We flew from one gig to the next in this 727 that was outfitted like a kind of low-profile shooting gallery/whorehouse. The "company physician," for example, was this young, extremely precocious, UCLA faculty member, who was so highly qualified that, in addition to his regular M.D. degree, he had a—dig this—a *license* to do toot-research. He could "requisition" oz. bottles of "fluffy flake Merc crystal" for about twelve dollars each. Fortunately, his Hippocratic Oath, and the strict rules of in-flight discipline, laid down by Jagger and Richards, precluded any abuse of the situation. HAW!

L.S.: *The other literary figure on board was Truman Capote, correct? He must have been an amusing companion.*

T.S.: One of the concerts was in New Orleans, so Tru and I made the rounds of his old gourmet haunts, ending up at the great Antoine's, where it was Red Carpet City—since Capote (next to Big Tenn Williams) is the most celebrated local weirdie-made-good in the annals of their neat ville. Consequently, we had one of the all-time "fab frog-feeds"—a phrase I used in passing, thinking only to amuse Tru-Baby for the briefest mo, little suspecting that he would seize upon it and shout repeatedly in manic glee: "*Mes compliments au chef! It's a fab frog-feed! Hee-hee-hee! It's a fab frog-feed!*" to the grand chagrin, one might imagine, of the management, but no notice was apparent—and, in point of actual fact, the chef (Jean-François Beauvoirs, if memory serves) *did* come out for the big hello with Tru.

L.S.: *Why—dare I ask—did it come to be called the "Cocksucker" tour?*

T.S.: The "Cocksucker Blues Tour" moniker was nothing, just silly PR hype—*not*, mind you, that there wasn't an almost *unbelievable amount* of actual, in-flight cocksucking going on (mostly hetero, in my view), it's just that it had nothing to do with the tour itself. "Cocksucker Blues" was the name of a Stones tune, and was the name Robert Frank chose for the film he made of the tour. "*Cinema verité,*" he kept calling it, but Keith was quick with a saucy rejoinder: "I don't want *verité*, you crazy galoot, I want *poetry*!" So that was pretty much that.

L.S.: *You did a stint writing* Saturday Night Live. *How did that work out?*

T.S.: That job o' work came about because of the great Michael O'Donoghue. He was engaged as head writer for the show, with *carte blanche* to get the best, so he was gracious enough to hire a certain yours truly. I would ask him, "Hey, are you really the *head writer?*" And he would say: "Yep." And I would say: "Well, why don't you give me some *head* then? Haw!" Anyway, the two of us—and Nelson "Big Nels" Lyon—wrote some funny stuff, but of course it was never used. "*Sleazy Gyno*" was an outstanding piece of that genre—given short shrift, natch. Then there was a solid, hard-hitting satiric skit called "*King Dong.*" And a really fabulous docudrama called "*Child Molestor! Or, It's the Little Things That Count.*" Nipped in the bud, I'm afraid. So now we're putting them all together, and they'll be released under the title "*Too Good For SNL!*"

O'Don had a falling out with the producer, and he left the show, and that was that. After that, everything went downhill. Into the toilet for good! *Kaput! Fini! Nada!* All hat and no cattle! Or perhaps more aptly, like Mark Twain said about a certain riverboat: "*All toot and no steam*" . . . if you get my drift.

L.S.: *In your novel* Blue Movie, *you more or less predicted the whole porn movie "revolution"—the addition of bigger budgets, story lines, a star system of sorts, the appeal to "mainstream" audiences. Would Boris Adrian—your Stanley Kubrick-type protagonist in the book—be pleased with the current state of the porn movie?*

T.S.: No, and it is implicit in your question. The fact that you say "porn" movie instead of "erotic" movie. A *porn* movie, by definition, cannot be good, because "porn" has very negative connotations. "Porn" is simply "erotica" which doesn't make it. In this magazine, for example, are photographs which one may find beautiful and stimulating; these are *erotic*. Others one may find gross and clinical; these are *porn*. But the kind of erotic film Boris Adrian was trying to create also involved the use of superior actors, a great director, and a really engaging story. This has never been attempted. One movie which *might* have achieved that was *Caligula*, with its use of John Gielgud and so on. But I don't think it even tried to be erotic; it merely tried to be gory, sensational, and sadistic. Eroticawise, it missed the boat.

L.S.: *What about doing a film of* Blue Movie *itself? Could real movie stars ever be convinced to go hardcore?*

T.S.: I have written a screenplay for *Blue Movie*, which was nearly produced a couple of times, but not as yet.

L.S.: *Kubrick would seem the perfect man for the job. Has he read it?*

T.S.: Stanley Kubrick had read the manuscript of *Blue Movie*—or rather had reached page 181, where Angela Sterling drops on the director. He called from

England, in the middle of the night, very excited. "You've written the *definitive blow-job!*" he kept shouting. "The *definitive blow-job!*" Made my day, in double-quick order.

L.S.: *Terry, as a man renowned to one and all for your sexual . . . curiosity, could you relate to* Puritan's *readers some edifying erotic experience of recent memory?*

T.S.: I recently had occasion to relate just such an instance. It was also, incidentally, a classic example of the "neo-nada" journalism you referred to earlier—since, under the guise of a "tribute to Kurt Vonnegut," I scarcely mentioned the great Von, but instead related at tedious length how, a few years back, a certain G. Ames Plimpton and I were treated by Sadruddin Khan (son of the Aga) to an evening at the most opulent whorehouse in Paris, *Le Maison du Langue* ("The House of Tongue"). The specialty of the house was called "*Le Circle des Enfants du Paradise*," and consisted of the patron being strapped to an elevated table, where his entire body was then "anointed" with banana oil, by the incredibly beautiful "Maitrix," statuesque in scant black leathers. When she had finished, one was in a state of "throbbing tumescence," as the porn mags like to express it; whereupon she would clap her hands and shout, "*Mes enfants! A table!,*" a signal for the entrance of four of the most darling eight- to ten-year-old girls imaginable, all dressed in diaphanous white chiffon—who proceeded to lick, with their precious pink tongues, the oil from one's body inch by maddening inch, though carefully avoiding the pent-up and pulsating member. Finally, when the tantalization had reached a nadir of near insanity, the Maitrix would gesture the fairy-children away, step to the table herself and voraciously engorge the pounding, soon spurting organ into her own hot, wet Sophia Loren–type mouth! *Hosanna!*

L.S.: *As one of the acknowledged masters of erotic lit, what books, films, would you cite as personal favorite turn-ons?*

T.S.: Nothing to compare with what is in my own head—fantasies which I can occasionally capture, at least to my own satisfaction, in writing. I don't mean this in any sense that has to do with "ego" or "arrogance," or even stylistic facility. It is rather that I am convinced that the most highly charged eroticism is so completely *personal* that it has to be created at the very source. This may account, to a large extent, for the universal phenomenon of masturbation, and in such extraordinarily high incidence. According to the *Hite Report*, for example, the majority of women actually *prefer* masturbation to intercourse. What this clearly suggests is that eroticism, even in women, is so totally *personal* that it must be "tailor-made" for the consumer.

L.S.: *But it would seem that most people need outside help—books, pictures, and so on—to think up their "personal" fantasies.*

T.S.: Obviously the vast majority of people have neither the imagination to formulate (or be seized by!) sexual fantasies, nor the skill and/or inclination to put them on paper. I am fortunate in that my own erotic fantasies—and the facility for putting them on paper—seem to have a certain general acceptance. At last count, *Candy* had sold over seven million copies, in languages too numerous to recall. Proof . . . o'*pudding*, if you get my drift.

L.S.: *And finally, by way of summary, could you reflect for a moment on the so-called "meaning of life"?*

T.S.: Gladly. Life is a sort of *parade* . . . wherein the participants are propelled by the beat of a distant drum; and by several varieties of Bolivian Marching Powder—figuratively speaking, of course. Or to take refuge in the words of the great Artaud: "We are all like victims, tied to the stake, signaling through the flames."

—1986 *Puritan*

Tales

Heavy Put-Away

or,

A Hustle Not Wholly Devoid
of a Certain Grossness, Granted

Recently I was researching an article for a woman's magazine, whose considerate editor had already entitled it—*Con Men: Their Games and Their NAMES*—aiming, with the final emphasis, for a bit of the old exposé mileage no doubt. I had assumed in front that, through editorial pressures, it might gradually get bent into the usual hacksville tom-foolery—a rehash of classic and clichéd hustles . . . and, for the most part, so it proved to be. Most, yes, but not all, for there was one conspicuous exception, and it was deleted, totally, from the piece—"because of," in the head-back closed-eyed words of the senior blue-coiffed lady-editor, "certain elements in the narrative which are simply too, how shall I say, er, uh, *gross* for our general readership."

I was really quite surprised. A prevalent real-life hustle "too gross" to be exposed? What a curious age we live in.

In my research I used a small unobtrusive Sony-600, obtaining verbatim recordings of every conversation. The following is the one which was deleted from the piece, and is, I submit, among the most intriguing (albeit outrageous) deceptions presently in vogue, in the U.S. of A.

The narrator—whom I shall call "Art"—is thirty-four, white, college-grad, unmarried, clean-cut and boyishly good-looking, a type seen mostly in beach-movies . . . a younger Jack Nicholson; and though he was careful to keep his story always in the third person, even slightly detached, as though describing someone else, I had the recurrent and distinct impression he was talking about himself.

The interview was taking place on the terrace of the "Sow 'n Merkin," a cafe-restaurant on La Cienega, about two blocks below the Sunset Strip. Only a moderate amount of pedestrian traffic on the sidewalk that passed our table, and whenever a girl would go by, Art's eyes would flick after her with a warm, somewhat carnivorous glint in them, without interrupting his story. He's also one of those "L.A. types" (no other way to say it) who do coke quite openly—

though with consummate discretion, natch—carrying it pre-chopped in an ornate antique-style snuffbox, dipping in with the little finger, for swift unobtrusive toots off the back of the nail . . . which Art did throughout his narrative, occasionally sliding the box to me across the table. The first time he passed me the box, I glanced around, super-casual, to check out the neighboring tables, but Art was quick to allay my concern.

"It's cool, man" he said, "no vigilantes here." He smiled and assumed a cracker drawl: "Hell, we done strung 'em all up."

I switched on the Sony-Six, and Art took that (as per intention) to be a signal to begin.

"Okay," he said, "now here's a funny number a couple of guys I know run from time to time—I've been saving it. I mean, it could be a little heavy . . . for, you know, certain tastes."

"No way, Art," I assured him, "you lay it down, and I'll pick it up."

He chuckled, somewhat cynically now that I think back on it, and then continued:

"Well, there was this chick—name of *Sally*—very cute, twenty-three, twenty-four years old, worked as a kind of hat-check cigarette-girl at a small club on the Strip. I forget the actual name of the club . . . it was like the *Crescendo*, one of those, you know, with a piano-player, and maybe a combo in for weekends—that kind of place, small but legit . . . just your 'average American bar.' Anyway, this guy—let's call him Al—starts coming in, almost every night. Nice-looking guy, about thirty-five, sharp dresser, leased Lincoln Continental parked outside. And he's always quite friendly—not pushy about it, just friendly—you know: 'Hi, Ted,' 'Hello Tom,' 'Hi Sally,' and blah-blah-blah. And so finally he's like a regular customer, coming in nearly every evening. Comes in before dinner, has a couple of drinks, and splits. Now he's gradually getting fairly tight with Sally, the hat-check cigarette-girl—no heavy come-on, nothing like that, just sort of a *pal*. And one night, a slow night, she's sitting at the bar with him, having a drink, and he lays this story on her . . . about a *friend* of his—an older guy, a terrific guy, friend of the family, a sort of 'surrogate father' is the way he put it—who's coming in from New York in a week or so. And he goes on to describe this guy, in very flattering terms—an important businessman, a well-known financier, a major executive of a huge corporation, on the board of directors of several big companies, seat on the New York Stock Exchange, private plane, and so forth. And he tells her how the guy comes to California on business two or three times a year, and that when he does, he likes to have a *discreet affair* with someone—*not a hooker,* he isn't interested in that at all—he wants someone, well, like someone to *talk* to, and to spend a pleasant evening with. 'He's good for a thou,' Al said, 'a thousand bucks for the evening, and usually a nice gift of some kind besides.' Al knows all about it, because he has arranged it for him before, several times—so he was able to assure her that it was 'strictly legit,' and what's more that if she didn't *like* the guy she could just split, she didn't actually have to make it with him. Naturally, he *hoped* it would happen, but it wasn't really critical, I mean it wasn't going to be a deal-breaker if she didn't let him fuck her—because he was happily married, had a wonderful family—wife, children, grandchildren, the whole bit—it was just that he liked the excitement of, you know, meeting a nice young girl from time to time, and so on . . . made him feel *younger,* whatever. Anyway, he went on to say that he, Al, knew that the guy would *like* Sally, and he wondered if she would be interested—a thousand bucks for a couple of hours, probably a nice present, and after she got there, if she decided she didn't want to make it with him, that would be okay, she could just leave. Well, right away she said *no,* it wasn't the sort of thing she would be interested in, *ever,* and he said 'Well, no offense,' and she said 'None taken,' and he took her to dinner, never mentioned it again, took her home, didn't hit on her in any way, didn't come in for coffee or a drink, said he had an early appointment, had to get to bed, and that was that. Saw her the next few nights at the club, never referred to it again.

"Now then, *parallel to this,* there was a young couple living in the Valley —the guy was a stunt man, or let's say an *ex*–stunt man, with a *broken back* . . . had taken a fall, a *big* fall, landed on a Chapman crane . . . crushed his back. So he's laid up—*totalled.* Now the tie-in is that the stunt man had married this girl's best friend, Sally's best friend, about a year and a half before this. Bill and Mary, that was their names, and they had this kid, and the kid was about *a month old*— a one-month-old kid—like an *infant.* Now the guy, Bill, had broken his back about six or seven months ago, so for the last four months they've been in heavy trouble. I mean, they bought a *house, furniture, two cars*—all the usual stuff— during the first six months they were married . . . and then he busted his back. But the studio wasn't liable, because it was some kind of unauthorized stunt, whatever, so he wasn't getting any workmen's comp. I mean, he really got ripped on the whole thing—wasn't getting *any* money. And they had all these *medical* bills—for his back, and for her having the kid, *plus* all the regular bills— the car payments, mortgage payments, insurance payments, *everything.* And, of course, she can't work because of having the kid, and he's lying around—they don't know yet if he's going to be a full-on paralytic or not—just lying there in a *full-body cast,* with the wife and the newborn baby, and they're *starving.* No bread at all, being dunned by everybody—about to get *killed* by the house-payments guy, the car-payments guy, the guys with the furniture, TV . . . all of it. *Murder. Wipeout.* Now the wife, Mary, she would call the other girl, Sally, and they could *talk,* on the phone . . . it was really the high point of her day, her conversation with Sally, the hat-check girl. You see, she could never get out of the house because she was stuck with the paralyzed husband and the kid. Actually, she was very much *in love* with her husband—which is what gives this whole story a certain *'je ne sais quoi,'* ha—I mean it wasn't like she was being a ball-breaker about it, it was just a *really terrible* situation. And so she was sort of living vicariously on the phone, through her friend Sally, who would tell her all about her day—her *night* actually—at the club . . . you know, who came in with who, et cetera . . . and so on that same level, of just interesting day-to-day trivia, she mentions the guy, Al, and the proposition he made—but only referring to it as something that happened at the club, no more than that. But a couple of days later, Mary calls and says that she's been *thinking* about that thing, that *proposition.* 'It's horrible, I know,' she says, 'but we're just *so* desperate that I think maybe I ought to *do* it—I mean, you know, if you think he would want to.' Well, Sally *knew* the guy would go for Mary, because she was even better looking than Sally was. But she said, 'Well, what about *Bill?* What's *he* going to say?' And Mary says, 'Well, he won't say anything, because he won't *know.* I mean, I'll just tell him I've got to go to this *meeting,* or something like that, and then maybe you can come over and pick me up, and you know, take me there—and when it's over I'll have the money and take a cab home . . . and well, he'll just never know anything about it. I mean, I realize it's terrible, and I hate it, but I just *don't know what else to do.'* 'Because she really *did love* the guy, of course, and that's the key to it, you see—of the whole caper—that she's this totally innocent person, this *very nice girl,* who is really in love with her husband, and had never *dreamed* of making it with anyone else, or with anyone for *money,* ever, but their terrible circumstances—and the *amount* of money being offered . . . well, it was *tempting.* Of course Sally was completely surprised, she could hardly believe it. 'Mary,' she says, 'I don't think you should do it—I mean it's too weird, it might affect your relationship with Bill—even if he *didn't* find out about it.' And Mary starts crying and says, 'Yes, I know, I know . . . I guess you're right, it's just that I'm so desperate . . .' And she cries for a little bit on the phone, and Sally cries, and then they drop the subject, and that's the end of it—except that a few days later, when they're about to *turn off the electricity,* Mary calls Sally and says, 'I know it's crazy, but that thousand-dollar thing—with the older man from New York—could you try to find out more about it?' And she tells her about the electricity, and everything. So the next time Al comes in the club, Sally asks him if he's found a girl yet for his friend. And Al says, 'No, as a matter of fact I haven't, and the guy is coming out in about a week, and I'm getting a little nervous about it.' And so Sally tells him about her friend Mary, who she says is sort of *thinking* about it. And she goes on to describe her—'a very beautiful, really *nice, nice* girl, who loves her husband very much,' and so on, but that they have these terrible financial problems, and she tells the whole story to Al—the guy's broken back, the electricity about to be shut off, and so on, and asks him, Al, to tell her more about the guy. So he lays this heavy rap on her again about what a wonderful, gentle, sweet, attractive, generous man this guy is. 'I mean, she's really going to *like* him, a lot,' he says, 'he's a *truly nice man.* And if she *doesn't* like him, you know, she can just leave.'

"So they set the thing up. The cover story, for Bill, was that Mary was going out for the evening with a girlfriend, to see a movie. She would go out at seven—the baby would have had its bottle by then, and she would put it next to the husband on the bed, because he can barely get around—he can *move,* but it wasn't the easiest thing to do, you dig, in this *full-body cast.*

"Now then, Al gives Sally full instructions about how it's to be done. *Discretion,* that was the main concern—you've *got to be discreet.* This was because the guy doesn't want to be *seen* in the lobby of the hotel, or anything like that. He's *staying* at the hotel, but he feels it will be more discreet and more comfortable, and so on, if they do their thing in a *bungalow.* So Mary is to book it, bungalow ten, a big mother, at the Beverly Hills Hotel, book it in her name, go there, sign in and register. Bring a bag, and in the bag have a couple of bottles of really fine Scotch, and a bottle of good brandy. Get some mixer—club soda, and some ice, wrap it all in a towel so it doesn't rattle, and put it in the best bag she's got, check in, and go to the bungalow. 'Listen,' she asks Sally, 'where am I going to get the *money* for the whiskey?' Well, Sally was short and couldn't come up with it, so she went to a neighbor, whom she barely knew, and said she was *desperate,* she *had to* raise fifty dollars, could *she* loan it to her. So the neighbor took the money out of her sugar bowl, but emphasized that she would have to have it back the *next day,* because it was the *household money* and so on.

And then Mary didn't have a really smart bag, so she borrowed that from Sally—who picked her up on her way to the hat-check joint, and dropped her at the Beverly Hills Hotel, where she had already called up and reserved bungalow ten. The boy took the bag to the bungalow, showed her in, and she waited there. See, the idea of bringing the booze in was that the guy didn't want anybody coming to the room while he was there, because of the big discretion thing—him being a famous person, well known at the Beverly Hills Hotel— and he just couldn't afford *any indiscretion at all*. So she, Mary, was instructed to get there at about seven, order a nice dinner for herself, anything she wanted—he recommended the pheasant, and a particular wine, very expensive—and he would eat elsewhere and then join her at about nine. And that way they would avoid the whole room-service scene and any risk of him being recognized. So she went to the hotel, about six-thirty, registered *her* name, went to the bungalow, had the pheasant, the wine, et cetera, signed the check, and waited. Then, at about nine, *he* called. 'Is everything all right?' trying to sound pleasant and cheerful. He says that he'll come down now, down from his room, and meet her, if it's convenient. She says, yes of course, and so he arrives in a few minutes—and he's a really *nice attractive* guy, very thoughtful and considerate and *cultured*. So the anxiety she had felt began to disappear. See, she had been getting sort of panicky about it. I mean, she hadn't been to bed with anybody in about *six months*, because of her husband's busted back, and then she'd had the baby . . . and so this was going to be the *first fuck* she's had in quite a while, and she was kind of uptight about it, about the whole thing, but he really put her at ease, and began to sort of draw her out, and she told him all about her husband and about the baby, and all the depressing stuff about their situation, and she cried a little bit, and he was terrific—perfect father-guy, and she found him attractive, and they drank some of the booze, and then they went to bed, and it was okay. I mean, it wasn't in any way sordid or vile, or anything like that, and she really dug him, and he was very interested in her and said that he understood there had been this money arrangement, this thousand dollars, and that was fine, but he didn't want that to be the main thing. He'd gotten to really *like her*, he said, and he wanted to take an active part in helping her and her husband out of this predicament, and maybe even take an interest in the *child*, the child's education and so on. And they talked some more and made love again, and now it was about *eleven o 'clock*, and he takes out this *ring*—this *beautiful diamond ring*—and he tells her that he bought it for his daughter's birthday, and he wants to know what she thinks of it. And she says, 'Well, it's really *beautiful*. Absolutely *fabulous*.' It's still in the velvet case, you know, and he says, 'Well, you see, I'd like *you* to have one just like it, because I think you're a blah-blah-blah wonderful girl and the ring really suits you,' and blah-blah-blah. It's a big stone, very impressive. 'Oh, I couldn't,' she says. 'Don't be silly,' he says, 'I insist.' Then he gets on the phone and calls the jeweler at the jeweler's home. 'Yes, you know the ring I bought this afternoon—well, I'm leaving first thing in the morning, and I want to get another one like it. Could you come over to the hotel now? No, I've got an early flight, and I just won't have any time at all tomorrow. Yes, the same ring exactly. Just call bungalow ten when you get here and I'll meet you in the lobby and pick it up. No, I don't know the size, so bring an assortment, and we'll determine the size when you get here. All right, see you soon. Thank you.'

"So, from her point of view, everything has gone just great—she'll have the *money*, she'll have the *ring*, she has this fantastic *new friend* who's going to be like a godfather to the child, and help them all out, and so on. *Now* her only concern is how she will handle it in terms of her husband, how to explain about the money and about the ring. And the guy advises her on that, too—he asks how well does her husband know her background. Is it conceivable, for instance, that she had an aunt or uncle, that Bill didn't know about, who could have died and left it to her? She thinks about this for a minute, and says yes it *is* possible, there could have been this aunt in *Youngstown*, or someplace . . . so that little problem is settled. Now it's about twelve-thirty, and the phone rings. It's the jeweler, down in the lobby. The guy starts out, to go meet him and pick up the ring, and just as he gets to the door, the instant before he goes out, he remembers about not knowing her ring size, so she takes off her wedding ring and gives it to him so he can match it for size. He says he'll have a quick drink with the jeweler, in the Polo Lounge, just to be sociable, pick up the ring and be back in ten minutes or so, probably less. So she turns on the TV, finishes getting dressed, and sits there waiting for him. Times passes. One-thirty, two-thirty . . . three-fifteen. She starts to get panicky, calls the Polo Lounge, the Lounge is closed. Calls the desk, asks for his room—he isn't registered, they never heard of him. *Never*. Now she calls Sally at the club. Closed. Calls Sally's house. No answer. So, she's sitting there, alone, four o'clock in the morning, no money, a hundred-and-ninety-five-dollar hotel bill . . . desperation time. Finally, nothing left but to bottom-line it—*call the husband*. She tells him where she is—bungalow ten at the Beverly Hills Hotel—he'll have to pick her up because there's no money for a cab, and there's no way to *get* a cab without alerting the hotel that she's about to skip. So—now dig this—the husband, Bill, wearing *his full-body cast,* moving like something out of a horror movie, has to *wake this neighbor* he doesn't even know very well, at four in the morning, *borrow his car,* put the baby on the seat beside him, *try* to drive from the Valley to Beverly Hills, cruise the hotel until she can sneak out—without the bag in case she's spotted—get in the car, and *drive back.* And on the way back, she has to tell him *what happened* . . . about the money she owes the hotel, the neighbor, the bag she has to replace, the wedding ring . . . and, you know, man, the *whole story."*

And with that, the sun sinking behind the Hollywood hills silhouetting him, Art gave me his All-American, boss-charm, hero-of-many-battles smile. "Now I ask you," he said softly, sliding the snuffbox across the table, *"wasn't that a heavy put-away?"*

We sat in silence then, watching the sun slowly go down, and having a few unobtrusive toots.

"Listen," I finally said, "those guys . . . they must have been really . . . well, one thing I'm a little *hazy* about is just how to characterize their *motivation."*

Art smiled, raising his brows, as in surprise. "Oh yeah?" He turned his eyes towards the distant hills, where the last rays of the sun bled out all along the horizon—but he didn't reply.

"Well," I went on, "I think you'll agree there *is* a certain ambiguity here . . . I mean, let's just run it down in a recap—what did they get out of it? Okay, *one:* the guy gets *laid,* by a beautiful young girl—*that's* a plus . . ."

"A *really nice* girl," added Art, nodding his head to emphasize that aspect of it.

"Right. A beautiful young *really nice* girl . . . who hasn't made it with anyone in six months. Okay, that's all a definite plus. But is that enough—to justify such an elaborate ruse? I mean, what *else* did they get out of it?"

He looked at me, with something close to pity. "I should've thought it was obvious," he said, a slightly pained smile on his lips.

"Well, let's see, there was her *wedding ring*—probably a simple, narrow gold band—what was *that* worth? Fifty bucks? A hundred?"

"A hundred tops," said Art, "probably less."

"Well, that doesn't seem like much . . . for all that trouble."

He laughed. "You've got a pretty *materialistic* slant on things, don't you?"

—1981 *The Paris Review*
Reprinted by permission of *The Paris Review.*

A Run of Dimes

It was one of those boxed-in government offices, containing, besides the standard olive-colored metal desk and its accompanying chair, a kind of school chair, for the part-time secretary, with a high, broad armrest for her writing. The death-white monotony of the neat box-walls was given striking definition by mounted photographs, all around, of American coins, greatly enlarged, which hung there, picturelike, in a series.

Nine o'clock, and Fred Merkle had been at this desk for an hour. Merkle liked the photographs around him. Against the devilish white of the walls, the great silver coins appeared, beneath their highlights, softly gray, almost malleable. Like huge cameos, there was something respectable, and vaguely academic, about them. Now, here was a man, Merkle, who had been with the Treasury Department for twenty-four years, one of that legion of conscientious, apolitical employees who manage to survive the ravaging spoils of administrative and policy change by dint of sheer, unambitious, hard work; and, by the concomitant fact that their positions are usually of a category below general, or rather, particular, notice. However, through twenty-four years of conscientious work, in any conceivable organization, one does attain, by degree, to positions of quasi-, and/or, momentary, authority. And so it was with Merkle. Today, for example, he was in charge of a run of dimes. His was the voice that would give the okay to start the casting run. It was routine actually, happening once or twice a month; but it caused him to be at his desk earlier than on ordinary days, because, lately, he had taken to reading the morning paper very closely. He had not been feeling too well either, and when he raised his head now from the flat-spread paper on his desk to look momentarily at the photograph of the dime, his eyes seemed all dark-circled and his features slightly drawn-in. A few days ago the doctor had told Merkle that he should rest more if he felt so nervous and irritable, that he was 'all right physically,' even making a little joke about being 'as sound as a silver dollar,' or some such. Merkle had hardly been able to smile, instead had vaguely brought up the subject of newspapers. "Lay off things like that for a while," the doctor had said grandly. "You're worrying too much. Sit in the park with a good book. *Fiction.*" But Merkle had subscribed to the paper, and it was there every morning, on his desk. At 9:30 now he was still over it, head in his hands. He had reread the lead article three times. It contained the text of a speech by the president. The banner read: PRESIDENT ASKS FAITH FOR NATION.

Merkle looked at his watch; he was feeling strange, his throat, and temples. He opened one of the desk drawers and drew out a thick, mimeographed directory which he began to thumb through.

Leaving the directory open on the desk, he picked up his phone and dialed. There was an almost immediate feminine response, "Good morning, Presidential Secretary's Office."

"Is the president there?"

"Who's calling, please?"

"This is Mr. Merkle. At the Treasury Department."

"Just a moment, Mr. Merkle." Followed by a man's voice, "Is the president expecting your call, Mr. Merkle?"

"No."

"I wonder if I could be of any help to you, sir; this is Mr. Reed of the Secretarial Staff."

"Well, we have a run of C-3 dimes on today, a considerable run, you see, and a question has come up . . . The Secretary of the Treasury is out of town, and—well, I'll have to speak to the president about it—it's in connection with something he said yesterday."

"That the president said yesterday."

"Yes."

"I see. Well, he's at the Executive Mansion right now. Shall I have him call you?"

"When will you see him?"

"Uh. He'll be at the Mansion until 10:30—"

"No, I have to speak to him before that."

"Well, the Mansion number is Capitol-7321. If you want to try there—"

"Yes. I will. Thank you."

Merkle penciled the number on the margin of the directory page. Before he could pick up the phone again, it rang. It was Harry, downstairs. "Fred? You coming down, or do you want us to go ahead and start?"

Merkle slowly traced the lines of the number he had just written, squint-
ing his eyes a little. "No, hold it up for a minute, Harry. OK?"

"You mean the C-3 run? Don't start it yet? What's up?"

"Well, nothing, I guess; but don't start it just yet. I'll call you back in a
few minutes. OK?"

"OK, Fred. Sure," said Harry, seeming slightly amused as he hung up.
Merkle dialed the other number. The response was less formal. "Hello."

"Hello. Is the president there?"

"Yes, who's calling?"

"Fred Merkle."

"Merkle. Is the president expecting your call, Mr. Merkle? This is his
secretary."

"I don't know."

"Uh. Just a moment, please, Mr. Merkle."

There was a moment of muffled conference, something about the 'Mansion number,' then the same voice again. "Mr. Merkle, this is Mr. George, the
president's secretary; perhaps I can help you—"

"Well, we're doing a C-3 run here at the Treasury this morning, and—
well, this is in connection with something the president said yesterday. If he's
there, I'd like to speak to him."

"Something the president said yesterday, you say. To *you* that is."

"Yes."

"Just a moment, Mr. Merkle. *Merkle*, that's right, isn't it?"

"Yes."

"Just a moment, please."

There was another moment of imperfect silence, during which Merkle
heard his name being pronounced several times, quite distinctly, and one or two
phrases like, 'conversation with you,' and 'talked to you yesterday'; then, a new
voice. "Hello."

"Mr. President?"

"Yes."

"This is Fred Merkle, Mr. President, at the Treasury. I'm sorry to bother
you, but I'm in charge of a run of C-3 dimes, and—"

"I'm sorry, but I'm afraid I didn't get the name—"

"Fred Merkle, sir. Frederick Merkle. I'm assistant to Mr. Fox."

"Fox? *Ted* Fox?"

"No. No, Arthur Fox. Section Five, Coinage Division. At the Treasury."

"And you say we *talked* together yesterday?"

"No. No, I read your *speech*—the speech you made yesterday. About faith? And I've been reading the newspapers, about the investiga—"

"Uh. Just a moment, please."

Merkle heard the voices go muffled again and the word '*speech*' being intoned with emphasis, and with tolerant good humor. Then, the first voice was on the line again, sounding brisk but rather exasperatedly amused.

"Mr. Merkle. Mr. Merkle, I'm sorry, I had the impression you had been *talking* with the president yesterday—from what you said—and that he had expressed an—I mean, you must realize, Mr. Merkle, that the president is extremely busy. He has a *particularly* heavy schedule today, and—well, don't you think it's possible for you to state in a letter—you say you're an employee of the Treasury department? I think you should address your—"

There was another break, as though the speaker had been interrupted, and Merkle thought he heard the words 'prankster,' or possibly 'crank, sir,' followed by a soft admonition, and the president's voice again. "Hello. Exactly what did you wish to speak to me about, Mr. Merkle?"

At that moment, Harry came into the office, looking wildly impatient.

"Excuse me a moment, sir," said Merkle covering the mouthpiece.

"We've got to start that run, Fred," Harry was saying, "the reading is point three eight *now*. What's going on? I couldn't get through to you."

"All right," said Merkle quietly, "go ahead and start it."

"Let me use that phone," said Harry coming forward. "There's no use risking any more time."

Merkle waved him away, frowning, and Harry stalked out of his office, looking aggravated.

"Hello? Mr. Merkle?" the president was saying.

"'Yes sir, I'm sorry. Well, what I wanted to say was that I've been reading the papers regularly now for quite a while—you know, about the investigations and so on? And this morning I read your speech—the speech you made yesterday about faith; I mean, with the emphasis being on *faith*." He paused, to take a breath, small breath, and the president's voice came firm, clear, and kind, edged only with a suggestion of tolerant good humor. "Yes, I see."

"Well, this morning we're doing a run of C-3 dimes, and somehow it didn't seem right to me—I'm the one, you see, who gives the order to start the run—and I was going to hold it up, because—I mean, after reading the papers, and your speech—"

"C-3 dimes," said the president.

"That's the regular dime, the one with the woman's head on it." Merkle looked at the large photograph on the wall. In these dimensions it had the majesty of some heroic bas-relief of another age; and, perhaps due to the lighting conditions at the time of the photograph, the unrelieved parts of the coin—the woman's cheekbone and temple, parts of her hair—gleamed as though faintly iridescent, while the raised letters *L-I-B-E-R-T-Y* seemed a foot high.

"It has the woman's head," Merkle continued, "and 'Liberty' around it, you know, in big letters; then, at the bottom, 'In God We Trust,' in small block, sort of balanced by the date of issue."

"I believe I know the coin," said the president with grand good humor.

"Yes. Well, from your speech, and the way things are going in the paper, it didn't seem right to me somehow having the emphasis—I mean, without asking you about it, before going ahead. I was thinking you might want to change the die."

"Pardon?"

"What I mean is we have other dime dies here. Experimental ones, of course. The only other current one is the C-12—you know, the Roosevelt dime. But it has more or less the same thing; it has a pretty big 'Liberty,' too, and a, little 'In God We Trust.' But there are others—do you know the C-8? Sort of like the A-2 penny? The Lincoln penny? Where the 'Liberty' and 'In God We Trust' are the same size lettering."

"Uh. Just a minute, Mr. Merkle" said the president. There was the sound of one or two muted remarks and some jingling, as though the president might be getting out coins. "The penny and the dime, is that right?"

"Yes sir."

"Now your suggestion is that we *change* the design of the dime to be more like that of the penny?"

Merkle looked uncomfortable and somehow saddened. "No. No, I was just thinking that in terms of *emphasis*—I mean, with the investigations and so on, and then your speech about faith—I was thinking that it might be more close to—well no, Mr. President, what I really wanted to say, now, is that we're going ahead with today's run." There was a pause, and Merkle got the impression that somewhere, faraway, at the other end or the line, the president was actually studying the coins. "I don't say that everybody notices it right away," Merkle said. "I mean, for example, a person in a foreign country will look closely at a coin, and probably even be thinking something about the country while he's doing it, but I think at home you more or less take a coin for—I mean, I doubt if I would have noticed myself except that it's part of my work, you see, I have to look at the different plates a lot, for flaws and so on, and then there are these big photographs on the wall."

"Yes," said the president evenly, "I think I see what you mean. In fact, I'm sure I see what you mean . . . I can only say we are doing the best we can."

"Well," said Merkle, "that's all I wanted to say. I mean, we've got a pretty good dime die in the C-8, it's sort of like the penny. I've seen some trial runs of it and they're all right. It's not like the C-3, of course, but it's a straight, clear cut—it's more like the penny."

"No," said the president, and Merkle had to strain to hear, "we—we don't want it like the penny."

"All, right, Mr. President, we're going ahead with the regular run then."

"Yes. Yes, of course."

"Good-bye, sir."

"Good-bye."

Downstairs, it was chaotic. Hot, noisy. Everywhere the molten silver fell in luminous, blade-thin streaks.

"What's the matter with you?" asked Harry crossly.

"Nothing," said Merkle.

"Who was that you were kowtowing to on the phone? 'Yes sir, no sir.'"

"I was talking to the president. I telephoned him."

"*Oh?*" said Harry, making a silly face. "And what did you tell the president?"

"I told him we were going ahead with the run," said Merkle.

—1950S

Fixing Up Ert

One of the creepiest guys in the world—I'm fairly sure about this: I mean, I know, for example, that he was the creepiest guy in our office (which, believe you me, was choc-a-bloc full)—was a guy named Ertegun Barff, doubtless shortened from something more nauseating, something even more attuned to his actual personality and heinous mien. Gangling would be a descriptive word of supreme flattery for the Ert; he was your traditional "six foot, two, eyes of blue"—although he was never actually seen at this height, so hideously craven was the slouch of his pinched shoulders, tapering up absurdly from his giant lard-ass, making up, no doubt, the bulk of his weight, which "varied" (he actually told me this one time, the self-centered prick) "between 130 and 132." Worse still, he wore those rimless glasses made out of thick plastic—and, in his all-too-frequent moments of lascivious reverie, he would snatch them off to rub with great urgency against his Hawaiian-print necktie, chortling, drooling, coughing phlegm all the while in what purported to be a form of laugh. His teeth, black with the rot of 10,000 *Baby Ruths*, jutted out crazily, like those of some weirdly mutated rodent—an Ichabod Crane with halitosis and a constant hard-on. He is the only person I have ever heard of (except for the late, great Bob Wadlow) who wore a size-14 shoe—while his hands, *paper* thin and *paper* white, like the rest of his body (cadaverous), seemed to flutter about his person, out of control, removing his glasses for no reason, caressing his legs, picking his nose, fingering his armpits, massaging his crotch, etc., etc., ad A-rab nauseam.

And yet it is *none* of these so-called traits, either singly or in gross combo, that led to the negative conclusion of yrs tly regarding the Ert. Indeed, I have never spoken or thought badly of a person due to his infirmities, either physical or mental; in fact, I count among my closest friends many persons who are so totally . . . well, no need to labor the point, "tooting one's whistle," as it were. Suffice it to say that when the old jug of compassion was being passed around up there, a certain *auteur* of our mutual acquaintance was not jerking off behind the door or otherwise playing the donkey-man. No, the alienating thing about this Ertegun, the basis for my low opinion, was simply his complete and profound shittiness—a shittiness, to the best of my knowledge, without parallel, and most flamboyantly apparent, if I may cite an example or two, in his senseless and authoritarian attitude regarding: *one*, my punctuality; *two*, the time and duration of my lunch hours; *three*, ditto my coffee (or, in some cases, "tea," hah, hah) breaks; and *four*, last though not by any means least, the old *wrapville*. I use the filmmakers' expression wrapville because I was at the time infatuated with the cinema, and the phrase "OK, boys, it's a *wrap!*" is used the world over to designate the end of the working day. The nature of our business (a crooked stockbrokerage—not actually crooked, in any heavy Watergate sense, just very slimy) was such that the working day ended, *gong*, at three P.M., with the closing of the grand old New York Stock Exchange, whereupon it was the duty of us *younger staffers* there at Davis, Fishbein, Carsten and Rowe to "tally up"—an antiquated bit of sordid and time-wasting nonsense involving such credit-and-debit ledger entries, à la Bob Cratchit, as might reflect the stock sales of the day; then these were checked against the grand totals.

The reason I say this was nonsense is that there already existed an unerring computerized version of the day's transactions. In the more than two years they had been using this system, it had never made a mistake; yet we were required to tally up our individual sales and purchases on an ordinary Mickey Mouse adding machine and see if they matched those of the boss computer. They always did.

As a rule, I can stand still with the best of them, like the proverbial Pavlovian dog, for the grotesque absurdities that are the warp and woof of daily life. On occasion, however, I just cannot hack it—or, in the words of the late, great Al Camus, "*Je m'emmerde.*" Such were my sentiments on a certain midsummer's day when, not feeling too well, I suggested, in the most artfully tact and reasonable way, that I might put off doing my tally until the following morning—and no harm to come because of it. Yet, despite all manner of persuasion, cajolery—indeed, downright groveling—the gross Ert, consummate asshole that he was, remained unmoved . . . except for an irrepressible sadistic glitter in his watery-blue fishlike eyes.

"You know the rules, Wilson," he said, "and the sooner you finish your tally, the sooner you can leave." Then he gave a lascivious grin, went into his glasses-polishing number and added, "What's the matter—got some hot nooky lined up for this afternoon?"

He had the habit of eavesdropping on my telephone conversations—not actually on the line but trying to make what he could of it by listening to my end and surmising the rest. So, in turn, I had started confounding him: I'd be talking to a young lady, for example—an innocuous conversation in subdued tones, aware that the Ert was straining to overhear—and then, when we said goodbye, I would ease the disconnect down with my finger and simulate a continuance of the conversation, hushed and secret. "Huh . . . oh, yeah, right . . . yeah, well, it was really, uh, *fantastic*, wasn't it?" I would squirm a bit and shoot a wink to Ert. "How many times did you, uh, you know, uh, *come?*" (Pause, soft whistle) "Oh, wow, baby, outa sight . . . yeah, well, I knew it was going *good*, but, wow. . . ." Later he would press me for details. Like most fastidious and puritanical types, he had a secret obsession for every bestial lust conceivable. *Sucking*, naturally, was quite high on his list of mind-bending taboos.

"Say, that girl you were talking to . . ."

"Yes, Ert?"

"Does she, uh, take it, you know . . . ?" He'd grin grotesquely, rolling his eyes and darting his tongue in and out of his cadaverous mouth—more in an approximation, or so it seemed to me, of clit-lick than of cock-suck. In any case, there was no doubt about what he intended, so sometimes I would give him a taste, maybe even spicing it up just a bit:

"Hey, now, you know it's funny you should ask that, because I would say, pound for- pound, she gives just about *the best head in the city*." And I might go on to describe her "fabulous ice-cube job," wherein she would have a small, round ice cube in each cheek, which, at the instant of climax, she would press firmly against the member with both hands.

"Huh?" Ert would query, knotting his roach brow in a show of Stone Age consternation. "What the heck for?"

"What for?" I feigned heavy surprise at his ignorance. "Why, to sustain ejaculation, of course! It's an Oriental technique. You see, the way it works is, the ice up against your cock acts like what they call a *repressant*—Christ, I've had orgasms that lasted for more than *three minutes!*"

"You're kidding."

"I swear to God! *Enormous . . . majestic . . . spurts* for three full minutes! And, what's more, you don't lose your erection, you can just keep going!"

"You mean . . . make her take it . . . in the *mouth* again?"

"In the *mouth*, in the *ear*, in the *flared nostril.* . . . No, man, the *second* time you really give it to her! Right between those incredible, smooth, bare, warm, rounded . . . luscious legs! The second time . . . *you fuck her brains out!*"

"*Haw!*" A manic guffaw from the Ert, followed by an almost spastic launch into his cough-polish-scratch-snort number.

It was during this period that I developed an inordinate love of *movies*. I decided it was my destiny not to be a stock-trading specialist in copper but to be a filmmaker—a *great* filmmaker—a sort of Fellini-Bergman-Bertolucci conglomerate. I was prepared to train rigorously to meet the exacting demands of my art; I was ready, as they say, "to pay my dues"—part of which, naturally, meant *seeing* as many films as possible. Now, it is nigh on impossible to give a fair viewing to a 90-minute film, *and* get something to eat, on a lousy one-hour lunch break. Ert was well aware of this, make no mistake, but he seemed to take an actual pleasure in reporting any tardiness on my part to Phil Davis—the president's son (a rabid Anglophile and another ultra-asshole)—who would, in turn, give me a sharp dressing down, along with thinly disguised ("I'll tell you one thing, laddie, we can bloody well muddle through without your services, if needs be!") threats to my tenure. It was also about this time that I made acquaintance with the Duchess Marleton—and a *gin-u-wine* duchess she was, too (if one may put stock in pesky *Burke's Peerage*)—widow to the late duke of same domain, and a very curious woman, indeed. She was about fifty-three (exactly fifty-three, if more stock is put in the *Peerage*), a tall woman, rapier-thin, with gaunt, assertive features—a veritable paragon of English aristocracy; you could practically see the blue blood coursing rampant beneath her skin of parchment white. It had fallen my lot to deliver certain stock certificates to her home and to pick up certain proxies.

"She's a bit eccentric," young Davis said, "but she's one of our best clients, so don't try running any of your bloody weirdo numbers on her."

He had no idea, of course, what he was saying; he was that way, would often say something just because he liked the sound of it. But I never bothered to argue the point. "Right and double-right," I would say, and get on with it.

So I went there after work—Park Avenue in the 70s—very swanky (two doormen) and very secure (three video monitors in the entrance, one scanning the fire escape, one in the elevator and one on the back door).

The duchess occupied the penthouse—a two-story affair, its vast living room looming upward toward a cathedral-like ceiling high above, and furnished (*totally*, as far as I could tell) in *white*. And therein her oddness: a consuming obsession with *purity*, beginning with the magnificent expanse of deep-pile white Angora carpet, like an unbroken snowfield. The chairs and divans were covered with ermine, the tables were white marble, alabaster, ivory, pearl—*everything* was white.

"Duchess Marleton?" I asked, after she'd opened the door; she stood looking at me for a moment, as though I were some sort of extreme weirdo—although, in actual fact, I was of quite smart appearance. But I silently cursed creep Davis for not having apprised me of the white scene, since I could have worn my supersmart *Our Man in Havana* white linen. *She* was in white, you can bet your sweet ass—long white satin, with lots of diamonds and pearls.

"Would you remove your shoes," she said, "before stepping on the rug?" and she indicated several pairs of paper sandals (*white*, naturally) neatly arranged next to the door.

"Certainly," I replied easily, determined not to let this bit of the unexpected spoil things between us. I stepped inside and onto a small vinyl mat, also white and immaculate, tucked my briefcase under one arm, adroitly slipped out of my right shoe and into the sandal, switched briefcase to the other arm and repeated same.

Then I gave her my best smile. "Wilson," I said, extending my hand, "Larry Wilson."

Almost imperceptibly, she recoiled. "I beg your pardon," she said in a toneless voice, with no change of expression. "I am not permitted."

What a weirdo! It turned out that her preoccupation with white was merely part of an extraordinary fetish regarding *hygiene*. Like Howard Hughes and Herman Wouk, she believed (no doubt rightly so) that germs were absolutely everywhere, and she would not risk the contamination of a handshake.

She led me to a table, where I waited, standing, while she signed the proxies. Before she finished, the phone rang and she answered it. After a moment, she said into the phone, "Wait. I'll take it upstairs," and she pressed the HOLD button, hung up and went upstairs. But, during her brief conversation in my presence, I had learned that today (Thursday) was her servant's day off, and when she left the room, I had a quick look at the phone number and made a note of it: The nucleus of an idea was taking shape.

Nothing of further interest occurred that evening. I guess we were not exactly each other's types. About two weeks later, though, it again fell my lot to deliver documents to the duchess. It was on a Wednesday, but I postponed it—decided to wait until the next day, Thursday, the servant's day off.

After the big gong, at three P.M., I was back in the office, doing my tally. Ert was there, of course, as zealously crummy as ever, watching me like a sick hawk.

At about four, I feigned a phone call—dialing, then disconnecting with an unobtrusive finger press, cupping my hand over the mouthpiece, talking *sotto voce extremus*, glancing anxiously about, squirming, chortling nervously, massaging my crotch, doing a full Ert and covertly watching his reaction. He was plenty interested, all right. When I finished, I gave a wag of the head and a deep sigh. "Wow," I murmured as though very privately, "that chick's *too much*."

The hideous Ert was all attention. He leered, grinning, snorting and coughing, spittle flying. "Another hot tomato, Wilson? Hah!"

"This one you wouldn't believe," I said. "I mean, I've had some fabulous suck in my time, but *this* chick . . . *wow*." I did a quick replay of my incredulity, the old wag of head, etc.

Ert wanted to be ultracool about not expressing excessive interest, but he gave himself away by momentarily not being able to find his voice and, at the same time, nearly falling out of his chair. "What's . . . er, uh . . ." He faltered and took another tack: "How does she *do* it?"

"*Per-fectly,*" I said, in measured tones, "It is *absolutely perfect*."

This must have conjured up something pretty weird in the mind's eye of the Ert. "Haw!" he guffawed and started picking his nose wildly.

"The thing is," I went on. "I can't make it tonight. I have to visit my dad at the hospital." I gave him a searching and formulative look. "You know, if *you* . . ." Then I shook my head in a gesture of dismissal. "No, she's too far out for you."

"Huh?"

"You see, when she gets in one of her *moods*—a 'sucky mood,' she calls it—well, she has simply *got* to give head and lots of it. Anyone or anything, and there's no stopping her. I mean, *you* could go in my place. . . . No, I guess not."

Ert stared at me, jaws agape, a thin glitter of saliva (as God is my witness!) stretching from left corner of mouth to bottom of chin. "Well, uh," he said, hesitating, "what makes you think she's . . . 'too far out' for me?"

"She's a perfectly normal woman," I began, "and, in fact, a really *superior* woman—except for this thing about sucking cock, whenever these moods hit her."

The great Ertegun was not put off by it. "Haw! That's OK with me!"

"Yeah, but . . . there's something else," I admitted.

"Huh? What?"

"I don't know how familiar you are with psychology, but she has what's called a 'catalyst syndrome.' In other words, it takes a certain *thing* to make it all right for her, and from there on she's fine."

"What is it?"

"Well, it's . . . what you have to do first is . . ." I faltered, searching for the *mot juste*, or the courage to say it. I couldn't. "Naw, it's too . . . I just don't think you could handle it."

"Haw! You just try me!"

I took a deep breath. "OK, this is the way it comes down. After she lets you in, she'll make some excuse and leave the room. While she's gone, what you have to do is go to the middle of the room, drop your trousers, squat down and take a big *crap*."

"Huh?" The Ert gave me his Neanderthal agog look, "You gotta be kiddin'."

"Nope, that's it. When she comes in, she'll pretend not to notice it, then she'll walk over and start copping your joint."

"Huh?"

"Yeah, she'll come right over and start *sucking* you. You don't have to do a thing, just lie back and relax."

"You mean you can, uh, *fix me up*?"

"Yeah, that's it, Ert, I think I can *fix you up*. The thing is, can you *handle* it?"

His grimace was the stuff nightmares are made of. "*Can do!*"

I handed him the big manila envelope.

"Park Avenue, huh?" His hand eased down to his crotch.

"That's right, very swanky—and all *white*, everything. Wait'll you see the fantastic rug."

"What's in the envelope?"

"Proxies and stock certificates. She's a client."

"Holy cow."

"Yeah, far out, huh? OK, now when she answers the door, tell her who you are, where you're from, that the other man couldn't make it tonight, blah, blah, blah, and she'll look you over, and then if she asks you to 'take off your shoes,' you'll know you're in."

"Take off my shoes?"

"Right. That's part of her kick, get the guy's shoes off, and it's a code way of letting you know she's *ready*. And then if she asks you to put on a pair of paper sandals that are near the door, that means *double-suck*."

"Yeah? That what you got? *Double-suck?*"

"Better believe it. Now, then, she'll take you over to a table, where you sit down and open the envelope. Then she'll make some excuse to leave the room—and the minute she's upstairs, that's when you do your thing. Right?"

"Can do!"

"Great! Now, one final and *extremely important* thing. *Punctuality*. Be there at *exactly eight o'clock*—not a minute before, not a minute after. She's got this thing about *punctuality*. I think she used to be a math major. One minute either way might blow the whole thing."

I had a look at his crappy, ostentatious wristwatch—or "chronograph," as he called it—with its three or four superfluous dials. "Is that thing accurate?"

"Huh? You gotta be kiddin'. A hundred and fifty bucks this cost me, it *better* be accurate!"

I did a quick time check by phone. Right on the button. Then I made sure it was wound.

"OK, I guess that's it," I said. "Any questions?"

The incredible Ert did have one. "Say—" He broke off momentarily to cough and splutter, leering grotesquely. I casually dabbed the profusion of spittle from my left cheek.

"Think I oughtta take along some jelly in case she wants to get pumped in the ass? Haw!"

"Uh, yeah . . . yeah, that's darn good thinking, Ert. Better safe than sorry, right?" I gave him a cheerful wink of conspiracy and he nodded with extraordinary vigor.

"*Can do! Haw!*"

At precisely 8:03, in the relaxed atmosphere of my posh and comfy flat, I telephoned the duchess.

"Hullo?"

Doubtless I flattered myself in thinking she might possibly remember my voice, so monumental was her unswerving egocentricity, but I took the precaution of placing a crumpled handkerchief in front of the mouthpiece.

"Duchess Marleton?"

"Yes, who's speaking?"

"It's Police Lieutenant Hank Barrow of the Ninth Precinct. Is there a young man there from the brokerage firm of Davis, Fishbein, Carsen and Rowe?"

"Why . . . yes."

Sotto voce: "Duchess Marleton, will you please take this call on another phone—I've something rather confidential to tell you."

Voce equally *sotto:* "Yes. Of course . . ."

I heard the HOLD button click and waited. Ten seconds, eleven, twelve and she was there, quite anxious. "Yes? What is it? What's wrong?"

"Duchess Marleton, I've no time to explain now, but will you please describe this person."

"*Describe* him? What do you mean, *describe* him?"

"His appearance—what does he look like?"

She seemed rather indignant. "I didn't *notice!* Why on earth should I?" A pause. "Yes, extremely *common,* that's how he looks—extremely common. Vulgar. Ugly. *Hideous,* really."

"Is he Caucasian?"

"Is he what?"

"*White,* is he *white?*"

"*White?* Yes, of course he's white! Good God, what *is* this all about?"

"Will you please see what he's doing at this very moment—it's quite important. I assure you."

I heard her immense sigh of exasperation as she put down the phone and moved toward the balustrade—the balustrade overlooking that vast expanse of immaculate white Angora pile. Silence. Then a distant, but superaudible, scream—a wail, a shriek, indeed a veritable *howl* of shock and maddened outrage, a *screech* of Homeric dimensions—and I gently cradled the phone and began carefully considering my next move.

—1975 *Oui*

Blue Movie
Outline for Novel

Boris Adrian, known to his friends as B. (and often referred to as King B.—as in King *Bee*), began making films when he was sixteen . . . using a rented camera and processing the film himself. He is an artist, and his work has always been the strongest factor in his life. Although, until recent years, his films were regarded as strictly art-house fare, he ironically finds himself at thirty-nine (which is where the story begins) at the very top of the industry. Of his last eight pictures, six have won the Golden Lion at Cannes, Venice, etc., and all have been smash box-office. His present power-status could only be compared to an exaggeration of a Bergman-Fellini composite. When stars, any stars, are invited to appear in a film of his, they don't ask "how much?" or "what's the part?," they simply start celebrating. He is very likable, and very good-looking, but he has seen too much of life, and a certain weariness, or bemused detachment, has set in—which only his interest in his work seems to relieve.

Harry Krassman, fifty-five, is a film producer, entrepreneur, and general hustler on a big scale. His schemes are as grandiose as they are sometimes absurd—such as his plan to beat Beverly Hills real estate prices and zoning laws by buying just enough land (2 sq. feet on each side of the hills) to anchor cables in, then string (condemned) cable cars across the canyon, with the idea that those could be made into a restaurant of the most exclusive private-dining-room type. However, no matter how high the fall, he always bounces back, because resilience is his forte. Harry's incredible drive and his compulsive deviousness are in sharp contrast to B.'s own laconic security and vague straightforwardness.

On several occasions the films of B. have been banned in certain places as "obscene," or have been otherwise interfered with. This, and the natural considerations inherent in his work, have given rise to his own private concern with the question: At what point does the aesthetically erotic, indefinitely extended, become offensive? Not offensive to the public, of course, but to himself.

As it happens, the only time he mentions this speculative notion is, by chance, in the presence of Harry Krassman. Harry turns up a couple of days later with his scheme for making a two-million-dollar pornographic movie. His plan is based on the fact that *Liechtenstein*, like Monaco, is a sovereign power, i.e., its internal affairs cannot be interfered with from without. Liechtenstein is a tiny (62 sq. mi.) country between Austria and Switzerland, with a population of about 11,000, German-speaking, and predominately Roman Catholic. Because of its rugged Alpine situation, it is relatively inaccessible—and for this reason, and the absence of interest otherwise, tourists have never shown an inclination to go there . . . although on occasion the government has attempted to attract them (building a casino, baths, etc.). The revenue of Liechtenstein is lower per capita than any of its neighbors. What Harry proposes is that the film be made there, and, under the protection of the government, *shown* there, exclusively. His reasoning is that people will come, especially tourists, from all over Europe to see this film, by the world's greatest filmmaker, which is to be seen there and only there. If the film, when completed, is thought by the authorities to be "immoral," then the populace of Liechtenstein can be protected from it, just as the residents of Monte Carlo are protected from the casino, by being refused entrance, and the same sort of security measures (presentation of passport, etc.) will prevail. In any case, the populace will not object to the presence of the film because (1) it is the work of a major artist, and (2) business will be booming. An airstrip will be built, a new hotel, new restaurant, shops, etc., to accommodate those staying over. The casino and opera house will be reopened. Outside capital will be attracted. Arrangements for group charter flights will be made with American Express, Cooks, etc. Liechtenstein will become as much a part of standard itinerary as a visit to Chartres. A social must. The revenue of the country will be increased ninety-fold.

In a conference between the Prince, lawyers, the professor of economics of the University of Liechtenstein, and a representative of the Church, these things are discussed and deemed to be true. (Note: this aspect of the story, and the financing of the film itself, are treated with the most exacting realism—that is to say, at no point is any detail, technical or otherwise, glossed over or ignored, so that the absolute feasibility of the undertaking can never be doubted.)

It is to be kept in mind that throughout the entire project, Harry is seeing it as a great moneymaker (admission price is $35) whereas B.'s interest is in the solution of the problem as stated, or which might be restated as: Is it possible to make an all-out erotic film on an acceptable (his own) level of aesthetics? In the big love scene in *Les Amants*, for example, the man's head slides down out of the frame. Why not follow his head? How far?

The film is called *The Faces of Love* and consists of episodes, each treating a different form of love—idyllic, profane, homosexual, incestuous, maternal, etc.

The very beautiful and internationally famous European actress, known simply as "Khaki," who happens also to be a notorious dyke (and proud of it), is signed for the lead in the lesbian episode. In a press conference she announces, with defiant pride, that not for all the money in the world would she consider using a stand-in for the intimate love scenes called for in the script. She even goes further, to Harry's embarrassment, to say that she has "always had zee eye" for Pamela Mills, the angelic English actress who is to play the weaker of the two. Khaki is the first to arrive. She and B. are old friends, having made many award-winning pictures together. They drive through the countryside, while he tells her about the part. At a passing vista, Khaki becomes ecstatic. They are near the place where she made love to a girl for the first time. They leave the car and walk through a wooded grove to a promontory of Alpine splendor. They sit beneath a gigantic pine and B. continues to tell her about the picture. A sylvan scene, and Khaki, in the warmth and camaraderie she feels for B., asks if he wants to make love to her (they never have, and she has not made it with a man for many years). B. smiles (wearily) declining, but he kisses her and gently brings her head to rest in his lap—where she very soothingly sucks him, while he strokes her hair fondly; but he is thinking about . . . *Grace*.

Grace Sanders is the world's highest-paid actress—an American Marilyn Monroe–type, or more specifically a sort of composite of Grace Kelly–Eva Marie Saint–Doris Day. She wants more than anything to be identified with Art, and to be taken "seriously" as an actress. She has been studying for some time, of course, at Actor's Studio. Naturally she is quite overwhelmed with joy at being offered a role in a film by the director she idolizes. She comes over at once, dropping previous commitments, etc. She is somewhat ambivalent, however, when she learns more about the role—a very serious one indeed, that of a blond negrophile nympho, an American heiress, who lives in North Africa for the single purpose of making it with as many gigantic Negroes as possible. It is a role which calls for "quite a few 2-shots," as B. smilingly puts it, and, in fact, a breakdown reveals four sequences of completely unbridled lovemaking, with four different giant blacks, and a final "orgy scene" in which she is spectacularly ravished by three Watusi tribesmen.

Her own natural feminine modesty causes her some disquiet about the requirements of the role, but she puts this down to naïveté and her secret fears that she may not recognize Art when she sees it. Her husband and agent, however, have a more definite reaction. They come over to find out what's going on, and when they do they blow their stacks. So that Grace is very much on the horns of a dilemma—she owes a great deal to her agent, and she certainly does not want to lose her husband; on the other hand, it is almost unthinkable to refuse this opportunity of working for B., which, in her mind, is everything she's been striving for, the chance of a lifetime, etc. (B., it should be noted, has a bemused contempt for the unquestioning adulation he gets, and for those who bestow it, and also for the overblown "seriousness" professed by Method actors—so that, for example, when he is explaining the part to Grace, and that the lovemaking scenes will be filmed in complete detail, he gently taunts her by saying that he supposes they can use a stand-in for some of it. "I mean, I doubt if they taught you how to make love at the Studio," he says with a mischievous smile.)

Before her husband and agent arrive, Grace's quandary is whether or not to actually get laid on camera—since B. has insinuated that it might be an artistic cop-out not to—or to use a double for the shots which show actual penetration, etc. With their arrival, however, the question becomes whether or not she will be in the movie at all. Grace, it has been previously brought out, is often high-strung and temperamental, has, in fact, suffered several nervous breakdowns in the past. So this is an especially difficult period for her because of her genuine ambivalence as to what decision to make. In the end it is her husband and agent who prevail, finally convincing her that no girl in her right mind would undertake such a role. When she informs B., he quietly puts her down as a Philistine, cornball, stupid cunt, etc., and with terrible effectiveness. Before she leaves, she learns that her replacement is to be Jennifer Lawrence, who is, in several respects, her arch rival with a growing reputation for "seriousness." Thus the devastation is complete, and Grace does away with herself, in a manner ironically feminine, by eating all of her lead-based cosmetics and then electrocuting herself with her hair dryer.

The major part of the story deals with the actual filming, where some amusing things happen. During a lovemaking scene, for example, B.: "Cut it . . . listen, Larry, it looked like you came then. Now let's take it from the top again, and just keep up a kind of steady, rhythmic . . . what? You *did* come? Oh Christ

. . . Okay (calls out to Makeup Dept.) Joe! Tissues, tissues! (pause) And bring that splint . . . yes, *of course* the black one!" Etc.

In terms of theme, a satiric line is developed against the hero-worship given (in this case) directors, and another line treating Method acting. The principle interest, however, should be in the characters and in the events which go to make up a project of this nature.

The film is finally completed and is shown as planned. It is even more success-ful than anyone had hoped, both critically and commercially. Certain groups, however, are outraged by its very existence, and the pressure mounts—chiefly from the Catholic Church. They organize an undercover "posse" of Vatican toughs, who, through a complex intrigue of bribery and cunning, gain access to the existing negative and two prints, and seize them in a dramatic 4 A.M. raid. A terrific skirmish ensues between the priests and the movie crowd, the men of the cloth finally gaining the upper hand, and absconding with the films in the Vatican helicopter. Thus do they "capture" the film (like getting Eichmann in South America) and impound it in the lower vault (the so-called Vault of Saint Anthony). Ironically, then, the Vatican becomes the only place where the film may be seen—if the rumor is true that it is, in fact, occasionally shown, as a sort of "exercise in temptation." In any case, certain privileged visitors—those with access to the balustrade overlooking the inner court—have reported see-ing curious processions moving slowly towards, or away from, the lower vault. Some such reports have come from persons who are known to be authorities on Vatican protocol and observances, and who say these processions do not fall within any prescribed practice. They can add little more, having observed the phenomenon from a distance; and almost nothing is to be deduced from the demeanor of the procession itself—moving slowly, almost contemplatively, faces shadowed by their ceremonial hoods, only the dim glitter of their eyes twinkling.

—*1966*

Letters

Dear Ms.

Editor
Ms.
370 Lexington Ave.
New York, N.Y.

20 November 1972

Dear *Ms.*:

Since the letters you see fit to print are so flagrantly and one-sidedly selective ("self-serving" is, I believe, the expression), I doubt this will find its way into those columns; we shall see. In any case, during your own innermost and private (and, needless to say, *unpublished*) quest for *the truth*, libbywise, you might consider the following suggestion: namely, that it is naïve in the extreme for women to expect to be regarded as equals by men (despite all lip service to the contrary) so long as they persist in a subhuman (*i.e.*, animal-like) behavior during sexual intercourse. I'm referring, as you doubtless know, to the outlandish *panting, gasping, moaning, sobbing, writhing, scratching, biting, screaming* conniptions, and the seemingly invariable "*Oh, my god . . . oh, my god . . . oh, my god*" all so predictably integral to the pre-, post-, *and* orgasmic stages of intercourse. Surely you're aware that such *extremes* of "expression" cannot fail to produce an ultimate and profound sense of alienation in the partner, and/or witness, to same.

I would further suggest to you that until women are able to exercise a modicum of self-control and restraint, and to maintain a semblance of *human dignity* during orgasm (clitoral, deep-vaginal, multiple, or whatever), they shall *never* gain from men the sort of respect they desire (again, the abundance of lip service to the contrary notwithstanding). Can you *seriously* imagine a man placing his confidence, his vote, or indeed any measure of real responsibility in the hands of someone he has just seen or heard (or *felt*) engaged in a *nail-digging, teeth-grinding, eyes-rolling, toes-curling, half-*

fainting demonstration more suited to the kennel, or *lair,* than to the bed-room. This is an "act of love" and, by definition, should be one of heartfelt tenderness and genuine concern. There is a considerable difference, I might add, between a *show of passion* and the *rutting of a wildcat.*

Yours sincerely,
Terry Southern
New York, N.Y.

Letter to Lenny Bruce

As Terry began working on the MGM movie The Loved One *with co-writer Christopher Isherwood and director Tony Richardson, he wanted Lenny Bruce to appear as the grotesque, drunken "Dear Abby" columnist Guru Brahmin.*

31 July 1964

Len Big Bopper—

Enclosed please find cine script by yrs truly and a crafty old fruit. It is our very real hope that you will consider the role of the GURU BRAHMIN— which can be altered and grooved up infinitely, natch, to your own outlandish specifications.

You will be rubbing shoulders, Len (if not, in fact, pelvic regions), with such star and feature players as: Sir John ("Jack") Gielgud (Francis), Jonathan Winters (Harry and The Dreamer), Rod Steiger (Joyboy), Liberace (Starker), Dana Andrews (Gen Schmuck), Keenan Wynn (Immigration Officer), and a host of other show-stoppers of equally curious persuasions. Director is tip-top Tony R., the oscar-copping madcap, and as I say, chief scripter is yrs tly.

Perhaps you are wondering about so-called material recompense. Well, Len, we have two schemes going here—under one, you can take your pay in straight top-drawer starlet sugar-scoop; under the other it is one bill (*big* bill, Len) per day. The GURU's lines appear on pages as per follows: 75, 76, 93, 119, 120, 141, 142, and 143. Please note that scene #131 gives you an excellent shot at the fantastic winner of our beautiful young girl star, whose name I will not reveal to you at this moment due to its effect of instant shoot-off.

We'll want to move fast on this one, Len—for reasons I shall explain later. Please let me hear from you by return of post.

Yrs. as per,

T.

Letter to the Editor of National Lampoon *aka Hard Corpse Pornography*

During the height of the Vietnam War, Michael O'Donoghue, the late editor of National Lampoon, *asked Terry to submit pieces to the magazine. O'Donoghue published this letter under the banner "#1 in a Series of Correspondence with Distinguished Authors."*

25 Jan 1972

My dear O'Don:

Many thanks for your kind letter—which, through curious misdirection, has only just come to hand. Your 'Nothing Sacred' issue sounds like a real winner, and I greatly appreciate the generous invitation to contribute. I should be most delighted to do so, but unfortunately have nothing suitable at the mo. The piece I'm presently working on is more or less straight journalism and would hardly suit your purpose—which I presume (correct me if I'm wrong) tilts more towards the 'satiric'. It is a piece, however, not wholly devoid of interest, and one which might well (and hopefully!) find a place in future pages of your good mag—since, though completely factual, it is not without an element of grim irony. Briefly then, it involves an organization of Vietnam veterans, of which you may or may not have heard (due to its somewhat clandestine nature), most often referred to as 'The SGR'. The SGR came into being, evidently, through the preservation and extension (in some cases, elaboration) of certain practices among the older members of a number of specific advanced field-units in the Nam. When these units, or their individual members, returned Stateside, they formed these small, highly secretive, groups, or "sharcoots" as they're called (in an apparent corruption of the French '<u>charcouterie</u>') and continued the nefarious and ritualized practices evolved in the Nam. The SGR, or "rimmers" as they call themselves less formally, is comprised of normal healthy American lads (or so they would appear) who "got hooked", as they explain it, on the rather unsavory (in my view) act of "stiff-gook rimming"—i.e., tonguing dead Cong assholes with such incredible fervor and abandon as to finally lose consciousness (and "the gamier, the better" according to them). Michael, you and I do not know each other too well, but I can assure you I am not, I believe, a particularly squeamish person, and yet I must say in all frankness that to witness their dervish-like gluttony when working Cong-rim is a mind-bender of considerable weight. Though developed, as I say, in the paddies of the Nam, they continue to practice this heinous 'art'—if, indeed, it may be so called—right here in heartland of USA, receiving packages of "cut-outs" as they're dubbed, straight from the deltas of the Nam, often via 'Diplomatic Pouch' (so highly placed are various elements of the member-ship). Mike, they say the stench of one of these so-called "rim-pacs" has an actual <u>impact</u> that will send an E-meter needle right through the side of the goddam box! Well, anyhoo . . . if you'd be interested seeing completed piece on the SGR (including action-pix of a <u>fairly</u> compromising nature) please let me know. Meanwhile all best for continued success of your good mag.

[Signed T. Southern]

National Lampoon, 1972
Reprinted by permission of *National Lampoon.*

A Letter to the Editor: Stiff Gook Rimming

Dear Sir:

I realize that *National Lampoon* is basically a "humor" magazine, or at least is so intended. Moreover, I'm quite aware that humor is a fairly *subjective* phenomenon. I don't wish to suggest, therefore, that there are, or should be, *guidelines* as to what is or is not "funny." What you consider to be humorous, I may not—and vice versa. That is your right. The so-called "letter" regarding the SGR which appeared in your last issue, however, is quite another matter.

Sex in heterosexual relationships is quite straightforward and represents nothing more, nor less, than another manifestation of intimacy, and/or of love and affection. By extension and/or reversal, the same may be said of "rimming" in heterosexual relationships, as indeed in bi-sexual, or group-sexual, relationships. One of my former patients, a woman of 37, could achieve deep vaginal (multiple) orgasm *only* through "rimming"— i.e., being "rimmed" and simultaneously manipulating her clitoris (manually). This is not as unusual as it may at first appear. There are many cases, both in my own files, and in the experience of my colleagues, where ejaculation is achieved *exclusively* through "rimming"—in either the active or passive role. All well and good. The nature of the cases, however, which *you* have seen fit to describe with such merciless shocking revelation is of a different order—different in two fundamental regards:

(1) necrophilia is involved (consorting with the dead—an illegal act in itself) and (2) the quasi love-object (i.e., "Cong-rim") is that of an *enemy*, a *mortal* enemy. Now this must be regarded as a *fairly rare aberration*. I use the word "aberration" with certain misgiving; in clinical psychiatry we have come to take a rather broad view of what constitutes the 'norm' and what may be considered a deviation from it.

My personal experience, however, with a number of SGR cases (both socially and clinically) led me to believe that such persons are deeply disturbed. Consider the case of Lt. Col. E. Thornton (not his actual name) of Military Intelligence, 1st Corps. A brilliant and sensitive man in most respects, his avidity for Cong-rim was so extreme that he insisted on wearing them like jewelry, and forced the men in his command to weave them together in profusion to form huge garlands and necklaces. It was their very abundance (and of course great stench) that brought the practice to the attention of Division HQ.

In another case—that of Brigadier General of 29th Brigade S. Green (again not the actual name)—the subject had an unrelieved compulsion to use Cong-rim as an infant's pacifier, and indeed, could not sleep without one or more in his mouth through the night ("my little donuts" as he called them). So unrelenting was the habit that he was known by the petty officers as "Baby Cong Suck"—reflecting an attitude which led to instances of insubordination and, in consequence, over 30 summary court-martials.

A final word about the spuriousness of your so-called letter. It implies that SGR membership is limited to persons who have actually served in Vietnam. This is not strictly true. It is a fact, for example, that at least two of the most highly placed officials of the present administration are among those with the deepest involvement in the practice of Cong-rimming.

Indeed, one of them (who shall, of course, in professional confidence, remain nameless) has been a patient of mine for the past three years; he acquired the habit *prior to visiting the Nam*, and by his own account, *has never tasted "Cong-rim in the field."* He had, however, already exhibited a proclivity for relationships which were primarily anal, and in fact his initial exposure to Cong-rim occurred when he stumbled over a diplomatic-pouch choc-abloc full of rim-pacs in the V.I.P. annex of the White House mail room, where he had come in pursuit of what he termed a "dirt road affair" with one of the young black mail-boys. In any case, his conversion was immediate and total—so overwhelming became his obsession with rim of the Nam that he actually tried to *become* it, as indeed he continues to do— donning snug-fitting jump-suits made entirely of Cong-rim, meticulously stitched together by his Senior staffers. Then, after cavorting in an eccentric and tarantella-like manner, while the rim jump-suit, due to the disintegrating nature of decomposed flesh, begins gradually falling apart, he will turn on himself—somewhat in the manner of a wounded scorpion—in a grotesquely frenetic attempt to *devour* the rim-pac jump-suit entirely, while shrieking "*I'm a rotten gook asshole! I'm a rotten gook asshole!*" In fact with such outlandish frenzy does he pursue this end that he has acquired the nickname among more impressionable SGR members of "THE CRAZY GREEK GOOK ASSHOLE."

I hope this will help to clarify for you the phenomenon of Stiff Gook Rimming, and to indicate to some extent how odd and erroneous you were in your original account. Next time get your facts straight.

Yours truly,
Thomas A Harley, M.D.
Walter Reed General Hospital
Special Advisor to the President

Letter to George Plimpton
aka Sports-Death Fantasy

This piece was written in the '70s in response to a form letter from George Plimpton requesting submissions for the ultimate "sports-death fantasy."

My dear George

Many thanks for your very kind 'letter' [if, indeed, a scrap of ragscap in memeo may be so construed—in which case old values are not merely crumbling, but have actually buried us more dead than alive. If there *is* a god (type) in heaven, it is my one hope and prayer to same that your Dad was spared the sight or knowledge of that heinously gross format!]

What then, running a bit *short*, are you? A bit of the old skimp-oh-roo, is it? Well, I am pleased to say that a certain yrs tly is delighted, indeed *flattered*, to serve as 'FILLER'—that *you* may meet your professional obligations and continue to 'walk tall' in the Quality-Lit World which we both know and love so well. So let's just give this one a couple of strokes and see if we don't get what Big Bill Becker used to call 'a touch of the old tumescence'.

Now then, my own 'sports-death fantasy' has always seemed to me a bit odd and perhaps even somewhat impressionistic. From what I have been able to learn so far (through hypnosis and drug-recall sessions, including the usual truth-serums, E-Meter, polygraph and various lie-detector type tests) as to the origin of the fantasy, it seems to have stemmed from early visits to *China*—not your mainland China, mind, but your tiny offland China. This was during the wondrous halcyon days of the perennially unbeatable Little League team of Taiwan (unbeaten in over 3000 games, unscored on in almost as many).

I would go there each year—'just for the ride', you might say—in the company of Larry Rivers and Gore Vidal, who made this annual 'trip to our own little Mecca', as they called it, under the rather shabby (in my view) guise of 'scouting 13-year-old lads for the majors'.

While Gore and Lar were 'doing their thing' with the lads, a certain yrs tly was into—or shall we say *trying* to get into, hee-hee—something quite different (namely, reportage for one of the quality slicks—*Pubes*, it was, if memory serves) covering the highly touted, though short lived, 'Great Ice Ping Pong Tournement.' As sports buffs will recall, the sport did not differ from ordinary ping pong so much *en principe* as in the actual mechanics of the game—making use as they did of rounded ice-cubes instead of the conventional hollow plastic-balls, and using foam-rubber padding on both table and paddle surfaces to afford the necessary resilience for the bouncing cubes.

I was attending the 'Young Ladies Finals' when the incident in question occurred. The contestants, ages 15 to 21, were clad, ostensibly to give them 'the maximum in freedom of movement', in what can only be termed the 'scantiest attire'. In fact, there was a thinly veiled aura of *pure sexuality* surrounding the entire proceedings, so it did not come as a total surprise when I was approached by one of the 'Officials', a Mr. 'Wong Dong', if one may believe him, who, with a broad grin and a great deal of ceremonious bowing and scraping, asked if I would care to meet one of the competitors. "Very interesting," he insisted, "a top contender."

I agreed, and soon found myself in an open alcove with 'Kim', a most attractive girl of 18 or so—attractive except for what I first thought of as 'rather puffy cheeks'. I soon learned, however, that the 'puffiness' was caused merely by the presence and pressure of an ice-cube in each cheek— this being the technique of preparing the ice-balls ('*le preparation des boules*') for play, holding the cubes in the cheeks until they melted slightly to a roundness.

The girl seemed extremely friendly, and Mr. D. now asked to examine the cubes. "Ah," he said, beaming, when she produced them—two glittering golf-ball size pieces of ice—one in each upturned hand. "We have arrived at a propitious moment," he continued, turning to me again, "the *boules* are now of ideal proportion for . . . '*la grande exstase du boules du glace*'!"

Not entirely devoid of a certain worldliness, I had heard of the infamous 'ice-cube job' as it was commonly known—the damnable practise, in my view, of *fellatio interruptus*, or according to other sources, '*fellatio prolongata*'—whereby, at the moment of climax, the party rendering fellatio, with an ice-cube in each cheek, presses them vigorously against the member, producing a dramatic counter-effect to the ejaculation in progress. As I say, I was aware of the so-called '*extase du boule du glace*', but had never experienced it—nor, and I would be less than candid if I did not say so, was I particularly keen—though, of course, I did not wish to offend my host—who then spoke to the girl, in Chinese, before turning to me.

"It is arranged," he exclaimed happily. "Allow her to grasp and caress your genitalia." And returning the cubes to her mouth, she extended her hand in a manner at once both coy and compelling, and with a grace charming to behold. Even so, I was not prepared to respond to this gesture without first working up a bit of heft.

I adroitly stepped just beyond her reach, though quite without ostentation so as not to offend. "Perhaps we should, uh, wait," I said, glancing about the room as though wanting more privacy.

"Ah," observed Mr. D., with a most perceptive smile, "you shall be quite comfortable here, I assure you." And so saying, he drew closed a beaded curtain, and then stepped through it, bowing graciously as he departed.

Alone with Miss Kim I felt immediately more secure, and a slight, unobtrusive squeeze assured me that a fairly respectable tumess was near at hand.

"Very well, Miss Kim," I told her, "you may, uh, proceed . . ." which she did, with, I can assure you, the utmost art and ardor. We had been thus engaged for several moments, and I was just approaching a tremendous crescendo—indeed was actually into it, when the beaded veil was burst asunder and in rushed the two madcaps, Vidal and Rivers!

"Get cracking, you oafish rake!" shrieked Vidal with a cackle of glee and inserted two large amyl nitrate ampules, one in each of my nostrils, and then popped them in double quick order. Simultaneous to this, Miss Kim pressed with great vigor the two ice cubes against my pulsating member, and the diabolic Rivers injected a heady potion of Amphetamine laced with Spanish Fly into my templer vein. The confluence, and outrageous conflict, of these various stimuli threw my senses into such monstrous turmoil that I was sent reeling backwards as from the impact of an electric shock, torn from the avid embrace of the fabulous Miss Kim, who bounded after me in hotly voracious pursuit, screaming: "Wait! *L'exstase du boules du glace COMMENCE!*" I now lay supine as she swooped down to resume her carnivorous devastation, while around us, obviously themselves in the crazed throes of sense-derangement, Vidal and Rivers pranced and cavorted as though obsessed by some mad dervish or tarantella of the Damned! Thus, my monumental and unleashed orgasm, prolonged (throughout eternity it seemed!) by the pressure of the *boules,* and intensified beyond endurance by *drogues variees,* caused me to expire, in a shuddering spasm of delirium and delight. Ecstasy beyond all bearing! Death beyond all caring! "I die!" I shouted (as I still do when I relive the experience), ". . . *FULFILLED*!!!"

Of course I did not die (oh no, Vidal and Rivers had *other* plans!) and persuaded a newly arrived member of our party, the near legendary 'Dr. Benway' (who later gained certain prominence as author using the name William S. Burroughs) to administer certain so-called 'remedial elixirs' (the exact nature of which I have never ascertained) and brought me around. In any event, I continue to relive (almost nightly, in fact) the sensations of that most memorable experience.

yrs as per,
[signed] T.

Best to the fab missus.

Worm-ball Man

In the early '80s Terry sent a ten-page letter written on yellow legal pad to Nelson Lyon, his Saturday Night Live *collaborator. Three* National Enquirer–*type articles came attached. Nelson calls it "The Worm-ball Man Letter" and has shared it with many people. Terry issued clear instructions to Nelson about reading this letter: "Read* after *having read, and understood—repeat, understood—the news items."*

[Synopsis of articles and Terry's editorial notes:]

    1) HUMAN HEAD TRANSPLANTED ONTO PIG'S BODY: describes the testimony of a Dr. Lewis Collins, of New York, who claims to have seen the hybrid beast. "Nels, I happen to know Lou Collins (Jns Hopkins, '62) and he's quite an able chap, so I can vouchsafe." *In the article, Dr. Ruben Smith, surgeon from Los Angeles, is cited as having observed one of the successful "human head to animal" transplant operations in China. Terry writes:* "Nels, will you please check out Dr. Smith—knowing your almost pathological cynicism, you'll not rest until you've done so!!"

    2) GIANT 13-FOOT WORM STRANGLES BABY: concerns the giant "Gippsland" earthworm, and how one "crawled into the mouth of a six-month old baby . . . came out through her nose, and wrapped so tightly around the child's neck, the baby strangled to death."

    3) ALBINO FRIES 3 TIMES: contains the following exchange with a prison guard: Q: "Did you ever electrocute children?" A: "No, but we did this one fellow, Humpy Russ. Hunchbacked little fellow. His arms went way past his knees. He was 5 foot and weighted 95 pounds . . . Old Humpy's head was too small for it and he was down too low . . . It took us 3 times to do him."

[TO NELSON LYON:]

    The real thrust of the piece, of course, will be *story* and *character*, i.e., the personality and the electrocution of Little Humpy Russ. The image of these hefty Texans not being able to get little Humpy's head up into the electrode-cap, or to bend the cap down far enough for a snug fit, is pivotal to the swelling of the progress of this extraordinary scene, I think you'll agree.

They also try to bend the cap down to make *adequate* contact but are unable to do so. Nevertheless, they continue to 'hit the juice'—and each time there is a 'sizzling' and a 'bacon frying' smell. This one guy claimed that there was (is?) a "different smell" to what he called 'albino cracklins' and 'regular nigger fry'. This is the same guy who told me about the 'worm incident' and gave me the idea for telling the true story—you know, sort of Woodward-Bernstein style. Well, it seems that after the second time they 'hit the juice' and Little Humpy was still 'alive and kicking', these 13-foot worms started coming out of his nose and mouth, apparently up through his body, trying to escape the extreme frits-city situation, coming out, as I say, of his nose and mouth, engulfing his entire head until it (his head) was about five times its ordinary size and was what this guy described as a "huge worm ball."

So here you have this extraordinary image, of this five-foot albino person, whose head now is a 'huge worm-ball,' writhing about in the chair, and these Slim Pickens types, cursing and trying to bend the electric copper-cap down far enough to encase his worm-ball head. If that doesn't strike you as bizarre, Nels, then your tastes are just a bit too jaded for me, sir. In any case, the next thing that happens (and so far, incidentally, this is *all straight fact*) is that this friend (or at least acquaintance) of mine, Lou Collins ('Dr. Louis Collins') whom I have known (casually, granted) for about 12-15 years (I would say about as well as I know Tone Goodstone, or maybe Van Dyke Parks, that sort of thing, know what I'm saying?). Anyway, Lou Collins happens to be on the scene, having just come back from China and his whole weird head-transplant experience. Well, to make a long story short, Nels, one of the Texas guys gets so pissed off at the way things are going that he takes out his bowie knife and cuts off the worm-ball head, so Lou has the 'bright idea' of keeping the worm-ball head alive and transplanting it on something at a later date. So he manages to persuade ('*bribes*' more like it, if you get my innuendo) one of the Texas lawmen to go out, catch an ordinary housecat and bring it back to the electric-chair room. There they cut off the cat's head and make the transplant—nigger worm-ball head onto housecat. Now the worms (and we are talking 13-footers, Nels!) go for the cat's body. Hey, talk about your ever-lovin' writing spectacle! Here's a page from Davie Lynch, maybe even H. Crews himself! Well, as you can probably imagine, this so-called 'nigger worm-ball head cat' was not the easiest thing in the world to handle, I mean this was not some kind of little goodie-two-shoes *lap-dog* that just wanted to bill and coo—this was a *very disturbed* critter!

Casting for Little Humpy? Hold it, Nels, I can already hear you saying: "Hey, this is a *natural for Mick*! I think not, Nels—with all due respect, ever since *Sugar Babies,* the Mick has borne the taint of 'comedian'. How about Little Mason Reece? Remember him? Or the guy who played Cyrano—what about him, he was short enough.

I think you'll agree that the article entitled HUMAN HEAD KEPT ALIVE FOR 6 DAYS is proof o' pudding positive that we are on *solid ground physiologically.* A documented case and your basic kraut micro surgeon is no *dummkopf*!! In other words there is *no way* the integrity of our piece could be questioned by any of the so-called 'gabardine brigade'! So it is quite feasible that the 'worm-ball head' could be kept alive until transferred to someone else—*OR* do you feel it should remain on the *cat,* and thus more creature-like and/or 'bestial', which seems to be all the rage now, am I right, Nels?

Correct me if I'm wrong, Nels, but here's one I think we'll want to be moving on in fairly quick order.

Yrs in haste,
T.

Best to the ultra-fab.
Letter follows.

Behind the Silver Screen

On Screen Writing

Q: *How does one get into screenwriting—or, more particularly, how did you happen to get into it?*

T.S.: Let me take the second part first. I was supposed to be doing an interview of Stanley Kubrick for one of the magazines—*Esquire*, probably—in New York, about 1962, alter he'd finished with *Lolita*. He was on his way back to London, and was just here for a few days. Well, it turned out that he'd read *The Magic Christian*, and dug it, so somehow or other we get into this rather heavy rap— about *death*, and *infinity*, and the *origin of time*—you know the sort of thing. We never got through with the interview, but the point is we met a few times, had a few laughs, and some groovy rap . . . and then about three months later, he called from London, and asked me to come over and work on *Strangelove*. So that was how *I* got into screenwriting—sort of through the front door— held open by the Fool on the Hill, you might say—or more precisely, by one of the Three Wise Men . . . Fellini and Bergman being the other two at the time.

Q: *But, as you suggest, that's hardly typical of how one becomes a screenwriter.*

T.S.: Right, absolutely non-typical. At that time, 1962 and earlier, practically *all* screenwriters—I would say there were about eight exceptions—were full-out *hacks*, completely incompetent in any other form of writing, and, of course, disastrous in their own. You've got to understand that it is *not easy* to make a bad movie—it requires a very special combination of non-talents and anti-talents . . . and that was generally the case, and unfortunately all too often still is. It used to be that the *people*—they were not *writers*—who would get into screenwriting would do so through talents much more appropriate to selling shoes than to writing . . . in other words, extroverted, hard-sell, bullshitting assholes. *Agents* . . . people like that. Hustlers . . . people who suddenly decided there was more money in selling "stories" to the studio than in selling siding or used cars, and since they had a brother-in-law already in the biz, why not give it a whirl? Once they had a *credit*, of course, there was no stopping them. The studios had rather employ a screenwriter with eight disasters to his credit than a William Faulkner with none. In fact, when Faulkner—who had the greatest ear for regional dialogue of his time—*was* finally used in Hollywood, his work was invariably *rewritten*, by hacks, simply because producers and directors were suspicious of anyone who had not written for films before—as if there was something special about it, or about the crap *they* were turning out. In short, it used to be there was *no way* to get into screenwriting, except through a brother-in-law process. Now independent production has changed this—but not as much as one might think. In the majority of pictures with budgets of five hundred thou or more, studio participation is involved, and wherever there is studio money, there is the dinosaur mentality and the apelike interference which are unfailingly part of the package.

Q: *Then what would you say is the most practical way to get into screenwriting?*

T.S.: There's only one sure way: write a full script—not an outline or a treatment—but as near to a completed shooting-script as possible. Choose or invent a story which adheres to these four principles:

(1) contemporary, to avoid costumes, 1929 Fords, etc.;
(2) all location-shooting, to avoid set-construction;
(3) no night exteriors, very expensive; and
(4) a story locale outside of either L.A. or New York City, in order to cool out the union problems that could otherwise come up with crippling frequency.

Now a script that meets these four requisites—regardless of its complexities otherwise—is automatically within the three hundred thou budget. This figure is crucial, because it is within this three hundred thou range that *private financing* may be had. The important things (aside from the *money*, natch) about private financing (as opposed to "independent production") is that it generally brings with it a somewhat less neanderthal mentality than the latter—that is to say, an investor whose prejudices do *not* exclude the possibility of using the script of a writer on his first time out.

Q: *Would you say that writing for films is a good or rewarding form of work for a writer?*

T.S.: Yes and no, but mostly no. Compared to other forms of writing it *is* highly rewarding, in the financial sense—*and* of course when things go as they should it is extremely satisfying creatively. In fact, when things are right, it is probably the most satisfying creatively of *all* the forms, because it is so much *stronger* than prose. Consider this: in establishing or creating *empathy*—which, after all, is what it's all about—the most effective sensory perceptions are those of *sight* and *sound*. In other words, to be standing on a street corner when someone is hit by a car . . . to *see* it—the look of surprise, of horror, of pain, and the blood . . . and to *hear* it—the brakes, the scream, the metal smashing against the body . . . well, that's considerably different to *reading* about it in the paper. To *see* it and *hear* it is to be only once removed from the *primary experience*—of being hit yourself—whereas merely to *read* about it is to be at least twice removed. In other words, when you succeed in getting what you have written onto the screen, exactly as you conceived it, then it is very satisfying indeed.

Q: *And when you do not?*

T.S.: Ah yes, when you do *not*, it is very frustrating. And that, of course, is the really monstro drawback and boss pain in the ass creativewise about screenwriting, because most of the time it simply doesn't happen the way you conceived it, and you—the writer, the *creator* of it—have to stand by powerless while some total schmuck director fucks it up. And that is why I would hesitate to encourage anyone to write for films—despite the great moments of creative satisfaction, and despite the financial rewards—because so much of your time will be spent in a creative wasteland. You see, the unfortunate thing, the *tragic imbalance*, is that *writers* are almost invariably more creative, more perceptive, and more sensitive than directors are, and yet they have no power on the set beyond simply power of persuasion, which, needless to say, isn't enough. When I refer to "directors," I'm not talking about *filmmakers*, you understand—*artists*, like Fellini and Bergman—I'm talking about the other 99.99 percent of the guild membership who practice the rather unsubtle craft of simply posing as a block of gross stupidity between the writer and the screen.

Q: *Could you be more specific regarding these negative experiences you've had as a screenwriter?*

T.S.: I could of course be *devastatingly* specific about it, but this would plunge us into the grotesque realm of badmouthery and personalities—whereas it is probably much more to the purposes of your project if we can somehow restrict it to the technical and practical aspects of screenwriting. I mentioned the negative side of it only because it would be misleading not to. Suffice it to say that with the exception of *Strangelove*, of the films I've worked on there isn't one which would not have been *infinitely improved* by the absence of the director.

Q: *Do you mean if* you *had been the director?*

T.S.: Or if the "director" had been satisfied to function in the proper and purely technical area of *transferring* the work to the screen—in other words, to *facilitate* instead of *interfere*. I mean, there's no mystery about what has to be done—it's all right there in the script . . . cuts, match-cuts, *sound* match-cuts, close-ups, *extreme* close-ups, *dialogue* . . . even the indication of which words in a passage require *emphasis*. If they would just *do* it, instead of falling into their own dumbbell ego-trip—going beyond their capabilities, trying to impose some of their own Mickey Mouse vision onto it . . .

Q: *Then just what is the proper function of the director?*

T.S.: In his present mode the director is wholly superfluous, an interfering parasite. His proper function—that is to say, a knowledge of lighting techniques and the use of lenses—has been taken over entirely by the Director of Photography. A good script, of course, does not leave room for interference—at least, not *legitimate* interference—it covers every move and every contingency, even anticipates those little areas where you *know* the director will go for overstatement, so you're careful to indicate that this is a CLOSE UP and the actor *doesn't need* to shout quite so loudly, or to grimace quite so weirdly . . .

Q: *Do you know of any directors who* do *function in this way?*

T.S.: Yes, well according to all accounts Rafelson (*Five Easy Pieces*) is able to do it—that is to say, he is sensitive and perceptive enough to recognize a good script when he sees it, and hip and capable enough to transfer it to the screen intact.

Q: *Is there anything the writer can do about protecting his work?*

T.S.: If a writer is sensitive about his work being treated like Moe, Larry, and Curly working over the Sistine Chapel with a crowbar, then he would do well to avoid screenwriting altogether. On the other hand, if he is *irresistibly* drawn to the medium of films, the wise thing, of course, is to become a *filmmaker*. Simply *insist* on being in charge of your material—don't give it up. In the end, they must relent—because without a story, without a script, without the *creative* element . . . there is no film possible.

Q: *Is this what* you *intend to do?*

T.S.: Yes, it's the *only* way to protect the work. For a while I thought it could be done by working with close friends, on a *co-directing* basis . . . people whose values you trust, and so forth—but too often it turns out you've allowed your friendship for them to exaggerate your notion of their talent. And you find yourself right back, if one may coin, where you started—the same old six-and-seven pearls before swine.

Q: *It seems that you're sometimes involved in arguments over who contributed what to the films you've worked on—how does that come about?*

T.S.: That comes about in three distinct ways: first, through a really monstro and misguided sense of generosity, it seems I invariably tend to *offer* sharing the screenplay-credit with almost anyone who happens to be around. You see, theoretically I believe that a film should have a *single credit*—"A Film By . . ." and then simply list, alphabetically, the principal creative people involved. Unfortunately, the Dickensian structure of the filmmaking labor organizations doesn't yet provide that possibility, so we are still faced with this primitive and irrelevant attempt to break it down into categories—like who's responsible for what—whereas in any really good film these things are bound to overlap.

You see, it is practically *impossible* for a director, or a producer, to get a screenplay-credit, because if a script goes to arbitration, the Writers Guild requires proof that they contributed *over 50 percent* of the total of the script. Now, whenever a director or producer wants a share of the screenplay credit, it *automatically* goes to arbitration, *unless* the writer—that is, the *real* writer—specifies otherwise, which is what I would always do. In other words I would *give them* the credit, which they could not possibly have gotten by any other means. So that's the *first* way it comes about—these arguments over who did what—by allowing their names to appear on the screen.

The *second* way it happens is that the *memory* becomes rather *selective* when one is trying to recall who wrote what in a script. This is even true of *writers*, so you can imagine how it is with *non*-writers—who tend to become pretty excited when they get into any writing heavier than a laundry list. And the experiences you refer to—these arguments over who contributed what—have always occurred with *non-writers*, that is to say "directors" and "actors" suddenly turned "writer." Fortunately—at least in some cases, including mine—

a writer can have a style which is unmistakably his own, so that anyone fairly knowledgeable in these matters doesn't have much difficulty recognizing whose work it really is, regardless of non-writer claims to the contrary.

The *third* way these disputes arise is through what is sometimes called the "one-shot syndrome," of certain parties involved. These are people of so little confidence—most frequently not without good reason—in their own abilities that they're inclined to regard any successful endeavor with which they're connected as a *fluke*, a *one-shot*, something unlikely ever to happen again—consequently, they're pretty anxious to make the most of it, and very loath indeed to share . . . it seems to be a kind of terrible *hunger* which brings out their worst, or at least most desperate, qualities.

Q: *What would you say is the role of "improvisation" in filmmaking—or, more exactly, in screenwriting?*

T.S.: Nil. Improvisation is a last resort to save an obviously sinking ship. The dialogue of a good script will have a *credibility* far beyond anything that could possibly come out of improvisation. This is not to say that actors like Brando, Olivier, Rod Steiger, Peter Sellers, Michael Parks, Rip Torn, Stacy Keach . . . cannot improvise on a poor or mediocre script, and thereby vastly improve it, *Or*, in fact, that they cannot make something out of nothing—something *good*, from scratch, just off the top of their heads—but so what? This is simply a facet of their genius—useful in emergencies, amusing in the living room—but can never produce anything comparable to the best written dialogue. The reasons for this become obvious when one considers the *characteristics* of good dialogue: *credibility* and *content*. For dialogue to be credible, it must have enough faltering uncertainty—or foolish certainty—to be *lifelike*. This is why the *best written* dialogue will often *sound* like the *best improvised* dialogue—and may be mistaken for such by people who don't know about such things.

As for the *content* of dialogue, it goes without saying that the most engaging, most relevant, most communicative content is achieved through a very strong combination of *creativeness* and *craftsmanship*, and not simply by somebody blowing off the top of his perhaps second-rate head. This is not to suggest, of course, that masterful dialogue cannot be improved during readings and rehearsals—just as the moves and action of a scene can be improved once the set exists and the actors are working—but this must be worked out between the author and the actor. It does not involve the director. Directors with an exceptionally strong visual sense may be useful in improving the moves and actions of a scene—but never in improving dialogue. Their ears are notoriously wooden. A *master* of dialogue, however—and there are extremely few—is able to *speak* an accent, or a dialect, as well as to *write* it, flawlessly. And equal in range to all but the king-thesps—like the ones I mentioned earlier.

Q: *Well now, aside from the things we've already covered, what other qualities would you say are important for the aspiring screenwriter?*

T.S.: What—you mean, just like that? Off the top of my head? *Improv?*

Q: *Right.*

T.S.: Well, let's see . . . how about: "The patience of Job, and a stomach of Iron, with a capital I fuckin-a-oroonie"?

Q: *Yeah.*

—1973
Movie People, edited by Fred Baker and Ross Firestone
Reprinted by permission of the authors.

Strangelove Outtake:
Notes from the War Room

1962. It was a death-gray afternoon in early December and the first snow of the New England winter had just begun. Outside my window, between the house and the banks of the frozen stream, great silver butterfly flakes floated and fluttered in the failing light. Beyond the stream, past where the evening mist had begun to rise, it was possible, with a scintilla of imagination, to make out the solemnly moving figures in the Bradbury story about the Book People; in short, a magical moment—suddenly undone by the ringing of a telephone somewhere in the house, and then, closer at hand, my wife's voice in a curious singsong:

"It's big Stan Kubrick on the line from Old Smoke."

I had once jokingly referred to Kubrick, whom I had never met but greatly admired, as "big Stan Kubrick" because I liked the ring and lilt of it. "Get big Stan Kubrick on the line in Old Smoke," I had said, "I'm ready with my incisive critique of *Killer's Kiss*." And my wife, not one to be bested, had taken it up.

"Big Stan Kubrick," she repeated, "on the line from Old Smoke."

"Don't fool around," I said. I knew I would soon be on the hump with Mr. Snow Shovel and I was in no mood for her brand of tomfoolery.

"I'm not fooling around," she said. "It's him all right, or at least his assistant."

I won't attempt to reconstruct the conversation; suffice to say he told me he was going to make a film about "our failure to understand the dangers of nuclear war." He said that he had thought of the story as a "straightforward melodrama" until this morning, when he "woke up and realized that nuclear war was too outrageous, too fantastic to be treated in any conventional manner." He said he could only see it now as "some kind of hideous joke." He told me that he had read a book of mine which contained, as he put it, "certain indications" that I might be able to help him with the script.

I later learned the curious genesis of all this: during the '50s I was friends with the English writer Jonathan Miller. I knew him for quite a while before I discovered that he was a doctor—of the sort who could write you a prescription for something like Seconal—at which point I beseeched him to become my personal physician and perhaps suggest something for my chronic insomnia. To encourage his acceptance, I gave him a copy of my recently published novel, *The Magic Christian,* which had been favorably reviewed in the *Observer* by the great English novelist Henry Green. Miller was impressed, at least enough to recommend it to his friend Peter Sellers. Peter liked it to the improbable degree that he went straight to the publisher and bought a hundred copies to give to his friends. One such friend, as luck would have it, was Stanley Kubrick.

At Shepperton Studios in London, Kubrick had set up his "Command Post" in a snug office that overlooked two wintering lilac bushes and, poetically enough, the nest of an English nightingale. Next to his big desk, and flush against it, stood an elegant wrought-iron stand that resembled a pedestal, and on top of the stand, at desk level, was one of the earliest, perhaps the very first, of the computerized "chess-opponents," which they had just begun to produce in West Germany and Switzerland. It was a sturdy, workmanlike model, black with brushed-metal lettering across the front: GRAND MASTER LEVEL

"I have perfected my endgame," Kubrick said, "to such a degree that I can now elude the stratagems of this so-called opponent," he gave a curt nod toward the computer, "until the proverbial cows come home. . . . Would that I could apply my newly acquired skill," he went on, "vis-à-vis a certain Mo Rothman at Columbia Pix."

Mo Rothman, I was to learn, was the person Columbia Pictures had designated executive producer on the film, which meant that he was the bridge, the connection, the *interpreter,* between the otherwise incomprehensible artist and the various moneybags incarnate who were financing the film. As to whether or not the "streetwise" Mo Rothman was a good choice for this particular project, I believe the jury is still out. Once, when Kubrick was out of the office, Rothman insisted on giving me the following message:

"Just tell Stanley," he said in a tone of clamor and angst, "that New York does *not* see anything *funny* about the end of the world!" And then added, not so much as an afterthought as a simple Pavlovian habit he'd acquired, "as we know it."

I realized he had no idea whom he was talking to, so I took a flyer. "Never mind New York," I said with a goofy inflection. "What about Gollywood?" This got a rise out of him like a shot of crystal meth.

"*Gollywood?*" he said loudly. "Who the hell *is* this?"

The Corporate, that is to say, studio reasoning about this production affords an insight as to why so many such projects are doomed, creatively speaking, from the get-go. It was their considered judgment that the success of the film *Lolita* resulted solely from the gimmick of Peter Sellers playing several roles.

"What we are dealing with," said Kubrick at our first real talk about the situation, "is film by fiat, film by frenzy." What infuriated him most was that the "brains" of the production company could evaluate the entire film—commercially, aesthetically, morally, whatever—in terms of the tour de force performance of one actor. I was amazed that he handled it as well as he did. "I have come to realize," he explained, "that such crass and grotesque stipulations are the *sine qua non* of the motion-picture business." And it was in this spirit that he accepted the studio's condition that this film, as yet untitled, "would star Peter Sellers in at least four major roles."

It was thus understandable that Kubrick should practically freak when a telegram from Peter arrived one morning:

Dear Stanley:
I am so very sorry to tell you that I am having serious difficulty with the various roles. Now hear this: there is no way, repeat, no way, I can play the Texas pilot, 'Major King Kong.' I have a complete block against that accent. Letter from Okin [his agent] follows. Please forgive.

Peter S.

For a few days Kubrick had been in the throes of a Herculean effort to give up cigarettes and had forbidden smoking anywhere in the building. Now he immediately summoned his personal secretary and assistant to bring him a pack pronto.

That evening he persuaded me, since I had been raised in Texas, to make a tape of Kong's dialogue, much of which he had already written (his announcement of the bomb targets and his solemn reading of the Survival Kit Contents, etc.). In the days that followed, as scenes in the plane were written I recorded them on tape so that they would be ready for Sellers, if and when he arrived. Kubrick had been on the phone pleading with him ever since receiving the telegram. When he finally did show up, he had with him the latest state-of-the-art portable tape recorder, specially designed for learning languages. Its ultrasensitive earphones were so oversized they resembled some kind of eccentric hat or space headgear. From the office we would see Sellers pacing between the lilac bushes, script in hand, his face tiny and obscured beneath his earphones. Kubrick found it a disturbing image. "Is he kidding?" he said. "That's exactly the sort of thing that would bring some Brit heat down for weirdness." I laughed, but he wasn't joking. He phoned the production manager, Victor Linden, right away.

"Listen, Victor," I heard him say, "you'd better check out Pete and those earphones. He may be *stressing*. . . . Well, I think he ought to cool it with the earphones. Yeah, it looks like he's trying to ridicule the BBC or something, know what I'm saying? All we need is to get shut down for a crazy stunt like that. Jesus Christ."

Victor Linden was the quintessential thirty-five-year-old English gentleman of the Eton-Oxford persuasion, the sort more likely to join the Foreign Office than the film industry; and, in fact, on more than one occasion I overheard him saying, "With some of us, dear boy, the wogs begin at Calais."

As production manager, it was his job to arrange for, among other things, accommodations for members of the company, including a certain yours truly. "I've found some digs for you," he said, "in Knightsbridge, not far from Stanley's place. I'm afraid they may not be up to Beverly Hills standards, but I think you'll find them quite pleasant. . . . The main thing, of course, is that you'll be close to Stanley, because of his writing plan."

Stanley's "writing plan" proved to be a dandy. At five A.M., the car would arrive, a large black Bentley, with a back seat the size of a small train compartment—two fold-out desk tops, perfect over-the-left-shoulder lighting, controlled temperature, dark gray windows. In short, an ideal no-exit writing situation. The drive from London to Shepperton took an hour more or less, depending on the traffic and the density of the unfailing fog. During this trip we would write and rewrite, usually the pages to be filmed that day.

It was at a time when the Cold War was at its most intense. As part of the American defense strategy, bombing missions were flown daily toward targets

deep inside the Soviet Union, each B-52 carrying a nuclear bomb more powerful than those used on Hiroshima and Nagasaki combined. Bombers were instructed to continue their missions unless they received the recall code at their
"fail-safe" points.

In my Knightsbridge rooms, I carefully read *Red Alert*, a book written
by an ex-RAF intelligence officer named Peter George that had prompted
Stanley's original interest. Perhaps the best thing about the book was the fact
that the national security regulations in England, concerning what could and
could not be published, were extremely lax by American standards. George had
been able to reveal details concerning the "fail-safe" aspect of nuclear deter-
rence (for example, the so-called black box and the CRM Discriminator)—
revelations that, in the spy-crazy U.S.A. of the Cold War era, would have been
downright treasonous. Thus the entire complicated technology of nuclear de-
terrence in *Dr. Strangelove* was based on a bedrock of authenticity that gave
the film what must have been its greatest strength: credibility.

The shooting schedule, which had been devised by Victor Linden and of course
Kubrick—who scarcely let as much as a trouser pleat go unsupervised—called
for the series of scenes that take place inside a B-52 bomber to be filmed first.
Peter Sellers had mastered the tricky Texas twang without untoward incident,
and then had completed the first day's shooting of Major Kong's lines in admirable fashion. Kubrick was delighted. The following morning, however, we
were met at the door by Victor Linden.

"Bad luck," he said, with a touch of grim relish. "Sellers has taken a *fall*.
Last night, in front of that Indian restaurant in King's Road. You know the one,
Stanley, the posh one you detested. Well, he slipped getting out of the car.
Rather nasty I'm afraid. Sprain of ankle, perhaps a hairline fracture." The in-
jury was not as serious as everyone had feared it might be. Sellers arrived at
the studio shortly after lunch, and worked beautifully through a couple of scenes.
Everything seemed fine until we broke for tea and Kubrick remarked in the most
offhand manner, "Ace [the co-pilot] is sitting taller than Peter."

Almost immediately, he announced that we would do a run-through
of another scene (much further along in the shooting schedule), which required Major Kong to move from the cockpit to the bomb-bay area via two
eight-foot ladders. Sellers negotiated the first, but coming down the second,
at about the fourth rung from the bottom, one of his legs abruptly buckled,

and he tumbled and sprawled, in obvious pain, on the unforgiving bomb-bay floor.

It was Victor Linden who again brought the bad news, the next day, after Sellers had undergone a physical exam in Harley Street. "The completion-bond people," he announced gravely, "know about Peter's injury and the physical demands of the Major Kong role. They say they'll pull out if he plays the part." Once that grim reality had sunk in, Kubrick's response was an extraordinary tribute to Sellers as an actor: "We can't replace him with another *actor*, we've got to get an authentic character from life, someone whose acting career is secondary—a real-life cowboy." Kubrick, however, had not visited the United States in about fifteen years, and was not familiar with the secondary actors of the day. He asked for my opinion and I immediately suggested big Dan ("Hoss Cartwright") Blocker. He hadn't heard of Blocker, or even—so eccentrically isolated had he become—of the TV show *Bonanza*.

"How *big* a man is he?" Stanley asked.

"Bigger than John Wayne," I said.

We looked up his picture in a copy of *The Players' Guide* and Stanley decided to go with him without further query. He made arrangements for a script to be delivered to Blocker that afternoon, but a cabled response from Blocker's agent arrived in quick order: "Thanks a lot, but the material is too pinko for Dan. Or anyone else we know for that matter. Regards, Leibman, CMA."

As I recall, this was the first hint that this sort of political interpretation of our work-in-progress might exist. Stanley seemed genuinely surprised and disappointed. Linden, however, was quite resilient. "Pinko . . . " he said with a sniff. "Unless I'm quite mistaken, an English talent agency would have used the word 'subversive.'"

Years earlier, while Kubrick was directing the western called *One-Eyed Jacks* (his place was taken by Marlon "Bud" Brando, the producer and star of the film, following an ambiguous contretemps), he'd noticed the authentic qualities of the most natural thesp to come out of the west, an actor with the homey sobriquet of Slim Pickens.

Slim Pickens, born Louis Bert Lindley in Texas in 1919, was an unschooled cowhand who traveled the rodeo circuit from El Paso to Montana, sometimes competing in events, other times performing the dangerous work of rodeo clown—distracting the bulls long enough for injured cowboys to be removed from the arena. At one point, a friend persuaded him to accept work as a stunt rider in westerns. During an open call for *One-Eyed Jacks*, Brando noticed him and cast him in the role of the uncouth deputy sheriff. Except for the occasional stunt work on location, Slim had never been anywhere off the small-town western rodeo circuit, much less outside the U.S. When his agent told him about this remarkable job in England, he asked what he should wear on his trip there. His agent told him to wear whatever he would if he were "going into town to buy a sack of feed"—which meant his Justin boots and wide-brimmed Stetson.

"He's in the office with Victor," Stanley said, "and I don't think they can understand each other. Victor said he arrived in costume. Go and see if he's all right. Ask him if his hotel is okay and all that." When I reached the production office, I saw Victor first, his face furrowed in consternation as he perched in the center of his big Eames wingbat. Then I saw Slim Pickens, who was every inch and ounce the size of the Duke, leaning one elbow to the wall, staring out the window.

"This place," I heard him drawl, "would make one helluva good horse pasture . . . if there's any water."

"Oh, I believe there's water, all right," Victor was absurdly assuring him when he saw me. "Ah, there you are, dear boy," he said. "This is Mr. Slim Pickens. This is Terry Southern." We shook hands, Slim grinning crazily.

"Howdy," he drawled, as gracious as if I were a heroine in an old western. "Mighty proud to know yuh." I went straight to our little makeshift bar, where I had stashed a quart of Wild Turkey specifically for the occasion, which I was ballpark certain would meet his requirements.

"Do you reckon it's too early for a drink, Slim?" I asked. He guffawed, then shook his head and crinkled his nose, as he always did when about to put someone on. "Wal, you know ah think it was jest this mornin' that ah was tryin' to figure out if and when ah ever think it was too early fer a drink, an' damned if ah didn't come up bone dry! Hee-hee-hee!" He cackled his falsetto laugh. "Why hell yes, I'll have a drink with you. Be glad to."

"How about you, Victor?" I asked. His reply was a small explosion of coughs and "hrumphs."

"Actually, it *is* a bit early for me in point of fact," he spluttered. "I've got all those bloody meetings. . . ." I poured a couple and handed one to Slim.

"Stanley wanted me to find out if you got settled in at your hotel, Slim, and if everything is all right." Slim had this unusual habit of sometimes prefacing his reply to a question with a small grimace and a wipe of his mouth against the back of his hand, a gesture of modesty or self-deprecation somehow. "Wal," he said, "it's like this ole friend of mine from Oklahoma says: Jest gimme a pair of loose-fittin' shoes, some tight pussy, and a warm place to shit, an' ah'll be all right."

We were occupying three of the big sound stages at Shepperton: one of them for the War Room set, another for the B-52 bomber set and a third that accommodated two smaller sets, General Ripper's office, including its corridor with Coke machine and telephone booth ("If you try any *preversion* in there, I'll blow your head off"), and the General Turgidson motel-room set. The B-52 set, where we were shooting at the time, consisted of an actual B-52 bomber, or at least its nose and forward fuselage, suspended about fifteen feet above the floor of the stage. They were between takes when I climbed into the cockpit area where they were doing "character shots": individual close-ups of the co-pilot scrutinizing a *Playboy* centerfold, the navigator practicing his card tricks, the radar operator wistfully reading a letter from home. Short snippets of action meant to establish the crew as legendary boy-next-door types. Conspicuously absent from the lineup was the bombardier and single black member of the crew, James Earl Jones, or Jimmy, as everyone called him. A classic thespian of high purpose, Jones was about as cultured and scholarly as it is possible for an actor to be, with a voice and presence that were invariably compared to Paul Robeson's.

Kubrick came over to where I was standing, but he remained absorbed in what he called "this obligatory *Our Town* character crap that always seems to come off like a parody of *All Quiet on the Western Front*," a movie that took an outlandish amount of time to focus on the individual behavioral quirks of every man in the regiment. "The only rationale for doing it now," Kubrick said, "is that you're making fun of that historic and corny technique of character delineation." Just as he started to go back to the camera, I saw that his eye was caught by something off the set. "Look at that," he said, "Slim and Jimmy are on a collision course."

Slim was ambling along the apron of the stage toward where Jimmy was sitting by the prop truck absorbed in his script. "Why don't you go down there," Kubrick went on, "and introduce them." It was not so much a question as a very pointed suggestion, perhaps even, it occurred to me, a direct order. I bounded

down the scaffolding steps and across the floor of the stage, just in time to
intercept Slim in full stride a few feet from where Jimmy was sitting.

"Hold on there, Slim," I said. "I want you to meet another member of
the cast." Jimmy got to his feet. "James Earl Jones—Slim Pickens." They shook
hands but both continued to look equally puzzled. They had obviously never
heard of each other. Somehow I knew the best route to some kind of rapproche-
ment would be through Jones. "Slim has just finished working on a picture with
Marlon Brando," I said.

"Oh well," he boomed, "that must have been very interesting indeed. . . .
Yes, I should very much like to hear what it is like to work with the great
Mr. Brando."

As if the question were a cue for a well-rehearsed bit of bumpkin business, Slim began to hem and haw, kicking at an imaginary rock on the floor.
"Wal," he drawled, his head to one side, "you know ah worked with Bud Brando
for right near a full year, an' durin' that time ah never seen him do one thing
that wudn't *all man* an' *all white*."

When I asked Jimmy about it later, he laughed. His laugh, it must be said,
is one of the all-time great laughs. "I was beginning to think," and there were
tears in his eyes as he said it, "that I must have imagined it."

The quality of Jones's voice comes through most clearly as he delivers
the last line of the *Strangelove* script before the bomb is released. The ultimate
fail-safe device requires the manual operation of two final safety switches, to
insure that the bomb will never be dropped by mistake. Major Kong's command
over the intercom is brisk: "Release second safety!" Jones's response, although
measured, is unhesitating. He reaches out and moves the lever. It is in his
acknowledgment of the order, over the intercom, that he manages to imbue the
words with the fatalism and pathos of the ages: *"Second safety . . ."*

Not long afterward, we began shooting the famous eleven-minute "lost pie fight,"
which was to come near the end of the movie. This footage began at a point in
the War Room where the Russian ambassador is seen, for the second time, surreptitiously taking photographs of the Big Board, using six or seven tiny spy-
cameras disguised as a wristwatch, a diamond ring, a cigarette lighter, and cuff
links. The head of the Joint Chiefs of Staff, Air Force General Buck Turgidson
(George C. Scott), catches him in flagrante and, as before, tackles him and throws
him to the floor. They fight furiously until President Merkin Muffley intervenes:

"This is the War Room, gentlemen! How dare you fight in here!"
General Turgidson is unfazed. "We've got the Commie rat red-handed
this time, Mr. President!"

The detachment of four military police, which earlier escorted the ambassador to the War Room, stands by as General Turgidson continues: "Mr.
President, my experience in these matters of espionage has caused me to be more
skeptical than your average Joe. I think these cameras," he indicates the array
of ingenious devices, "may be dummy cameras, just to put us off. I say he's got
the real McCoy concealed on his person. I would like to have your permission,
Mr. President, to have him fully searched."

"All right," the president says, "permission granted."

General Turgidson addresses the military police: "Okay boys, you heard
the president. I want you to search the ambassador thoroughly. And due to the
tininess of his equipment do not overlook any of the seven bodily orifices." The
camera focuses on the face of the ambassador as he listens and mentally calcu-
lates the orifices with an expression of great annoyance.

"Why you capitalist swine!" he roars, and reaches out of the frame to the
huge three-tiered table that was wheeled in earlier. Then he turns back to General Turgidson, who now has a look of apprehension on his face as he ducks
aside, managing to evade a custard pie that the ambassador is throwing at him.
President Muffley has been standing directly behind the general, so that when
he ducks, the president is hit directly in the face with the pie. He is so overwhelmed by the sheer indignity of being struck with a pie that he simply blacks
out. General Turgidson catches him as he collapses.

"Gentlemen," he intones. "The president has been struck down, in the
prime of his life and his presidency. I say massive retaliation!" And he picks up
another pie and hurls it at the ambassador. It misses and hits instead General
Faceman, the Joint Chief representing the Army. Faceman is furious.

"You've gone too far this time, Buck!" he says, throwing a pie himself,
which hits Admiral Pooper, the Naval Joint Chief who, of course, also retali-
ates. A monumental pie fight ensues.

Meanwhile, parallel to the pie-fight sequence, another sequence is occurring. At about the time that the first pie is thrown, Dr. Strangelove raises himself from his wheelchair. Then, looking rather wild-eyed, he shouts, "Mein
Führer, I *can valk!*" He takes a triumphant step forward and pitches flat on his
face. He immediately tries to regain the wheelchair, snaking his way across the
floor, which is so highly polished and slippery that the wheelchair scoots out

of reach as soon as Strangelove touches it. We intercut between the pie fight and Strangelove's snakelike movements—reach and scoot, reach and scoot— which suggest a curious, macabre pas de deux. When the chair finally reaches the wall, it shoots sideways across the floor and comes to a stop ten feet away, hopelessly out of reach.

Strangelove, exhausted and dejected, pulls himself up so that he is sitting on the floor, his back against the wall at the far end of the War Room. He stares for a moment at the surreal activity occurring there, the pie fight appearing like a distant, blurry, white blizzard. The camera moves in on Strangelove as he gazes, expressionless now, at the distant fray. Then, unobserved by him, his right hand slowly rises, moves to the inner pocket of his jacket and, with con-siderable stealth, withdraws a German Luger pistol and moves the barrel to-ward his right temple. The hand holding the pistol is seized at the last minute by the free hand and both grapple for its control. The hand grasping the wrist prevails and is able to deflect the pistol's aim so that when it goes off with a tremendous roar, it misses the temple.

The explosion reverberates with such volume that the pie fight freezes. A tableau, of white and ghostly aspect: Strangelove stares for a moment before realizing that he has gained the upper hand. "Gentlemen," he calls out to them. "Enough of these childish games. Vee hab vork to do. Azzemble here pleeze!" For a moment, no one moves. Then a solitary figure breaks rank: It is General Turgidson, who walks across the room to the wheelchair and pushes it over to the stricken Strangelove.

"May I help you into your chair, Doctor?" he asks. He begins wheeling Strangelove across the War Room floor, which is now about half a foot deep in custard pie. They move slowly until they reach the president and the Rus-sian ambassador who are sitting crosslegged, facing each other, building a sand castle.

"What in Sam Hill—" mutters General Turgidson.

"Ach," says Strangelove. "I think their minds have snapped under the strain. Perhaps they will have to be *institutionalized*."

As they near the pie-covered formation of generals and admirals, Gen-eral Turgidson announces gravely: "Well, boys, it looks like the future of this great land of ours is going to be in the hands of people like Dr. Strangelove here. So let's hear three for the good doctor!" And as he pushes off again, the eerie formation raise their voices in a thin, apparitionlike lamentation: "Hip, hip, hooray, hip, hip, hooray!" followed by Vera Lynn's rendition of "We'll

Meet Again." The camera is up and back in a dramatic long shot as General Turgidson moves across the War Room floor in a metaphorical visual marriage of Mad Scientist and United States Military. The End.

This was a truly fantastic sequence. In the first place it was a strictly one-shot affair; there was neither time nor money to reshoot—which would have meant cleaning the hundred or so uniforms and buying a thousand more custard pies. The studio representatives, who were skeptical of the scene all along, had been excruciatingly clear about the matter: "We're talkin' one take. One take and you're outta here, even if you only got shit in the can!"

So it was with considerable trepidation that we screened the results that evening. It must be recalled that each branch of the military service—Army, Navy, Air Force, Marine—receives a separate budget that determines the welfare and the lifestyle of its top brass. The pie fight, at its most contentious and prolonged, was not between the Russian ambassador and the United States military but between the rival branches of the U.S. military, and it represented a bitter and unrelenting struggle for congressional appropriations. This continuing jealousy between service branches, which causes each one to exaggerate its needs, precludes any chance of reducing our absurdly high defense budget.

The style and mood of the sequence should have reflected these grim circumstances. Kubrick's major goof was his failure to communicate that idea to the sixty or so pie-throwing admirals and generals, so that the prevailing atmosphere, as it came across on the film, might best be described as bacchanalian—with everyone gaily tossing pies, obviously in the highest of spirits. A disaster of, as Kubrick said, "Homeric proportions." Needless to say, the scene was cut.

It was about this time that word began to reach us, reflecting concern as to the nature of the film in production. Was it anti-American? or just anti-military? And the jackpot question—was it, in fact, anti-American to whatever extent it was anti-military? This "buzz along the rialto" was occasionally fleshed out by an actual Nosey Parker type dropping in from New York or Hollywood on behalf of Columbia Pictures. They usually traveled in pairs, presumably on the theory that sleaze is more palatable if spread somewhat thin.

"I feel like Elisha Cook in one of those early Warner films," said Stanley. "You know, when you learn there's a contract out on you, and all you can do is wait for the hit. They're ruthless," he went on, carried away by the film noir image, "absolutely ruthless."

The early visits of those snoopers (with their little high-speed cameras and voice-activated recorders, which they would try to stash on the set and retrieve later) were harbingers of stressful things to come about nine months later, when the first prints of the film were being sporadically screened at the Gulf and Western Building in New York, and word came back to Old Smoke that the Columbia head honchos, Abe Schneider and Mo Rothman, were never in attendance.

I overheard Stanley on the phone to New York. "Listen, Mo," he said, "don't you think you ought to have a look at the film you're making?" Afterward he told me: "Mo says they've been too busy with the new Carl Foreman film—the one with Bing Crosby singing 'White Christmas' while a soldier is being executed. He said, 'It's not so *zany* as yours, Stanley.' Can you believe it? And that isn't the worst. He also said, get this, he said, 'The publicity department is having a hard time getting a handle on how to promote a comedy about the destruction of the planet.'"

It was the first time I had seen Kubrick utterly depressed, and during the ride back to London, he said, "I have the feeling distribution is totally fucked." The next day, however, he was bouncing with optimism and a bold scheme. "I have learned," he said, "that Mo Rothman is a highly serious *golfer*." In a trice he was on the phone to Abercrombie & Fitch, Manhattan's ultraswank sporting-goods emporium. Some fairly elaborate manipulations (plus an untold cash outlay) got him a "surprise gift" presentation of the store's top-of-the-line electric golf cart, to be delivered to the clubhouse of Rothman's Westchester Country Club.

It is a sad anticlimax to report the negative response on Rothman's part. "The son of a bitch refused to accept it!" Stanley exclaimed. "He said it would be 'bad form.'"

It soon became apparent that no one in the company wished to be associated with the film, as if they were pretending that it had somehow spontaneously come into existence. Kubrick was hopping. "It's like they think it was some kind of immaculate fucking conception," he exclaimed with the ultrarighteous indignation of someone caught in an unsuccessful bribery attempt. It was difficult to contain him. "'Bad form!'" he kept shouting. "Can you imagine *Mo Rothman* saying that? His secretary must have taught him that phrase!"

In the months that followed, the studio continued to distance itself from the film. Even when *Strangelove* received the infrequent good review, it dismissed the critic as a pinko nutcase and on at least one occasion the Columbia Pictures publicity department *defended* the company against the film by saying it was definitely not "anti–U.S. military," but "just a zany novelty flick which did not reflect the views of the corporation in any way." This party line persisted, I believe, until about five years ago, when the Library of Congress announced that the film had been selected as one of the fifty greatest American films of all time—in a ceremony at which I noted Rothman in prominent attendance. Who said satire was "something that closed Wednesday in Philadelphia"?

—1994
Grand Street
Reprinted by permission of Jean Stein and *Grand Street*.

Proposed Scene for Kubrick's Rhapsody

In the early '80s, Stanley asked Terry to help him adapt a book he had been striving to make into a movie for more than a decade: Arthur Schnitzler's Rhapsody, A Dream Novel *(the basis for* Eyes Wide Shut*). After reading it, Terry challenged Stanley to "go the comedy route."*

Dear Stanley:

Were you serious about the protag-physician being a *gynecologist?* How about this (*indication of a*) possible exchange (after they've returned from an evening out, but *before* she lays her heavy 'ready-to-give-you-up-for-the-boy-on-the-beach' reminiscence on him):

CYNTHIA

But, darling, surely in your profession, you've had your share of . . . (*averts her eyes*) *amorous adventures.*

BRIAN (FORBES?) (*smiling*)

In my profession? You mean as a physician? Or as a *gynecologist?*

CYNTHIA

Both. Women are notorious for becoming infatuated with their doctors, aren't they? And as for their *gynecologists* . . . well, of course *I've* always had a *female* gynecologist—and I should think any woman in her right mind *would* have. (*pause*) But I can well *imagine* what might go on . . .

BRIAN (*playfully wagging a finger*)

You're not suggesting I violate the sacred trust of doctor-patient confidence, are you, my dear?

CYNTHIA

Don't tease me, Brian. I answered *your* questions about the tall dark man at the party tonight—now you can answer mine.

BRIAN *(shrugs)*

Darling, I'd be delighted . . . if there were anything of interest to tell.

CYNTHIA *(slightly annoyed)*

Oh Brian! Please!

BRIAN *(gets up, pours a drink)*

Well, there *was* this one case—more amusing than amorous, I'm afraid—but rather . . . *intriguing* even so.

CYNTHIA *(impatiently)*

Go on.

BRIAN

It was before we were married, about twelve years ago, just after I came down from Boston. This woman made an appointment for the . . . the 'examination and testing of her clitoral reflexes'.

CYNTHIA *(frown of surprise)*

Her 'clitoral reflexes'? *Really?*

BRIAN *(nodding)*

Seems she—or perhaps her husband—didn't feel she was sexually responsive enough, so . . . *(shrugs)* she came in for this examination.

CYNTHIA *(slightly exasperated)*

My god. How old was she?

BRIAN

Oh I don't know. Twenty-six or -seven.

CYNTHIA *(coolly)*

Was she attractive?

BRIAN

Attractive? Hmmm . . . *(recalling)* yes, I believe she was.

CYNTHIA

Was she *beautiful?*

BRIAN (*smiles*)

Yes, she was *extraordinarily* beautiful . . . (*leans over, kisses her cheek*) but not nearly so beautiful as *you* are, my darling.

CYNTHIA (*vexed*)

Was she blonde? Brunette? Redhead?

BRIAN (*recalling*)

She was blonde. Yes, long blonde hair . . . (*indicates*) Below her shoulders.

CYNTHIA (*narrowly*)

Was she . . . a *natural* blonde?

BRIAN

You mean . . .

CYNTHIA (*trying to sound matter-of-fact*)

Yes, her pubic hair, was it blonde?

Brian sighs, puts his head back, half closing his eyes, as if making an effort to remember.

BRIAN

Yes . . . yes, as a matter of fact, it was.

CYNTHIA (*brow furrowed in irritation*)

You can remember *that*? After *twelve years*? You still remember *that*? (*half turns away*) My god . . .

BRIAN (*shrugs*)

I could be wrong . . .

CYNTHIA (*glaring at him*)

Well, what happened . . . with your so-called 'examination and testing of her . . . her clitoral reflexes'? You actually *did* it, I suppose?

BRIAN (*shrugs*)

I couldn't exactly *refuse*, could I?

CYNTHIA (*coldly*)

No, of course not. (*glares*) So?

BRIAN

She had a condition known as '*clitori cloturum*'—more commonly referred to as 'hooded clit'.

CYNTHIA (*half turns away in exasperation*)
'Hooded clit'!

BRIAN

You've never heard of it?

CYNTHIA (*emphatically*)
No.

BRIAN

I'm surprised. It's really not that uncommon. It's a condition where the normal membrane extends down farther than it should—that is, than it should for full erotic stimulation.

CYNTHIA (*icily*)
I see. You've known a lot of those women? 'Hooded-clit women'?

BRIAN

No, no, I mean *statistically* it isn't uncommon. I've seen it in the casebooks . . . the figures on it.

CYNTHIA

Well, go on, tell me about your . . . your *relationship* with her. Your 'Miss Hooded Clit' *of twelve* years ago!

BRIAN (*frowning*)
There was no 'relationship' . . .

Etc., etc.

—c. 1980

Plums and Prunes

This short screenplay was written for a hardcover compilation of so-called risqué scripts by Jack Gelber, Arthur Kopit, Bruce Jay Friedman and others, called Pardon Me Sir, But Is My Eye Hurting Your Elbow? The collection was to be made into a motion picture, but was never produced. The piece debuted, however in Playboy.

EXTERIOR. APPROACHING THE BRAD JEFFERY HOME. DAY.

It is an ideal "suburbia home" in Westchester. White, with well-kept lawn, shrubs, etc. It is the contemporary and eastern counterpart of the house in the Andy Hardy pictures. CAMERA MOVES UP the drive, STOPS ABRUPTLY.

CUT TO:

EXTERIOR. A BUICK CAR (OR SIMILAR) IN THE DRIVEWAY. DAY.

BRAD JEFFERY is getting out, briefcase in hand. We realize that the approach has been from his POV. BRAD is a dapper and handsome man of 40–45, a Madison Avenue advertising executive at the top of his profession. There is bouncy anticipation and assurance in his manner as he walks toward the house. We realize that BRAD is very much "with it."

CUT TO:

INTERIOR. LIVING ROOM. DAY.

Westchester contemporary: a long pearl-gray room; fireplace; bar; a couple of smart prints (Braque guitar and Modigliani nude) and a semiabstract original or two; on the wall nearest the door are a pair of African masks, spaced well apart, with a decorative crossbow mounted slightly above and between them. MUSIC from the phonograph is soothingly, harmlessly modern jazz. Door opens ON CUT and BRAD enters. At the far end of the room, by the bar, is DONNA, his wife, gingerly emptying ice-cubes into the ice-bucket. She is about 38, trim, tanned, and very attractive in her hostess-length skirt. Behind her we can see the kitchen area from which she has come. As BRAD approaches she looks up, giving him a smile filled with warmth and a hint of sexual promise. (Note: Besides the kitchen door and the entrance door, there is another leading to the downstairs bedrooms and bath. This door is opposite the bar, and through it can be seen the staircase as well.)

DONNA (CU)
Hello, darling.

There is a confident smile on BRAD's face as he reaches her, places briefcase on floor, puts arms around her.

BRAD *(tenderly sexual, with rich,*
masculine Princetonian modulation)
Hello, baby.

They kiss, very warmly. She finally draws back slightly.

DONNA *(teasingly)*
Mustn't muss.

BRAD *(soft, masterful insinuation)*
You know, sometimes I think you're psychic . . . *(caresses her)* That happens to be *exactly* what I feel like doing.

DONNA (CU) *(momentarily yielding, closed-eyed)*
Hmmm . . . *(sighs, begins to withdraw, whispers)* Debbie will be home *any* minute. *(gives him a seductive wink)* Why don't you make us both a nice martini?

BRAD
(also sighs, somewhat theatrically)
Right. *(shakes his head good-naturedly as he turns to drink preparations)* A child-centered home! Who would've thought it could ever happen to us?

DONNA *(happily)*
Thank goodness she didn't hear you say *that!* She's a young *lady* now, darling. *(in mock confidence as she squeezes his shoulder)* She told me so herself!

BRAD, busily engaged in martini preparation, chuckles in bemusement at the notion. DONNA adds, seductively:

> Besides, we *do* have our moments, don't we, darling. . . .

> BRAD (*in mischievous sex-threat*
> *as he hands her her drink*)
> You can count on *that.*

> DONNA (*flushes, pleased, starts to*
> *withdraw toward kitchen*)
> I won't be long, darling. I just have to speak to Sarah about the Thursday dinner.

She leaves. BRAD looks after her momentarily, then turns back to pour his own drink, (CU) a smug, virile smile on his face.

FADE OUT AND IN:

A few minutes later. BRAD is sitting in an Eames chair, coat off, tie loosened slightly, reading *The New Yorker,* and sipping his martini. He is still looking as youthful and dapper as before—black knit tie, tailored shirt, etc. The door opens and in comes DEBBIE.

DEBBIE is sixteen, and is cute as a button—pert derriere and pert breasts—all freshness and innocence. She's wearing a pleated skirt, white sweater with school-letter "F" (or "C") on it, saddle shoes and bobby socks, and carrying a small notebook and a couple of texts.

> DEBBIE
> Hi, Daddy.
> (*crosses to him, kisses his forehead*)

> BRAD
> Hello, cutie. How's the team spirit?

> DEBBIE (*sighs, sitting down on the arm of his chair*)
> Oh, it's *awful,* Daddy. Mulie broke his *ankle* again!

> BRAD
> Mulie? Which one is he?

> DEBBIE (*despairingly*)
> The *full*back! Gosh, if it had only been someone *else!*
> (*gets up*)

BRAD (*laughs*)
Preferably someone on the *other team,* I suppose.

DEBBIE (*laughs too*)
Oh, Daddy! (*kisses him again*)

BRAD (*gives her behind a fatherly pat*)
You go and get ready for dinner.

DEBBIE (*crossing room*)
Tonight's the club *dance,* Daddy—remember? (*looks at her watch*)
Good grief, Tommy's picking me up in twenty minutes! I've got to
shower and *everything!*
(*at the door*)
Remind Mummy I'll be eating out, will you, Daddy?
(*rushes through other door*)

BRAD shakes his head in bemusement, gets up, goes to the bar, pours another
from the mixer. DONNA comes in from the kitchen.

DONNA (*sigh of relief*)
Well, that much is done.
(*brightly*)
Did I hear Deb coming in?

BRAD (*mixing another batch, chuckles*)
Hmm. Not for long, though—she's got to change, and *everything*
. . . whatever that may mean.

DONNA (*smiling*)
It *means* that she's a young *lady,* darling, and that she's going to the
club dance.

BRAD
Where's your glass? Ready for another?

DONNA
Not just now, dear. I think I'll rest for a bit before dinner—it's such
a trial getting things straight with Sarah.

BRAD (*with mischievous insinuation*)
Say, you know *I* wouldn't mind a little rest myself . . . before
dinner.

DONNA (*smiles, flushed and pleased, starts out*)
Oh, do say hello to Tommy for me, darling—and tell Debbie to
behave herself.
(*hesitates, adds coquettishly*)
Perhaps you'll . . . wake me with a kiss, as they say.

BRAD (*in a charmingly masculine sex threat*)
I might just *do* that.

They exchange meaningful looks, and DONNA leaves. BRAD'S eyes follow her as
before; his POV, her handsome tushy as she goes up the stairs; then CU, his
smugly virile smile as he turns back to his drink and adds a bit of fresh to his
glass. He crosses the room toward his chair. The telephone RINGS. He gets it.

BRAD
Hello. (*glances toward* DEBBIE'S *room*) Yes, who's calling? Oh, hello,
Tommy, how are you? Sorry to hear about Mulie—doesn't look too
good, does it? (*pause, chuckles*) Yes, that's the spirit. . . . Hold on a
minute, Tommy, I'll call her. (*covers phone, calls*) Debbie! Deborah!
Telephone!

We hear a distant response, indistinct but vaguely affirmative in tone. BRAD
shrugs, speaks into the phone again.

BRAD
She'll be right with you, Tommy . . . (*chuckles*) I *think*.

He puts down phone, picks up his drink and crosses to his chair, sits down, picks
up *The New Yorker* again. His POV, DEBBIE comes in, picks up phone. (The
phone is about 25 feet away from where BRAD is sitting, so that her remarks are
indistinct, have a purring sensuous quality, and her movements are coordinated
with the sounds). She is wearing panties and bra, and as she talks she absently
fingers them, smoothing the side of the panties, idly toying with the edges, waist-
band, checking the bra straps, etc., as though she is subliminally being undressed. These movements and gestures should have an extremely sensual and
erotic quality, though performed quite absently and reflexively. She is bare-
foot, and occasionally raises one leg and draws her toes slowly up and down
the back of her calf and knee. This is all shown from BRAD'S POV, though the
CU's give it an effect of INTERCUT, and her remarks on the close shots are

clearly audible to the audience, though presumably indistinct to BRAD. Their effect, however, is by no means lost on him.

> DEBBIE
>
> Hello? Hello, Tommy . . . yes, I'm almost ready. . . . Um-hmm, I bet you would. (*laughs shyly*) Tommy, don't be silly. . . . Yes, I'm listening . . . Where? Indian Lake? You mean after? (*shakes her head*) Uh-uh. . . . Sure, that's what you said *last* time too—remember? And the time before that. (*pause*) Tommy, you *promised* then too! . . . I couldn't anyway—it would make it too late getting home. (*pause, looks interested*) They are? Kathy and Jean? (*hesitates*) Well . . . wait a minute. . . . (*covers phone, turns*) Daddy, some of the kids are going up to Indian Lake for a cookout after the dance. It would only make it about an hour later getting in. Would it be O.K.?

As she turns, BRAD lowers his eyes, then raises them at her voice. There is an almost imperceptible pain in his look of nonchalance.

> BRAD (*slightly strained*)
> Sure, don't see why not. (*takes a sip of his drink*)

> DEBBIE
> Gosh, Daddy, that's swell.
> (*back to phone*)
> It's O.K.! (*softer*) But remember what you said, Tommy. (*pause, doubtfully*) Uh-huh, I'll bet. . . . Yes, in about ten minutes. O.K., bye now. (*hangs up, crosses to Daddy*)

> DEBBIE (*leans over to kiss him*)
> Thanks a lot, Daddy—you're a darling.

When she leans over we get (his POV) a nice CU of her well-defined young cleavage, enticingly marked at the edge of the bra by a tiny crossed ribbon, almost, it might seem, in invitation.

> BRAD (*as though absorbed in his magazine*)
> Sure, kitten, sure.

> DEBBIE (*turning away*)
> Gosh, I've got to hurry!

She crosses the room again, and BRAD raises his eyes, following the provocative twitch of her pert rump as it recedes in the distance. CAMERA MOVES
SLOWLY STRAIGHT INTO HIS TROUBLED EYES, THROUGH THEM
TO BLACK. CAMERA PULLS QUICKLY BACK on a KNOCK at the door.
He rises, walks slowly toward the door, a slight tic (CU) appearing on his right
jaw. He opens the door on TOMMY—17 or 18, leaning insolently on the casing,
hands in pockets, a matchstick dangling from the corner of his mouth, his head
cocked to one side. His appearance and demeanor are a mixture of the ultimate
in sneakiness and arrogance. He surveys BRAD with amused contempt, finally
speaks—in a revolting nasal whine of indifference.

TOMMY
How 'bout it, Pops? That chickie got her pants on yet?

BRAD slowly, wordlessly, beckons him inside. TOMMY shrugs, as if to say "What a
kook!" then saunters in. BRAD carefully closes the door, faces TOMMY—who is now
standing about five feet in front of the door, slouched, a repulsive sexually demented leer on his face. BRAD casually sets himself, then delivers the most powerful right haymaker in the history of cinema—a blow with an effect more like those
of Popeye than of Duke Wayne. This should be so staged that it is shattering even
to the audience . . . a blow of such FORCE that when TOMMY hits the door five
feet behind him, he seems to be a couple of feet off the ground (VOLUME should
be UP HEAVILY on both the sound of the blow and on his slamming against the
door). It is obviously a mortal blow, obviously a blow which crushed every bone
in his head. He goes sacklike to the floor, out of frame. (During the entire living
room sequence he remains OUT OF FRAME.) BRAD moves with a sense of great
urgency, crouches over him, and throttles him powerfully. His expression is not
one of anger but of a strange nameless urgency. Near at hand is the edge of the
fireplace, with a wrought-iron stand holding poker, tongs, etc. Having choked
the life out of him, BRAD rises, draws the poker from the stand and smashes it with
incredible force against his adversary (O.S.), then he picks up the entire stand,
raises it on high, and slams it down with tremendous power. He looks about the
room, an expression of extreme urgency; his eye falls on the crossbow on the wall,
he walks quickly, takes it from the wall, removes safety clasp as he returns, stands
directly above the body (O.S.) and shoots; then, without hesitation, he holds the
crossbow like a club and splinters it in a blow of fantastic power against the adversary (O.S.). He turns, crosses the room to a side table, opens the drawer, and
takes out a .45 automatic (or .44 magnum—the bigger the better), turns up the

phonograph, walks back, working the action of the gun and slamming a shell into the chamber, picks up a cushion from the davenport on the way, cups it over the gun, and standing directly above the body, empties the clip. This should be done with full-load blanks, so that the recoil of each shot is tremendous, jerking his hand up, realistically conveying the power of the weapon and the outlandish excess of BRAD'S efforts at destruction. When the hammer clicks on an empty chamber, BRAD stands momentarily gazing down, as though the job may be finished; then he realizes it isn't. He bends over and starts dragging his adversary toward the kitchen. Here we merely glimpse the form (LONG or MED SHOT) of Tommy.

CUT TO:

INTERIOR. KITCHEN.

A large, modern kitchen, very clean. BRAD has gotten the BODY into the sink. He presses down on it; then he reaches over, flicks into operation the garbage-disposal unit, which comes on with a loud grating SOUND, and BRAD raises himself on tiptoes, pressing down with both hands. His expression is one of earnest urgency and high purpose, no trace of mania or anything negative.

CUT TO:

Same. Motor is off; BRAD bends down, opens cabinet door beneath sink; there is the familiar trap receptacle; he stares at it momentarily, then reaches in and wrenches it off in a powerful motion; he stands holding it, looking around the kitchen, then walks quickly back toward the living room.

CUT TO:

INTERIOR. LIVING ROOM.

BRAD comes striding in, with the receptacle under one arm, places it on the floor, goes to closet, takes out a heavy oblong cardboard container, tears it open, draws out a 16-pound sledgehammer. He raises the sledge on high and begins to smash the receptacle, tremendous blow after blow. CU his face, guiltless, earnest resolve and heroic effort.

WAVERING DISSOLVE AND MATCH-SOUND CUT BACK TO:

Beginning, where BRAD was on his way to the door. Sound of KNOCKING synchronized to sound of SLEDGE BLOWS, which grow rapid toward the end as we discover that this killing sequence has all taken place in an instant in BRAD's mind.

BRAD now is still on his way to the door, opens it on TOMMY. It is the same TOMMY, except that his manner is extremely normal.

> TOMMY
>
> Hello, Mr. Jeffery.

> BRAD (*unsteadily*)
>
> Good evening, Tommy . . . I think Deb is—

At that minute DEBBIE appears, hurrying across the living room.

> DEBBIE (*brightly*)
>
> Who says girls aren't ready on time!
> (*gives Daddy a peck*)
>
> Bye, Daddy!

> TOMMY
>
> So long, Mr. Jeffery.

They go down the steps, DEBBIE taking TOMMY's hand. BRAD stares after them; DEBBIE's flouncing skirt and pert derriere. He slowly closes door, face still away from camera. DONNA calls down from upstairs, seductively.

> DONNA (O.S.)
>
> Brad . . . darling . . .

BRAD slowly turns. (CU) His face has transfigured into that of an eighty-five-year-old man. He moves slowly.

> BRAD (*looking vaguely in* DONNA*'s direction,*
> *speaks in a voice ancient with age*)
>
> Yes, darling . . . I'm coming . . .

FADE OUT.

—1967
Playboy

New Journalism

Fiasco Reverie

In January of 1963, Esquire published Terry's "Recruiting for the Big Parade or, How I Signed Up at $250 a Day for the Big Parade Through Havana, Bla, Bla, Bla, and Wound up in Guatemala with the CIA—a Hipster Mercenary's Version of the Cuban Affair." It was the first story to detail the extent and depravity of the United States' "Bay o' Peeg" operations in both Latin America and Cuba. The "hipster mercenary" was Boris Grgurevich—a friend of Terry's in New York.

Shortly after the aborted 'Cuban Invasion' (May 17, 1962) I did some research into the affair and an interview(*Esquire*, January 1963) with one of the participants.

In light of the additional recent outlandish disclosures regarding the C.I.A., I went through my files again, and discovered, among other things, the enclosed letter, from an old school and service buddy, which might be of certain interest to students of that curious period of our history.

Boston, Mass.   21 July, 1962

My dear Ter:

Good to hear from you and to know that all is well.

In your letter you asked what was my *"idea"* in participating in the so-called 'Cuban Fiasco.' If, by *idea* you mean, as I assume you do, *ideal*, I am sorry to say there was none—at least not in the usual, commendatory, sense of the word. My participation was more the result, I believe, of an unusual confluence of some rather ordinary circumstances. In the first place, my wife and I had just failed in an attempt to reconcile our broken marriage—a failure all the more unfortunate since the lives of two small children were involved. Secondly, I had become dissatisfied, to the point of an almost

crippling boredom with my job; as you may recall, I am an architect, and for
several years I had then been employed by a firm of builders whose single
interest was (as it doubtless remains) in making as much money as possible
in the 'urban renewal' field. We had just taken on another mammoth
'project' and the prospect of endless months of tedious, unimaginative labor,
with substandard materials, cynical superiors, in constructing what would
soon afterwards inevitably become an even worse slum than before, was, for
me at any rate, only slightly less heartbreaking than the plight of my own
two abandoned children. The third, and most decisive, factor, was my friend
Juan H., whom I had known since childhood, and perhaps a word about his
own background is called for. Juan was born in this country, of well-to-do
Cuban parents, attended the best schools, and enjoyed every advantage (as
well, perhaps as the disadvantages) of being the only son in a wealthy home.
Spanish was spoken a good deal in and around the household, and Juan
achieved a fluency in the language at an early age; any interest he may have
had in Cuba itself, however—aside from it having been the birthplace of his
parents—was rather superficial. His tastes inclined more towards places like
Bermuda, Nassau, and the French Riviera; he was, in fact, something of a
playboy, having never married during his thirty-five years, nor in any other
sense 'settled down.' He was always a fine companion though, for an
evening on the town, or a weekend of skiing, and I saw him often throughout the years following our days together in school, but, of course, considerably less after my own marriage.

     Juan frequented the Spanish-speaking sections of the city, and it was
there, of course, that he learned about the plans for the Cuban 'invasion'—
recruitment for which was then being carried out quite openly, both in NYC
and Miami. I ran into him one night, in a West Side restaurant, and he told
me all about it. He claimed, and it is not unlikely, that he was extremely close
to the man who, if the invasion succeeded, would be made the new President, and that *we*—if we got in 'on the ground floor'—would receive posts
of the cabinet level. There was a good possibility, he said, that I would be
made Minister of the Interior, in charge of all housing and building, and he
. . . well, I believe at this point he was still undecided between being something he called 'First Secretary' and the Ambassador to France. While I did
not, of course, put any stock whatever into this pipe dream of his, I *was*
intrigued by the *general* proposition—that is, the one which seemed to apply
to *all* recruits, irrespective of family ties with the high command, namely: a

salary of $300 a month and round-trip transportation; more informal was the assurance that the living quarters and food were excellent, and finally, that there would not be much training involved—at least not the rigorous sort of which I had had my fill in the early days of World War II. Then, as a sort of clincher, was the promise that anyone who didn't like it could leave any time he wanted to. I don't recall whether, under these circumstances, your return transportation was to be provided or not—but with the 300 a month this would not seem to present a problem. Moreover, knowing Juan as I did, and his concern for his own well-being, and the elaborate precautions he would take to safeguard it, I felt confident that he had looked into the matter with some care. Suffice it to say that, after several evenings of discussing it, we did, in fact, decide to go—something which I very much doubt either of us would have done alone, and certainly not I.

I promptly gave notice at my job, along with a short speech on 'irresponsibility in high places'—and exactly one week later, received a call from Juan, saying we were to meet at Idlewild the next evening for the 10 o'clock flight to Miami. We were pleasantly surprised to find we held first-class accommodations on one of the regular super-jets; I recall very little of the trip down, except for a superb filet mignon with a sauce of artichoke hearts —after which, following the promptings of the hostess, we proceeded to consume what must have amounted to about a quart of cognac.

In Miami we had a four-, or possibly five-day layover—which was spent in the suite at the Ritz-Carton, or more often than not, lying on the edge of the splendid hotel pool, drinking, ironically enough, *Cuba Libres*. It was during our stay at the Ritz-Carlton that I began to sense the enormity of the wealth and power which must be behind the project. The fact is, we were living, like the proverbial prince; not only did Juan insist on our having meals sent up to our room, and at all hours, but there would usually be several guests on hand, both to enliven the festivities of the moment and to sharpen the prospects of later on—all of which, of course, was charged to our bill. At the same time Juan was maintaining a number of serious flirtations in New York City, by telephone, and he must have made three dozen such lengthy calls during our stay.

What was somewhat surprising, at least to me, was that there were not more people taking advantage of this singular opportunity—so far, at least, we had met only one other whom we definitely knew to be a 'comrade-in-arms.' He had been at the hotel for two weeks, and he and Juan had ex-

changed a few words the day we arrived. He was a man of about 50, a Latin
bon vivant, and evidently having the time of his life; whenever we chanced
into him in one of the hotel corridors, he invariably had a young girl on each
arm, one of whom was usually carrying a big bottle of rum. Upon seeing us,
he would break into a rhythmic cha-cha, chanting '*Yankee si, Cuba no*' as he
and his retinue shuffled past.

Then one morning the ball was over, as abruptly as it had begun, when
we received a telegram, curiously enough, sent from another part of the city,
instructing us to be at the Municipal Airport at 8:30 that evening. We had
gotten up at noon, and Juan spent the rest of the day trying to devise some
scheme whereby we could be entertained by a succession of $100 call girls,
and have it put on the bill—but we could get no cooperation in this, from
either the girls or the management. A couple of interesting sideline prospects, however, did materialize in the late afternoon, and in the end we were
half an hour late reaching the airport—only to find, with a mixture of
surprise and vague disappointment, that the plane was waiting for us. It was
a regular passenger transport, though considerably less luxurious than our
previous one. There were about twenty-five other men on the plane, occupying less than half the seats; almost everyone was asleep, and the air of
collective depletion and satiety in the plane was quite striking. As we went
down the aisle, I noticed the fellow from our hotel, sleeping, and we took
two seats nearby.

It was already known, at least insofar as one *can* know in these matters,
that we were bound for Guatemala, and this, unlike ordinary military
movements, left very little to discuss or speculate about, so Juan and I were
soon asleep, too.

It was still dark when I half awoke. The plane had landed and everyone
was getting off and into a bus waiting next to it, like sleepwalkers, and Juan
and I finally joined them. The bus appeared to be a new one, painted olive-
drab, with white numerals along the side, and the driver, an extremely
affable Spanish type, was wearing summer khaki. At last things were
beginning to take on the military aspect I had so long anticipated. Juan and I
were almost the last to get on the bus, by which time everyone appeared to
have dropped off to sleep again. We took seats not far from the driver, and
as he closed the door, he turned to me with a huge grin and said, "Guatemala!" nodding vigorously, and we were off. He drove very fast, and quite
expertly, though not without some apparent difficulty in certain gear

changes. A couple of times there was a resounding clash and grind from the transmission and the bus abruptly slowed to a crawl; at the second of these slowings I noticed that we seemed to have passed through a large, dimly lit gate, and although not much could be seen, I soon began to sense that we were inside the camp—that quality peculiar to military establishments everywhere, unforgettable to anyone who has known it . . . a sparse, flat quality, the low buildings, uncluttered lines and an absence of curvature of any sort, barren, a curious mixture of spaciousness and economy. Then the bus, as we were approaching a small area of light, slowed, and stopped; the door opened and I could see that a man was getting in. Like the driver, he was wearing summer khaki, though decked with ribbons and various insignia; he was a small man, with glasses, and a tight little smile. The driver turned to the occupants of the bus, and said, first in English, then in Spanish, "Boys, this is Captain Mack!" Somehow it was apparent to me that this was the commandant of the camp—or, as it actually turned out, co-commandant, since the chain of command here proved to be both shifting and nebulously defined. At any rate, I experienced a moment of remote panic, trying to recall military procedure under such circumstances. I knew I should call attention, but did one salute in a bus? Or stand? Before I could decide, however, Captain Mack did a remarkable thing; *he* saluted, then spoke, in a noticeably terse tone: "We're fighting for freedom here, men—glad to have you aboard." It struck me at once as odd that an army man, as I had some-how presumed him to be, would use this latter expression, but then he went on: "Now here's the scoop—there's hot chow waiting in the mess for those who can use it, and a good bunk-down for those who can't. Brief you in the morning." And so saying, he saluted again and stepped off the bus. I looked around me and saw that everyone seemed to be asleep, except for one man who was in the midst of a gigantic yawn and stretch. "Is he in command?" I asked the driver as we started out again. "Yes, yes. Captain Mack!" he answered with a show of enthusiasm. "*Commandanto!*"

Very soon we stopped again, and the driver indicated we should all get out. We were in front of a barracks, evidently quite new, a prefabricated affair, and smelling freshly of paint. The driver led us inside. It was a moderate-sized barracks, as those things go, with about 100 bunks. At first it appeared that the barracks was completely empty, but on closer look one could see that toward the far end of the barracks, beyond where the single light was burning, several of the bunks were occupied. As there was no further mention of 'hot chow,' and still being very tired myself, I quickly got into a pair of pajamas and into the nearest bunk.

I awoke the next morning in a flood of sunlight, glanced at my watch and saw it was 11:30. I jumped frantically out of bed, aware that I had badly overslept, but was relieved to see most of the other bunks still filled, including Juan's next to mine. I dressed hurriedly and went outside, where I immediately ran into the bus driver. "Chow?" he asked. "Wash?" I said, "Yes, wash." He took me back inside and showed me where the lavatory was—at the far end of the barracks, past where I had noticed the other men sleeping. In walking past, I observed that the bunks were now empty, but were unmade, the covers just sort of pulled up, as you might do in a hotel room, and the whole end of the barracks in great disorder, at least by any military standards I had known: civilian clothes—slacks and sport coats—were hanging about, and what appeared to be two huge cooking pots were sitting atop hot plates on chairs between two of the bunks. Moreover, the whole end of the room was heavy with the smell of food, in no way unpleasant, but somehow strangely out of place. I went on into the lavatory, and was glad to find it a most adequate one, modern in every respect, the hot water quick and plentiful. I noticed, somewhat disconcertingly, that two of the ten or twelve basins were stacked with dishes—quite a lot of them. Evidently the boys at this end of the barracks had been doing some cooking on their own.

When I went back in, Juan had awakened and was sitting on the edge of the bunk. I told him I was going to try to get something to eat; he wanted me to wait, but I said I would meet him at the mess hall, and I went out. I have found that my discoveries in a new place, or my first impressions, always seem sharper and more enjoyable if made alone. It may be that, alone, I don't feel burdened by the obligation of having to register or express a reaction, and yet at the same time somehow take a keener, or more concentrated, interest.

Outside, the bus driver was again on hand, and he pointed out the mess hall, or its general direction, and I headed that way. The camp now, in full daylight, already seemed familiar. It was like one of those newly built camps that one would hit every so often in being shuttled about in America during the days of 1943. There were quite a few people in sight, some in khaki, others, like myself, in civilian clothes, walking about, singly, or in groups, talking, all rather leisurely. What the camp was most like, in my own experience, was the officers' section of an ordinary camp; this was further borne out, happily enough, at the mess hall, where the food was quite good, and served on regular plates, rather than in the cafeteria style more common to military establishments, or at least to that part of them given over to enlisted men.

Sitting in the mess hall, alone at the end of a table, I became somewhat contemplative, musing, taking stock, as it were, of my situation. I was aware of a strange, and gradually growing, sense of well-being which was quite unaccountable. I recalled the numerous prior occasions when I had sat in army mess halls, swearing to heaven I would *never*, in a thousand years, be in one again of my own volition. And now, here I was, in an army mess hall, in a strange country, committed to a project of which I knew little or nothing—and yet feeling fairly good about it. Then, slowly, the reasons behind it all began to be clear. They related, of course, to the disordered state of my life at home—that my life there had become, almost without my knowing it, purposeless and without direction. What I was now doing was a sort of quietly desperate attempt to give these things back to my life, even if only for a moment—an almost purely instinctive act, like a man whose stomach has been shot away, asking for food with his last breath. I wished suddenly that I knew more about the issues involved; I had taken practically no interest whatever in Cuban affairs, merely following accounts in the press and in the weekly news magazines, so that my ignorance of the matter was fairly abysmal. But now I was ready to learn; I wondered if there would be a program of lectures—'indoctrination,' it used to be called—certainly they would not find a more willing listener than I. I could literally *feel* my receptivity, my complete openness, and more, my actual hunger for the thing, whatever it was, the cause, the reason, something anyway to really identify with and to fight for. It seemed to me now that I was on the threshold of an emotion which I had not known for many years—not since 1943, to be exact—an emotion which at that time arose out of being a part of the horrors of the bombs which fell on London, an emotion of *purpose* and *direction* . . . of 'togetherness,' if you like. What I had done in coming here, of course, was to seek a *family* to replace the one—my wife and children—I had lost. I realized that, and I thought about the notion of *camaraderie*. Would it really be possible to know that feeling again? Of course I had been very young then, but still . . . Or was I now being merely maudlin and self-indulgent—trying to escape life's realities in a sham of sentimental clap-trap? I thought about it carefully. I was sorry now I had sat down alone; I wanted very much to talk to someone about the issues involved, I wanted very much . . . to be a part of things. I glanced about the room, seeing the different groups, and individuals, wondering if, and whom, I could approach. And then, Juan arrived. I started to try to explain my feelings to him—about wanting to identify and so on, but then thought better of it. He could not possibly have understood; after all, his own life was more or less consecrated to the very opposite—flitting about, enjoying himself, taking an interest in various things, but with no particular need or desire, apparently, for the kind of stability and sense of purpose I had in mind. I don't say it critically of him, nor did I think of it in that way at the time, for in many respects I have always admired Juan for these traits—certainly his self-sufficiency in them is admirable, or at least enviable—I simply recognized that we were different in our basic needs, so I said nothing about what I had been thinking. But, I must say, I was very pleased when the conversation took the turn it did.

"I've just met our leader," he said, "I think you'll like him." And he went on to explain how the men were divided into groups of fifty, each under the charge of what was called a 'leader'—this being the only break-down of rank, in the ordinary sense, except for that remote echelon of very high-ups, such as Captain Mack whom we had met last night.

"*Good*," I said, "is he American?"

Juan nodded. "He's part of the cadre here."

"Yes, of course," I said. I noticed, or almost noticed, that my voice had slipped about half an octave lower and that my manner had become com-mensurately more serious. I wondered again if I were forcing this, and moreover, if it was apparent to Juan. It was a good feeling though, and I decided to tolerate it, but, of course, keep it within bounds. I knew that one could get away with only a certain amount of pomp and ceremony around Juan; he was a very exceptional person, but he avoided matters of 'high seriousness' like the plague.

"When do you think we'll be seeing him again?" I asked, in a more casual tone now. "I've been wanting to talk to someone . . . you know, about what' s happening and so on."

"We can see him after we finish eating."

"What's he like anyway?" I asked, immediately regretting that I had, thinking certainly Juan would spoil it all by saying something inadequate or cutting. He surprised me though by not replying at once, but gazing in a sort of abstracted way, as though he were carefully considering it.

"Well, he's pretty interesting, actually," he said, with the kind of absolutely objective ingenuity of which he was capable. Then he added, more conversationally, "I told him about you—he's looking forward to meeting you." Then he smiled, somewhat shyly, as though having said the wrong thing, and concluded: "You can talk to him about architecture or something—he seems like the kind of person who would know about things like that."

"*Good.*" I believe I made a reasonably strenuous effort to conceal my impatience while Juan picked at his food and speculated as to what fantastic obscenities his New York girlfriends were engaged in at the moment. Then, at last, he was done, and we left the hall.

I cannot, when I think back on it, remember any previous anticipation of meeting and talking with someone which would at all rival the keyed-up intensity I felt on this occasion. Well, it was a meeting which was not long in coming, and one which I shall not be forgetting in a hurry. It occurred, in fact, only moments after we left the mess hall. Juan had gotten into a conversation with a couple of Spanish-speaking persons, and we were just passing the dispensary when this fellow rushed out the door and fell in alongside us. Juan, it appeared, did not see him come up, although he did so with considerable gusto—a short and extremely fat man, bald, and with a very red face. He was sweating profusely, mopping his face with a huge crimson handkerchief, and grinning like an absolute moron. He came directly up to me, actually blocking my way, and said in a very loud voice: "*Eee otta ʒinna igras piʒan hogus!*" or something phonetically equivalent. What it was, I learned later, was the really incredible accent of the Louisiana bayou country. It was, at any rate, a form of English with which I was not yet familiar, and it was so outlandish, or so it seemed then, that I immediately assumed it to be some obscure Spanish dialect.

"I'm sorry," I said, turning to Juan, but could not get his attention.

"Nah, nah," the man shouted, pulling at my arm. "*Eee otta ʒinna igras piʒan hogus!*" he repeated at the top of his voice, pointing at the sun now, still grinning. It was obvious that he was saying something about the weather, the extreme heat, but for the life of me I could not make it out, though he must have repeated it at least ten times. We had been at a halt for minutes on end before I finally *insisted* that Juan give the matter some attention. "Do you understand what he's saying?" I asked.

"Don't you understand what he's saying?" asked Juan, in great grave innocence.

"No, I do *not*," I said shortly; I was beginning to feel the heat myself, standing there under the blazing noon sun.

"He is saying," said Juan carefully, "that 'IT'S HOTTER THAN A NIGRA'S PUSSY IN AUGUST!'" And then, before he exploded with laughter, actually doubling up, he added, pointing gleefully at the man: "That's Fats Cracker—our *leader!*"

Well, that was the mentality of the man—Fats Cracker. I mean, really; to *say* something like that, *once,* and then pass on to other things, is all right (I suppose) as some sort of tasteless joke—but to do as he did, repeating it in a shout, *laboring* it, delaying several people in the heat of the day, and so on, struck me as odd in the extreme.

At first I could *not* believe that this man, Fats Cracker, was really our group leader, nor, moreover, that he was actually a representative of the C.I.A. I found it fairly inconceivable that a person of his apparent limitations could have risen to a position of power—outside, say, guard duty on a Georgia chain gang. My second thoughts, however, were deeper; perhaps this was not, in fact, his real personality—after all, it could be an adroit stratagem, towards a purpose as yet hidden to me, that he would pretend to such exaggerated coarseness.

"How did you happen to get into this sort of work?" I asked casually, as soon as we were alone.

"What, this 'telligence work?" he said in his incredible dialect, and with an expression of genuine surprise that I should ask. "Shit, it ain't too bad a deal." He gave a short snorting laugh. "Beats shotgun and dog work, I can tell you that!"

And so it was actually true, that what had occurred to me merely as a poetic image—Fats Cracker as a chain-gang guard—had, in fact, been his last job. Not in Georgia as it turned out, but Louisiana.

"What're *you* doin' here?" he asked, and added, amiably enough, "you don't look like no spic."

"Yes, well, I'm beginning to wonder about that myself," I said. And after a few minutes of his garbled warnings about 'them greasers, boy, they all got knives,' we parted.

Returning to the barracks I discovered the far end of it half filled with smoke and conviviality; two or three guitars were playing, and a couple of card games were in progress. Almost everyone seemed to be smoking a cigar. I learned from Juan that a sizable proportion of the men did not like the new mess hall, despite its relative luxury and wholesome American fare, and had made arrangements of their own—taking ample quantities of canned stores from the quartermaster and trading them in town for red beans, rice, chicken, and fish, and then cooking meals there in the barracks. Evidently they had just finished a rather hearty breakfast.

I sat down next to Juan on his bunk and he immediately handed me a thin sheaf of papers he was holding. "Here," he said, "sign this."

"What is it?" I asked, noting his faint look of amusement.

At the top of the first page was a paragraph in Spanish, and the rest of the space was given over to signature—several hundred of them.

"It's a petition for doubling the ration of cigars and rum," Juan said.

I gazed around the barracks, and I was suddenly struck by a very odd sensation indeed—at least half the men were wearing beards, and each with a cigar, so that in the dim light of the smoke-filled room, they looked like several dozen Castros.

"What is the present ration?" I asked.

"Who knows?" said Juan, and added with a smile. "I would sign it if I were you."

I signed, and Juan passed the petition to a man sitting on the next bunk, who, I noticed, simply signed it without looking.

"We are going to be in *cryptography*," Juan announced then, "we will be decoding officers."

"I see," I said, "did you locate your friend then, the one who's going to be President?"

Juan sighed and shook his head. "No, I'm afraid he's not with us any more—a sad story—he was one of the first to arrive, about two months ago, and he was wearing a beard. Well, he got into an argument with the C.I.A. people about the beard—they wanted him to shave it off and he wouldn't; finally they insisted that he shave it off, and he told them to go to the devil.

They said he was a communist and put him in the stockade, and that's where
he is now."

"Well, that policy must have changed," I said, "look at all the beards in
this room."

"Yes, they're a good deal more indulgent now—and the commanding
officer, of course, is a different one. The commanding officer, I understand,
has been replaced about six times since then."

"But your friend is still in the stockade?"

"Yes, he refused to come out—he said the whole experience did, in
fact, make a communist out of him. Now he won't even discuss it—they
keep asking him why he's a communist, and he says: 'Because *you're not!*'
Curious, isn't it?"

"It's very curious," I said.

"I'm going to write my lawyer about it," said Juan. "I'll bet he can sue
them for deranging his mind."

The first scheduled event for the day's training was an 'orientation lecture.'
The bulletin board described it, in English, as: "Emil Zopek, formerly
connected with the Warsaw Red Police, who chose Freedom to Red Tyr-
anny, will speak on 'The Conspiracy of International Communism.'" Mr.
Zopek, it developed, had been a hairdresser in the building opposite what
was once a precinct station of the Warsaw police, so that his observations
were fairly vague. Moreover, they were delivered, not in Spanish, but in a
pidgin-English that was only occasionally comprehensible to the most astute
listener. Most of the men began wandering off before the lecture was half
through. Fats Cracker and several other members of the cadre who were
roaming around made no attempt to stop the exodus, but did appear to be
noting their names on paper—a difficult, if not impossible, job, due to their
great number. Once, Fats Cracker, in passing near where I was sitting, nodded
his head at the general departure and whispered tersely, "Commie tamales!"

Our training began in earnest, however, that afternoon when we were taken
to the rifle range. Most of the men had never fired a gun outside an amusement park, and it was refreshing to observe the childlike eagerness which
they brought to the new experience of firing an M-1 rifle. The instructors
were all speaking in Spanish, and there was a great deal of argument and

horseplay going on between them and the men on the firing line, and always a round of backslapping whenever someone hit the bull's-eye. Curiously enough, though, as soon as one of the men had managed to hit the bull's-eye, his interest immediately began to wane, and, almost invariably, he would get bored before completing his score and would move over to the line where the .45 pistol and the Thompson submachine gun were being fired. The Thompson was the great favorite, though everyone seemed surprised that it kicked and jumped so violently—unlike the silky-firing ones in the movies—and, after a couple of clips, they lost interest in that as well and then wandered back to the barracks.

Juan and I were the last to leave the range, and when we got back to the barracks, at about four o'clock, there seemed to be some sort of festival under way. It was a bedlam of music and dance—a number of girls were present, and most of the men had changed into their sharp civilian outfits. Radios were blaring three different mambos, and the place was jumping. Someone immediately put a water glass full of rum in my hand; I took a drink of it and sat down on my bunk in a slight daze, when Juan, after a few minutes' conversation with one of the other men, said that I was to report to the C.O.'s office at once. After making some adjustments to my ill-fitting uniform, I preferred my drink to Juan.

"Why not take it with you?" he suggested with a wry smile.

From what we had so far seen of the affairs of the camp, it would not have been entirely out of the question; however, I contented myself with another swig, and then set out for headquarters.

The C.O. was, of course, the same nautically minded person we had met the night of our arrival. He was a man of striking appearance—very tall, with crew-cut hair, and blue eyes that were extremely light in color; despite the fact that he appeared to be in his late forties, or even older, his hair was as blond as a schoolboy's.

"Stand easy, M.," he said when I had reported. He gave me half a minute of shrewd appraisal before he continued: "I wanted to talk to you, M., because you're a fellow American. That's right, isn't it?"

"I'm an American, yes sir," I replied.

"By birth, or by naturalization?"

"By birth, sir."

He was seated at his desk, his swivel chair half facing the door, and he stood up now and walked to the door, opened it and casually looked into the

outer office. Only the clerk was there at the far end of the room. The C.O.
shut the door carefully and faced me again.

"We've got a 21-gun problem on our hands here, M., I suppose you
realize that."

I assumed he was referring to the problem of general discipline in the
camp, or the complete lack of it, and buoyed up by the rum I was tempted to
say, "You're not kidding, skipper," but wisely let it pass. In any case, his
remark was purely rhetorical, because he immediately supplied the answer
himself, intoning it with a certain dark drama:

"*Security?*"

He returned to his desk and picked up some papers, which I recognized
as the rum and cigar petition I had signed earlier.

"You've seen this before, of course," he said, either suspecting a
forged signature, or testing my sanity.

"Yes sir."

He dropped the papers back on the desk. "I don't drink myself," he
said, rather awkwardly, "nor do I smoke cigars. This is not to say, however,
that I expect the rest of the world to follow my example—and here I'm
speaking on the policy level of command. I mean, in the light of present-day
psychological realities, we are prepared to recognize that *our* way is not
necessarily the *only* way. After all, the *British Navy* has a rum ration—the
cigars, well, that's something else. Still we've got to be realistic, we've got to
recognize these cultural differences and be prepared to accept them—indeed,
be prepared to turn them to mutual advantage. Do you see my point?"

"Yes sir, I do."

"Now, in the case of this petition however, G-2 has reason to believe that
something else is afoot." He took up the papers again and leafed through them.
"Now, your friend, J.*66*—he's not by any chance a Russky, is he?"

I was somewhat taken aback, not so much by the notion, as by the use
of the word 'Russky,' which I don't believe I had heard since World War II.

"No sir, he's an American . . . by birth," I added, anticipating him,
correctly, too, because he gave a tight smile and lowered his eyes.

"Yes, of course," he said with heavy irony, "J.___, fine old American
name, isn't it?" He sighed, shaking his head, and replaced the papers on the
desk. Then he cleared his throat, frowning slightly, as though distracted
from his original line of thought. "G-2, as I was saying, has reason to believe
that these supplemental rations—of rum and cigars—are not going to be

consumed, but are going to be sold at black market in the town, and that the funds so derived are to be used to step up communist infiltration and espionage in this garrison. In short, Russky mercenaries—under the direction, of the number-one Russky mercenary, *Fidel Castro*."

From his challenging look it was apparent that he expected a comment, and I tried to manage one.

"It's a possibility, sir, which I hadn't considered."

"M., we happen to *know* that supplies—stolen from Q.M.—have been sold in the town. Are you going to say you've heard nothing about that?"

"Nothing, sir."

"Nothing at all?"

Still uncertain of my allegiance, and wanting to do the *right* thing, I said:

"I understand that supplies may have been traded in town for food—and the food prepared outside the mess hall. But I've heard nothing about . . . the other."

But this was evidently old hat to the C.O., and he made a grimace of impatience. "Yes, yes, we know about *that*—all that business about not liking the food—that's merely a . . . a *diversionary tactic*, a smoke screen to conceal the real operation. Surely you see through that ruse?"

"No, sir, I think they're probably quite sincere about that—I mean they certainly seem to enjoy the food in the barracks."

It was, of course, a mistake to say this; it was not what he wanted to hear. It seemed to anger him profoundly—not against me, but against the men themselves. He stared rigidly out the window, one hand working over a clenched fist at his chest; he appeared to be doing a slow burn.

"Hypocritical bastards," he said softly, between grinding teeth. "Christ, we're *paying* them enough, aren't we?" And he turned to me, an expression of childlike bewilderment in his faultless blue eyes; it was a genuine plea: "Why can't they just . . . just *eat the food*?"

This matter of security, however, was to plague the rest of our days in the camp. It got increasingly worse, and it reached its high point towards the end, shortly before the "invasion," when it was rumored that Castro himself, in a feat of devilish daring and mockery, was in the camp—that he had personally come to taunt the piteous forces against him. The C.I.A. thought it probable that he was disguised as a *woman*. "He's a sexual pervert, you know," the Captain had said and they began trying to ban all women visitors from the garrison; this caused a hell of a row because the presence of the camp-following hookers was an integral part of the scene. The disturbance reached such proportions that there was a new change of command.

In retrospect, one sees that these anxieties were not wholly without foundation. Our 'attack plan,' if it may be so called, was apparently well known and analyzed in advance, down to the minutest detail, and with considerable evidence of internal subversion. For example, when D-Day rolled around, we could not get the supply ship *started*, actually could not get the motor turning—everything seemed to have gone wrong with it: the fuel tanks were filled with water, the compass was riveted on upside down, the rudder was missing. Sabotage? Of course, but on the most monumental and contemptuous level; after all, it would have been much more clever to do something more subtle, or more straightforward simply to have blown up the ship at its moorings. Obviously they were toying with us. In any case, after an interminable delay, the supply ship did manage to chug out of the harbor under quarter-power. I was in one of the L.S.T.s [Landing Ship Tank—ed.], but a friend of mine was aboard and described the following: At the forerail was a man wearing two life preservers who kept asking the mate, with a grin, what his last sounding was. When the mate's reading was 14 fathoms—which give or take a few feet was the distance from the keel to the top of the stack—the man pulled out a handkerchief, and there was an almost immediate explosion from below decks, and the ship promptly began to sink. Through a curious diversionary tactic of our own we had put *all the supplies* on that one ship. (That strategy, I later learned, was based on a chess theory called "King Forward," well thought of at C.I.A. headquarters, but apparently not yet fully developed.) It was disheartening to watch her go down; but the L.S.T.s plowed ahead—G-2 had promised quick capitulation of the adversary at the first show of strength. High-powered reconnoitering, plus the latest in positive-objectivist analysis in depth, clearly indicated that the people would rise as one, march solidly into the marketplaces, the town halls, the churches . . . and take down Castro's photograph.

On our own L.S.T. things were rapidly coming to a head. Fats Cracker, under the pre-battle strain, was beginning to lose his bearings. On the pretext of whipping up enthusiasm among the men, he was trying to work his way to the back of the landing craft, so as to be the last one off—or, more likely, not get off at all. The men were on to this, however, and crowded him well forward. This crass insubordination under actual battle conditions must have almost snapped his mind, because when the ramp finally dropped in the surf of the beach, he screwed his courage to the sticking point and lunged to the fore with a thunderous battle cry:

"GIT THEM NIGGERS!"

He missed his footing, though, and went headlong into the water at the base of the ramp, and thereby became a sort of continuation of the ramp for those who followed, many of whom seemed to revel in the notion, heavy footing it with gleeful abandon. In any case, by the time Juan and I reached that point, he must have been pressed fairly deep into the sand, because I felt nothing as I stepped past, no trace of bodily countour. Not that there weren't certain distractions—above each landing craft the air was bristling with the cross fire of several dozen machine guns, scarcely a foot over our heads, with a high percentage of tracers so we would be sure and notice. Apparently they were so accurately zeroed-in that they didn't have to shoot *at* us, merely over us. Everyone—except Fats, of course—immediately dropped their rifles and raised their hands. There was really nothing else to do.

As we climbed the dunes, hands over our heads, like you see in the World War II newsreels, the victorious adversary rose as one from his emplacements ahead of us, doubled up with laughter. Castro himself was there and personally gave a swift kick in the ass to each of the invaders. Then, with no fanfare, or even further ado, we were taken to Havana.

Thanks to some string pulling on Juan' s part, the two of us were released after a couple of totally uneventful days in a very ordinary barracks-compound with a minimum of security. In short, we were not even accorded the respect of mistreatment. We went back to Miami and tried to check in at the Ritz-Carlton on the same dodge, but no soap, the movement had folded. Juan went back to New York, and I set out for Europe. So that was that.

As for the others, I had a letter from one of them recently—H., the bon vivant at the Carlton—and he said they're doing all right, except for a few kamikaze types. He said Castro isn't really mad at them any more, but does have to keep up the appearance of it because of the tractor deal and other considerations. Most of them, apparently, have come around to seeing things his way, which didn't surprise me much. I mean, why shouldn't they see it his way—after all, *they're* Cuban, too. Right?

—1970s

Grooving in Chi

In the streets of Chicago during the National Democratic Convention the chant "The whole world is watching!" erupted as peaceful protesters were pummeled and gassed by the police—live on the six o'clock news. Esquire magazine had dispatched a "hard-hitting investigative team," as Terry described it, which included himself, Jean Genet, and William Burroughs. During the Chicago 8 trial, Terry testified on their behalf, and provided an eyewitness account of how an FBI agent-provocateur initiated the Lincoln Park police riot.

The Year of Our Lord, 1968

Chicago. On the way to the hotel this afternoon, coming from the airport, I saw something right out of a Buñuel movie; in a desolate section that resembles the Jersey flats, four boys each about ten years old and armed with small sticks were flailing wildly at a huge crippled black man who reeled and staggered drunkenly among piles of debris in a deserted lot. The taxi passed within fifty feet of the scene, slowing down as the driver looked directly at it, with no other apparent reaction.

"Wait a minute," I said as we continued past, "they're beating the hell out of that guy back there. We'd better help him."

The driver shrugged and brought the cab to a gradual stop. "The coon's loaded," he muttered, craning his head out the window to look behind us.

"Just back up a little," I suggested, "they'll probably take off."

"Uh-huh," he started slowly backing up, "what if they don't?"

"They're only kids for chrissake," saying this with an almost total lack of conviction as we drew nearer—but as it happened my analysis was correct; after one last flurry, and amidst mucho high-pitched prepuberty screeching of obscenities, the children abandoned their prey and scurried pell-mell across the lot.

"Are you okay?" I asked the Negro, much closer to the curb now, still staggering, but seemingly unscathed. Instead of a direct, or indeed a verbal reply, his response was to seize a large, empty and battered ashcan, to raise it over his head, ready to slam it into the side of the taxi.

"Wait," I started so explain, "me friend . . ." but the driver had by now definitely lost interest in the case, and he lurched the car up and away.

"Boy, was that coon ever loaded," he said matter-of-factly about five minutes later.

A curious tableau—did it augur well or mal, conventionwise?

Six P.M. Rendezvous of our hard-hitting little press team—Jean Jack Genet, Willy Bill Burroughs, and yours truly as anchor man, trying to lend a modicum of stability to the group. Also on hand, Esky editor young John Berendt—his job: straighten these weirdos, and K.F.S. ("Keep Flying Speed!"). We met in the queer little Downstairs Lounge, one of several bars in our hotel, the Chicago-Sheraton—and John Berendt was quick to charge us with our respective assignments: "You Jean Jack Genet, on the alert for all manner of criminality and perversion in high places! You, Big Bill Burroughs, let your keen and experienced eye discern any sign of sense derangement through the use of drugs by these delegates, the nominees, and officials of every station! Now then, you, T. Southern, on double alert for all manner of *absurdity* at this convention!"

Thus charged, we drank steadily for the next two hours before going to visit grand guy Dave Dellinger, head of National Mobilization to End the War in Vietnam and one of the chief coordinators for the planned demonstrations. Before our meeting, I thought this so-called Dellinger must necessarily be some kind of old-fool-person—a kind of leftover leftist from another era who didn't know where it was at right now, just a compulsive organizer . . . maybe even a monstro-commie-spade-fag. But no, a groove and gas he proved to be.

"Our demonstrations shall be entirely peaceful," he explained (with a certain lack of prophecy) and then went on to describe the coalition and its program. The other two principal groups were the S.D.S. (of Morningside Heights fame) and the fun and ever-loving Yippies. A wise and gentle man, it was this same Dave Dell, editor of *Liberation*, who led the Pentagon March last fall, and so we sat talking in a bare and harshly lit room, the windows of which had been blown out the previous day in some ironic industrial explosion, the glass replaced with a flimsy plastic cloth which flapped absurdly now in the Chicago (Windy City) night breeze, lending a surreal quality to the scene. "We are not seeking a confrontation," said Dave—a term incidentally which proved the most meaningful, both in theory and in fact, of any concept put forward during the convention—"we simply wish to protest the foregone conclusion that it is a closed convention, that there is no possible alternate to Humphrey, as a candidate, and more importantly, of course, to express our continued opposition to the war in Vietnam."

"What's happening with Lincoln Park?"

Early in the afternoon an announcement had been issued by the Office of the Mayor—Richard Daley—to the effect that everyone would have to be out of the park by eleven that night. This edict was fairly inopportune, because about two thousand young yip-yip Yippies had just arrived from various U.S.A.; and with absolutely no other place to go, all hotels full for proverbial months on end, they had ensconced at the Link.

"We're hoping the Mayor will reconsider his decision," said Dellinger, ever boss-reasonable, "that perhaps he will understand the best way to deal with a situation like this might be to accommodate it . . . not to defy it."

This truth was obvious and it immediately brought to mind my own John Jack Lindsay, and how *he* would have handled it, to good advantage, god bless him, strolling down there in shirt sleeves, with some hot dogs to roast, a nice little Panasonic transistorized cassette unit blasting a fine sound, and maybe even a taste of, hrrumph, hee-hee, *Chicago* Light Green! It was all so apparent how Dumbbell Dick could have cooled it—and not merely have cooled it, but turned it to gross P.R. advan. I began to think of myself as some sort of lean and hungry Pierre Sal, as I grooved there with Dave Dellinger—just grooving on Big Dave and his son, Ray, both too beautiful to be believed—son boss-physical-spiritual, wearing a blue beret, circling catlike bodyguard-style around his father . . . knowing Dad Dave was something else, and that certain lewdies and sick weirdos might venture harm against him.

Suddenly Mister John Jack Genet, knowing no English at all, demanded of our ace trans (Richard Dick Seaver—of Evergreen-Grove fame) if Hugh Hefner was a fag.

Well, really. I mean I'm no prude myself, but when some weird frog starts blasting the Hef, that's when I begin to get a bit uptight. Unfortunately I had nothing at the moment to get up on, much less tight, so I simply lay back, and sort of dropped out, so to speak. Dellinger, of course, knew nothing about Hef sex, nor could (I warrant) care less. In any case the subject was soon dropped in favor of more serious matters—namely where we could find Allen Ginsberg. Allen, it developed, was staying at the Lincoln Hotel, just opposite the park itself; so with Dick Seaver at the wheel, we zoomed across town—toward the very heart of the action, for it was now ten minutes till curfewville, eleven P.M. And quite apparent it was, too, when we reached the scene—the baby-blue police already massed in rows of three . . . nightsticks and Mace at the ready, also gas masks, smoke grenades, and riot guns, a weird sight I can tell you. They lined the sidewalk bordering the park, which was completely dark, except for two or three bonfires glowing in the distance. In the midst of the police formation was a huge armored van, on top of which were several banks of large searchlights; in front of the still dark lights stood three men—the ones on either side holding riot guns, the kind used to fire tear-gas shells, while the man between them made announcements over a gigantic bullhorn:

"This is a final warning. Clear the park. Disperse. You have five minutes to disperse. You have five minutes to get out of this park!"

About then we spotted big Ed Sanders, of Fug and E.V.O. fame, threading his way along the periphery of monstro-fuzz before knifing into the darkness.

"Where's that loony fruit Al Ginsberg?!?" I shouted, rushing to overtake him. Fortunately, just before lowering the boom on me, Ed recognized the remark for the clever and good-natured jibe it was.

"He's doing his thing," he said, pointing, "over by that fire."

We all started walking in that direction. As our eyes became accustomed to the dark, and in the eerie light of the approaching fires, we could now make out figures and faces where before it had been an empty blackness. It is difficult to estimate the number of persons there, but they were everywhere—probably more than two thousand, milling around, seemingly about half of them moving toward the street to get out of the park, the other half just wandering uncertainly in the half-light.

We found Allen, seated in the center of a group of fifty or so, doing his thing. Which in this case was the "*Om*"—leading the others in chanting the word "Om" with varying intonation, pitch, and volume. Sanders explained that at eleven o'clock a rumor that the police were moving in had caused panic and started a general and chaotic fight. Ginsberg however had restored calm by gathering these people around him and doing his Om thing. Now they appeared to be serenity itself, while behind us the bullhorn droned on:

"Final warning. The Officers are moving in in five minutes. Anyone in the park will be arrested."

We sat down with the others, and joined the Oming, which especially delighted Genet; we stayed there for maybe half an hour, while the circle grew steadily larger, and the "final warnings" were repeated. It was now nearing midnight. Burroughs looked at his watch, and with that unerring awareness of which he is capable, muttered, "They're coming." At that instant, the banks of searchlights blazed up on the armored van which was already moving toward us. Fanned out on each side of the van were about a thousand police.

"Well, Bill, I think we'd better pursue another tactic," I suggested, getting to my feet. What the hell, we were supposed to be here as *observers*, not as participants in any of Allen's crackpot schemes. That the entire reportage team should be bested the first time out was unthinkable. Genet was the most difficult to persuade, but finally, on Ginsberg's insistence, we all went up to his hotel room. By this time the police had made their first contact with the crowd— persons who were actually trying to leave the park, but had been driven back in the opposite direction, so that now people were fleeing all around us. Advancing in the distance, silhouetted against the wall of light, moved this incredible phalanx of strangely helmeted men, swinging their nightsticks as they came. Once it was decided that we should leave, we moved with unfaltering gait— odd how infectious panic can be. Near the street, I glanced back in time to see them reach the place where we had been, and where a dozen or more were still sitting. They didn't arrest them—at least not right away; they beat the hell out of them—with night-sticks, and in one case at least, the butt of a shotgun. They clubbed them until they got up and ran, or until they started crawling away (the ones who were able) and then they continued to hit them as long as they could. The ones who actually did get arrested seemed to have gotten caught up among the police, like a kind of human medicine ball, being shoved and knocked back and forth from one cop to the next, with what was obviously *mounting* fury. And this was a phenomenon somewhat unexpected, which we were to observe consistently throughout the days of violence—that rage seemed to engender rage; the bloodier and the more brutal the cops were, the more their fury increased.

Witnessed an amusing, and perhaps historic, confrontation this P.M. when in the lobby of the Hotel Drake, we chanced across a dramatic encounter between Louis ("I have nothing to hide") Abolafia, the nudist-ticket candidate, and testy Babe Bushnell who's running on the S.C.U.M. (Society for Cutting Up Men) ticket, whose founder, it might be recalled, tried to assassinate Andy Warhol. It was a curious meeting, a sort of "battle of the sexes," you might say. While the Babe shouted her diatribe about the "cutting up" of men, and where exactly the process should begin, Abolafia attempted to detract from her remarks by executing what appeared to be a nude dervish or tarantella. Both candidates had to be dragged from the lobby.

Right after lunch we very dutifully piled into the car and headed for the Convention Hall. It is exactly like approaching a military installation—barbed-wire, checkpoints, the whole bit; Genet was absolutely appalled, I was afraid he was going to be physically sick; Burroughs, of course, was ecstatic; it was all so grotesque that at one point he actually did a little dance of glee. He has a tape recorder, and he applies his cut-up and fragmentation theory to its use—recording speeches by the delegates and committeemen, then putting blank spaces in them, and filling the blanks with pieces of other speeches, and finally playing back this composite of clichés and inanities in such a way as to sound like live radio coverage—a possibility which was enhanced by the fact that this particular recorder looks exactly like a portable radio. It was Burroughs's belief that if these tapes were played constantly in the Convention Hall, the subliminal effect—of the repetitions, the non sequiturs, and the general idiocies—would so confound any chance listener as to possibly snap his mind, and thus become a profoundly disruptive factor in the overall "Convention profile."

We had one hell of a time actually getting admitted to the hall, despite all the proper credentials. Burroughs and I, of course, are veritable paragons of fashion and decorum—but Ginsberg and Genet, it must be admitted, are pretty weird-looking guys. In any case the cluster of door cops took one look at our group—which now also included Michael Cooper, an English photographer with shoulder-length hair, a purple suit, and sandals—and then simply turned away, as though we had never arrived. The lieutenant in charge looked at us, though, and just sort of shook his head, a tight little "Who-are-you-kidding?" smile on his lips.

"Our accreditation is all in order, officer," snapped Esky's John Berendt, indicating the door passes around our necks.

"It is, huh?" said the lieutenant, not even bothering to look.

"How about *his* creditation?" he said, pointing to Ginsberg, "is it in order too?" And he gave a derisive snort.

"It certainly is," said Berendt, "show him your pass, Allen."

The lieutenant ignored Allen's attempt to show his pass, and fixed on Cooper. "And *he's* got creditation? Hell, he ain't even got any *shoes!*"

This drew some appreciative snickers from the cops in the doorway. Just then another lieutenant arrived and wanted to know what the trouble was, whereupon the first lieutenant simply indicated us with a nod, as though it was that obvious.

"They got passes?" asked the other, and reached out to examine the nearest one.

"You wantta handle this?" said the first lieutenant in a highly annoyed tone, "you handle it. I don't want no part of it." And he turned away, arms creased, a sullen little-boy expression on his fifty-year-old face.

The other one watched him for a minute, then looked at us again, with perhaps only one iota less suspicion than his colleague.

"Okay, let's go," he said, "I'll take you up to Security."

The Security chiefs were typically F.B.I., C.I.A.—cop-types, but a shade less stupid; at least they made a slight effort to disguise their arrogance. In any case, after a thorough checking they let us go on our way, and into the hall. Not that it was necessarily worth it—because, aside from Burroughs's tapes, and an occasional hoodlum act on the floor, the events were without interest. It was so flagrantly obvious that the fix was in, and that there was no possibility of altering the outcome. It was in the air; you could see it, you could feel it, you could almost smell it. Worse, like the cheapest sort of wrestling match, where even the *staging* of the deception is inept. The spectacle of grown men behaving like children at a birthday party, cavorting in colored hats and streamers, jumping up and down, standing on chairs, screaming and waving, did not lessen the nausea.

Riding back to the hotel everyone felt depressed, as if the absurdity of it might not be enough after all. We listened to the tapes.

"I wonder what can be in the mind of a politician," someone mused. Seaver translated it for Genet, but he was not intrigued. "*I* wonder," he said, staring as the dashboard of the Ford car we were in, "what can be in the mind of someone who names an automobile 'Galaxie'?"

* * *

Near the hotel we passed a procession of about five hundred Yippies, a red flag flying at the fore, and all chanting "Pigs must go! Pigs must go!" We learned that they were parading to the police station to protest the arrest of two of their leaders, Tom Hayden and Wolf Lowenthal. Ginsberg was apprehensive about the growing tension. One of the reasons he had come to Chicago, he explained, was to try and dissuade certain of the more militant leaders from pursuing a program of violence. An hour or so later we went to Grant Park, opposite the Hilton Hotel, where a meeting concerning the Lincoln Park situation was in progress. The parading Yippies had arrived, and one of them had climbed atop a large marble statue commemorating a Civil War hero. A large number of police, guarding the Hilton, watched the boy with smoldering antagonism— and finally a contingent of them abruptly crossed the street and pulled him down, so forcibly that it broke his arm. A tremendous wave of resentment swept through the crowd, and things might have gotten out of hand at that moment, but everyone started leaving for Lincoln Park. They had decided that tonight they would hold it.

We got there around eleven and immediately sensed that there was a different atmosphere from the night before, an air of determination, and about twice as many people—including twenty or thirty priests and ministers. A few helmets were in evidence, and a number of the medics, dressed in white with Red Cross armbands, were on hand—but the park was not yet the armed camp it would become. At midnight the police began to appear; they arrived on the opposite side of the expressway which forms the north boundary of the park— it was a solid line, shoulder to shoulder, five blocks long. Their gas masks were quite conspicuous. About twelve-thirty, one officer crossed the expressway and started issuing "final warnings" on the bullhorn. A few minutes later, a patrol car occupied by four cops with shotguns slowly moved off the expressway and down the sidewalk, through the crowd. Somebody in the crowd threw a brick through the windshield, probably a cop. Incidentally, one of the most insidious aspects of the entire police operation was the use of "confrontation provocateurs." These were cops dressed like hippies whose job it was to incite the crowd to acts of violence which would justify police intervention or, failing that, to commit such acts themselves. It is curiously significant that their artfully dressed undercover men were so flagrantly conspicuous as to be impossible to miss— not due to their appearance, which was indiscernible from the rest of the crowd, even the fact that they were encouraging violence, but due completely to the loud, lewd, tasteless stupidity that characterized their every remark and gesture.

In any case, when the brick hit the windshield, it seemed to me that was our cue to get the hell out of there, so we began a leisurely withdrawal. Behind us now the crowd had surrounded the car, and was rocking it, trying to turn it over. That's when the police charged. They came very fast, clubbing everyone they could catch, and firing tear-gas shells ahead of the fleeing crowd—so that it was a question of going through the gas or waiting to get clubbed. Most people chose the gas, and emerged into the street on the south side of the park, groping blindly, face streaming with tears. Our fun party was well ahead of the clubs, but not the gas; no one seemed to escape the gas—the wind was right, and they were using a lot of it. We reached the street adjacent to Allen's hotel, and assumed we were safe—they had wanted us out of the park, and now we were out. But we continued to walk away from it because of the fumes. About three-quarters of the way down the block, we heard yelling ahead and the approach of frantically running footsteps, then the appearance of several dozen people tearing along the sidewalk toward us. "They're coming!" screamed a girl in absolute terror as she passed; running behind her was a boy of sixteen or so, blood covering one side of his face. Now, at the rear of the crowd, we could see the cops, chasing and flailing. We started running with the rest, down the middle of the street, but almost immediately encountered people running in the opposite direction.

"Don't go that way, man," one of them said, "it's a very bad scene back there." We were trapped, and for a moment it was sheer panic, then someone (Berendt or Seaver no doubt) had the inspired thought to try one of the apartment-house doors we were passing, and so the next moment we were all huddled in this small hallway, just as one wave of police swept past, wiping out everyone in its path. Now we had to crouch so as not to be seen through the glass front of the door, because from the other direction they were rushing into the doorways and halls and routing them out. We could hear it happening next door in no uncertain terms. And then it was our turn and, sure enough, in charged four of the finest, with expressions of rage such as I have never seen. In fact, Genet later jestingly insisted that they had not been cops at all but actors who were overplaying their roles.

"You Communist bastards!" one of them snarled, "get the hell outta here! Now move!" And he raised his club at the nearest person, who as it happened was Genet—but the latter, saint that he is, simply looked at the man and shrugged, half lifting his arms in a Gallic gesture of helplessness. And the blow didn't come. Another tribute to Genet's strange power over people. Instead, they pushed and prodded us out onto the street where they talked about taking us to the station; but they were soon distracted by activity farther down the block, and they rushed away. Because it wasn't really us they wanted to get— it was the children.

I talked with Ed Sanders at the park this afternoon. The Yippies have brought a pig, which they are going to try to place in nomination if they can ever get near the hall. The pig is pink, and weighs about a hundred pounds. They keep it in a burlap bag.

Tonight we went to the L.B.J. Un-Birthday Party at the Chicago Coliseum. It was a swinging affair, with a groovy audience who responded very enthusiastically when our brutality statements—prepared earlier in the day— were read to them.

Tonight's scene at the park was certainly the strangest yet. About one hundred priests were there, having earlier announced that they would conduct an all-night religious service. A large cross (about ten feet high) had been erected, and several fires burned nearby. The pattern of events was identical to what had transpired on the previous evenings. Only the presence of the cross, after the smoke and tear gas came rolling in, slowly engulfing it, lent the spectacle an unreal and cinematic quality. As we fled from the park, I witnessed a curious incident, near the lake. A young boy on a bicycle, of apparently no connection whatever with the demonstration, was peddling along the outer path, past six or eight police who were stationed there. They grabbed the bicycle and pushed it and the boy into a lagoon, laughing uproariously the while. By chance a photographer was standing not fifty feet away, and he got a picture of it— published the following day (Wednesday, the 28th) in the Chicago *Daily News*.

Wednesday, August 28th. This was our biggest, most outlandish day. The plan was to march to Convention Hall, so the crowd began early to form in Grant Park. By four o'clock there must have been seven or eight thousand people. Mayor Daley had refused to issue a parade permit, and the order was that anyone who attempted to march would be arrested forthwith. By now, of course, the National Guard was there in great strength, massed three deep along the Michigan Boulevard side of the park, while on the opposite side, in front of the Hilton, were the police—or "the Pigs" as they were now known by all. Again the order to clear out of the park was given. Under the circumstances (of not being allowed to parade) it was decided that it might be best to regroup elsewhere, so what was intended as a general exodus was begun. And this is where the logic of the Chicago authorities can be proved either insane or sadistic, perhaps both, because the park is joined to Michigan Boulevard by several bridges, and these are the only means of egress; but when the first of the crowd reached the nearest bridge, we found it blocked by soldiers with fixed bayonets. As the crowd continued to accumulate near the bridge, the order to disperse was given again.

"Hey, why don't you stick those bayonets up your ass?" someone suggested—a quip which was answered with several quick rounds of tear gas, and the crowd began to scatter wildly across the park. The same thing was experienced at the next two exits—here was a case of *containment* and *dispersal* all in one. "Somebody's wig has snapped," observed Burroughs drily. But it was patently a harassment tactic of the shabbiest order, and one which was to backfire badly. The only way out of the park now was to walk around on the lake side by the expressway, a very long route indeed—so that by the time the bulk of the crowd reached Michigan Boulevard, and the Hilton Hotel, they were hopping mad. So were the cops, and you could see adrenaline rising.

We had all gotten separated during the confusion at the park, so now I found myself alone outside the locked doors of the Hilton, caught up in a seething crowd, and a rapidly growing malaise. I pounded on the glass.

"I'm a guest," I insisted.

"Let's see your key."

"It's at the desk."

"Sorry."

Then by the sheerest chance I spotted a guy I knew, just as he was dangling his key in front of the glass. He was able to get me in, and we immediately went to the hotel bar on Michigan, the windows of which afforded a grandstand view of the melee which followed. By now it had all become like some strange, and sickening, spectator sport.

Bill Styron and John Marquand Jr. were also in the bar and there was a certain undeniable decadence in the way we sat there, drinks in hand, watching the kids in the street getting wiped out. Tear-gas fumes began to permeate even the locked doors, and at the height of the slaughter five or six kids were pushed through a plate-glass window on one side of the bar. The cops rushed in after them.

"Get the hell outta here!" a cop was yelling, which they were trying to do as fast as possible. But something was wrong with one of them, a thin blond boy about seventeen.

"I can't walk," he said.

"You'll walk outta here, you little son of a bitch!" said the cop and clubbed him across the side of the head with his stick. Two of the others seized him by the shirt and started dragging him across the floor of the bar and through the lobby.

Next to me a middle-aged man, wearing a straw hat with a Hubert Humphrey band, watched the incident with distaste.

"Those damn kids," he muttered, "I haven't seen a clean one yet." Then he looked back out into the street where, at that moment, a flying squad of blue helmets and gas masks, clubs swinging, charged straight into a crowd obviously of bystanders.

"Hell," he grunted, "I'd just as soon live in one of those damn police states as put up with that kind of thing."

—November 1968
Esquire,

Reprinted courtesy of *Esquire* and the Hearst Corporation.

The Straight Dope on the Private Dick; Including Certain Previously Undisclosed Facts About the Persecution of the Late Lenny Bruce

One recent P.M., I dropped in on my good friend, James 'Big Jim' Goode, top staffer at one of the country's better mags. Big Jim was brooding over a manuscript on his desk which he said was "too hot to handle."

"Then why not let a certain yours truly have a look at that M.S." I suggested, ". . . perhaps a bit of tightening up, brightening up . . ."

"No, no," said Big Jim, rather brusquely, but he pushed it across the desk towards me, "this may be a question of *libel*."

I leafed through the pages thoughtfully, paused from my perusal to give Jim a straight look. "The defense against libel," I reminded him, "and correct me if I am wrong, is . . . *truth*."

"Um-hum," mused Jim, not overly impressed—in fact, not even bothering to look up, stirring the papers on his desk instead, with a thinly disguised show of impatience.

Well, the long and short of it was that this Mister 'Top Staffer' then stalked off to lunch (to 'Elaine's', or some other posh eatery no doubt!), leaving me to ponder the damnable pages "at your leisure," as he had phrased it. *And* a curious M.S. it was—*book-length 'memoirs' of a private detective*—written in a primitive style, but chock-full of weird info. One section dealt at length with a case with which I was vaguely familiar, a case which involved the tailing and stake-out of a celebrated female film star, and included an infamous incident which became known as '*The Night They Bust Down the Wrong Door Awready.*'

It seems that her husband, a British stockbroker, suspected his wife of having an affair, in fact, he was abso-*tootly* (if you get my drift) *certain* that his darling star's fabulous cooze was being deeply penetrated *and* voraciously gobbled by two, three, perhaps more, persons unknown—including, or so he believed to his great chagrin, 'a man from the motor trade'—a used Mercedes salesman. What he required, however, to really nail her to the cross, was proof positive . . . '*proof of pudding* positive,' one might say! And to this end he en-

gaged the services of a sleazebo private eye, who, at the critical moment—the
moment when the clandestine lovers were doubtless going at it like a pair of
maddened warthogs in rut—accompanied by a couple of hood-types, smashed
through the motel door in question, and started snapping photographs with fast
lens and infrared apparati. "Then," the story continued, "someone turned on
the lights, and there, lo and behold, we seen this *old lady*—maybe sixty-five—
like them pictures you see in the *True Detective*, with the sheet grabbed up to
her neck, and she couldn't say nothin', just '*Aaaahhh*', like she might be *croakin'*
outta shock, and right away somebody says, '*Hey, we bust down the wrong door
awready!*'

I decided then and there that a full report on the so-called *ethics* of the
profession might make good copy for a sensitive readership. Would these 'private eyes,' for example, take on a case which clearly had no substance? Would
they fabricate evidence? To what depths of deception would their avarice take
them?

Next step—front money for expenses. I sounded Big Jim in that regard.

"We'll go two hundred," he said at last, grimly writing out a check,
". . . but let's make damn sure it's an *in-depth* report, not just run-of-the-mill
crackpot gibberish."

"And *not*," I took the liberty of adding, "*devoid* of *human interest*."

"That's the idea," he said, handing me the check, "tight and bright, but
with plenty of *meat!*"

"Shall we play it for pix?" I asked, casually stashing the loot.

"No, no, let's shoot for *substance* on this one. An *in-depth* report! The
straight dope on the private dick! Say, that might even be our lead—'The
Straight Dope' . . ." he began repeating it to himself, jotting it down.

"Now you're *talking story*, Jim," I said with marked enthusiasm, easing
towards the door. My familiar use of his own vernacular seemed to reassure
him tremendously, and I was able to exit without further question.

'*In-depth*,' as the semanticists have suggested, derives from the expression '*low-
down*'—so after giving a bit of thought to the matter, I had a couple of tall-ones,
a change of clothes, double-Dexed it, and hit the street. My first stop was a
shabby building on lower Broadway, about two blocks off the Bowery—dingy
offices shared by a real estate broker, an insurance salesman, and the private-
eye outfit I'd selected: "*Proof City*—Action-Pix A Speciality." Each man had

a partitioned space which was not much larger than the room of a dentist—so small, in fact, that all transactions were conducted in hushed tones, lending the atmosphere a curiously sinister ambience, but for no other particular reason.

For the occasion I had worn a western shirt, a leather drawstring tie, a Stetson hat, and I reverted to the cracker drawl of my youth:

"Looky heah," I said tersely, "ah got my boy in *school* up thah in the South Bronx borough. He's a Negra, you unnerstan, an' ah got good reason to believe thah is some *de*scrimination goin' on up thah! Ah want *you* to look into it!"

The detective, a middle-aged man, small of frame, narrow of brow, but with an oddly florid face—a man who had doubtless heard many strange things in his time—had evidently never made room in his philosophy for a white-cracker with a black child, complaining of discrimination against him in a predominately black area. His face went into a twist of agonized consternation, like a Frenchman hearing his language garbled in some monstrous way. He leaned forward, as in involuntary fascination by a terrible hydra-head. "*You* . . ." he began, obviously without any control over what he was saying, "you *want* . . ." Then he seemed to get hold of himself, leaned back, cocking his head slightly to the side. "*Who* referred you to us, Mister . . . Mister . . ."

"Johnson," I reminded him, "Ed Johnson—we pushed up here from Chattanooga last fall. Ah work out at the Sperry-Rand Corporation. Ah'm a *in*-ventor. But we live in the Bronx borough, you see, an' like ah say, this trouble come up . . . an', well, ah jest looked in my yeller pages an' thah you was. Bein' in this *lo*-cation an' all I figgured you must have prutty dang *low oveahhead*—an' ah tell you frankly ah'd like to keep the cost of this operation down to bedrock minimum. Oh, ah got the money awright . . ." And saying this, I extracted a wad of fives from my western-shirt pocket and clutched them meaningfully. The gesture did not go wide of its mark.

"Well, now just a *minute*, Mr. Johnson," the detective said, then cast a quick look at the other occupants of the room, "it would be a big mistake, *hurumph*, indeed a *major* mistake, to judge our overhead by appearances." He patted the top of the desk near the edge. "Why, if I were to show you the *files* in that drawer—the private and personal dossiers of some of the various cases that we have handled through this office . . . well, I think you would understand why our clients prefer *anonymity*."

This was apparently such a touchy subject that he could not treat it without getting emotionally involved. With a show of indignation, he lit a cigarette and took a few quick drags.

"Oh well," I hastened to reassure him, "ah knew you was awright the minute ah seen you in the yeller pages!" And I gave him a completely open and trusting smile, which seemed to put him at ease once more. But only for a moment, as his mind then began to reconstruct the case at hand, and the torn look of anguish and bewilderment again took hold. He put out his cigarette and cleared his throat. "Now you say," he began unsteadily, "that you have a Negra . . ." he corrected himself, ". . . a *Ne*-gro child? In the South Bronx? I mean, just let me get this straight . . . it's *your* child, is that right, that . . . that you're interested in, and he's . . . he's . . ."

"He's up there in *school*," I said, and gave the number of a public school in the South Bronx, "an' ah have reason to *be*-lieve that thah's some 'scrimination goin' on up thah, an' ah want you to in-vestigate this, to git on up thah with tape recorders, camera, whatevah you got, an' git some *documentation* of it! Ah'm gonna *sue the damn city!*"

He cast an artfully surreptitious glance at the wad of bills in my hand and cleared his throat. "Uh, tell me, Mr. Johnson, just how *deeply* did you want to go into this?"

"Oh, ah could go a hunnert, ah reckon," I said, following his eye down to the bills and then beginning to smooth them out. "What's your *re*-tainer?"

He cleared his throat again. "Well, in a case like this, a case of discrimination—let's say . . ." he threw another quick look at the bills, "fifty down, and fifty when we *wrap it up*. Uh, how's that sound?"

"Fair enough," I said tersely, and began counting out the fives.

He gave me a receipt and then took some data on the case—the child's name and so on.

"Now, uh, this is *your* child, I take it . . . I mean, your wife is . . . is . . ."

"My wife is Negra," I explained, "she's a lil' ole colored gal ah met in Chattanooga, an' we pushed on up heah because of the *de*-scrimination, you see."

"Uh—huh . . . and this is your child?"

"This is our boy, yes."

"Yes, well, uh, now perhaps you could tell me about the . . . well, I mean it's sometimes helpful to know about the . . . the *home* situation, in cases like this. Is, uh, everything all right there?"

"What, you mean with *Thelma-Jean?* Oh, well, now she's jest about *perfect!* Why ah mean she's just about the best lil' ole *home*maker, cook, an' so on you could imagine—an' a real *cutie* too, ah tell *you!* Hee-hee!"

"I see . . ." He nodded gravely, then continued to nod, staring at me, or more or less through me, you might say, so entranced by the strange case that he failed to note that a small fly was moving slowly across the bridge of his nose.

We agreed that he would call me when his 'investigation' was complete—and so, we shook hands and I took my leave of these modest offices to broaden my research elsewhere.

A change of costume, and my next call was at a Lexington Avenue office in midtown, '*The Dalton Agency—Private Investigations,*' a considerably more prosperous looking setup, with a receptionist who tried to augment this impression by asking, with a trace of irritation (though feigned, to be sure), if I had an 'appointment.'

"No, I do not," I said firmly, having assumed for the purposes of this encounter an eccentrically straightforward Ivy League–Joseph K. manner, garbed accordingly in a somber Brooks Brothers outfit.

"I'll ask Mr. Wilson if he can see you," said the girl with a small haughty toss of her curls as she lifted the phone.

"Yes, do that," I said, softly indifferent, not looking at her but glancing around the office, sniffing lightly as though detecting some interestingly unpleasant odor, then I added with a bemused chuckle: "Tell him you may have a 'live one' out here."

She ignored this bit of con-game argot, and after several seconds of private communication on the inter-office phone, said, scarcely looking at me: "Yes—Mr. Wilson can give you a few minutes now. Through that door," she added, indicating with delicate disdain the only door in the room, other than the one I had just entered.

The girl was getting under my skin—and a veritable cutie-pie she was too . . . a willowy blonde, quite like Mike Hammer's secretary, in fact . . . full, wet, petulant lips, and in the wide gray eyes the tiger-trace—a petulance which I knew could be changed to abject adulation with a bit of the old you-know-what.

My encounter with Wilson was of a more subtle and intricate nature than had been the case on lower Broadway. A middle-aged man with rimless glasses, hair surrounding his very round head in sparse, whitening tufts, he resembled one of those vice presidents of a large bank—a bank with many vice presidents. After a rather strained exchange of amenities, and having admitted that I came by his name through the Yellow Pages, I said, quite frankly: "Wilson, I suspect my wife of . . . *having an affair.*"

Here I had imagined he might express certain reassuring doubts as to the improbability of this—or at least a "*Why* do you think so?" Instead he merely nodded, as though it were the most understandable thing in the world. This was fairly disquieting, ID-wise; it also put me at a momentary loss as to how I might gracefully present my reason for the suspicion. "An *affair,*" I repeated with feeling, "*definitely* an affair."

Mr. Wilson nodded again. "And what would you like us to do about it?" he asked.

So, here was an insensitive fellow indeed. "Perhaps," I said, after clearing my throat, "I'd better give you a little *background* on this."

Mr. Wilson seemed to settle a bit. "By all means," he replied, with an expansive gesture to proceed.

"Well," I began, "one afternoon, about ten days ago—an afternoon when my wife was *supposedly* at her bridge club—I gathered up some discarded magazines, and I cut out several dozen *letters*—letters of the alphabet—from ads, titles, and so on. With these letters I composed a *message*, which I pasted on a piece of paper—then I put the paper in an envelope. Again using the letters—which, of course, represented a variety of type-faces—I spelled out my name and address, and pasted them on the envelope . . . which I then mailed. A curious business, granted—something I had read in a novel—by H. Nemerov, if memory serves. In any case, the letter arrived the next day; it was with the rest of my morning mail, by my breakfast setting, where it had been placed, as usual, by our maid. Now, Edith—my wife—had not come down yet, so I waited until she arrived, meanwhile opening the ordinary letters. After she came in I uncovered *the* letter, then opened it. A disconcerting conglomeration of typeface, large and small, block, script, what-have-you."

And then I took from my pocket a piece of paper, unfolded it, and handed it to Wilson. "This," I said, "is the letter in question." He read:

YOUR WIFE IS TOO MUCH ALONE—THOUGH PERHAPS SHE IS *LEAST* ALONE WHEN YOU BELIEVE SHE IS *MOST* ALONE.

A FRIEND

While Wilson studied the letter, I continued with my story: "I read, or pretended to read, the letter several times; then I replaced it in the envelope and put it with the others. 'Anything of interest?' my wife finally asked, as she often does. I carefully folded my napkin, saying nothing, got up and walked to the window. 'No, no,' I said, in a theatrically casual way, 'not really . . . ' saying this in such a tone, you understand, that only a fool would fail to sense that there *was*, in fact, something of very real interest indeed. My wife, let me assure you, is *not* a fool. However, she merely gave me a curious look and continued with her breakfast. I left for the office shortly afterwards—quite as though nothing unusual had occurred. That evening I found the letter, along with the others, on my desk. This is customary—that when the maid clears up after breakfast, she puts my letters on my desk. So far, so good; now the plot thickens. I put the letter on *top* of the pile . . . this was almost a week ago. Now then. My wife, you see, has occasion to pass my desk several times a day; she could hardly fail to notice this odd letter, with its blatant hodgepodge of typeface, a veritable *crazy-quilt* of type-face—and so noticing, could hardly resist opening it. Yet she has said nothing of its content. How does one account for that? Isn't it all too obvious?"

Mr. Wilson had listened to this narrative with great patience, only once or twice frowning down at the pencil in his hand, which he turned slowly, end over end—and then staring at the letter, which he continued to do now, for about half a minute after I had finished. Finally he coughed, leaned forward to rest his head on one hand, elbow on the desk. "I think you may be going about this the wrong way," he said, quite deliberately. "It seems to me that *personal surveillance* for, oh, say a week or two, would be the best approach to a case . . . like this." He glanced at the letter again, folded it, and returned it to me.

"But you do agree that I have *fairly* sound reason here for suspicion."

Mr. Wilson cleared his throat, leaned back, and gazed at the ceiling. "Now from what I know of this . . . *case*, from what you've told me, and on the basis of whatever, uh, *suspicion* you may have otherwise . . . *intuition* we sometimes call it, or educated guess, if you like . . . I would say quite definitely *yes*, that here's a matter that warrants . . . looking into. Yes, I can put a man on this, this very afternoon—right now, in fact . . ."

I stayed his hand from reaching for the phone, and asked what the cost would be. One hundred an hour it was, plus expenses.

I told him I'd think it over. "I'll have to see if I can borrow the money from *Dad*," I said—which seemed to surprise him momentarily, but then he suggested that I do this by phoning right from his office.

"I think not," I said, getting up. "Personal contact is usually best—you know how dads are," I added with a pleasant chuckle. Wilson's smile in return was not without a trace of rue—minutely assuaged when I promised to call him within the hour.

"Yes," he said, reluctantly opening the door for me, "we'll want to move fast on this one. These affairs don't last forever, you know."

From a booth outside, I phoned in a 'progress report' to the editor. Just as I was getting warmed up to a really dramatic presentation of the coverage so far, he interrupted with a disgruntled snort.

"Listen, that's all *crackpot* stuff," he said, then continued impatiently: "Now look, I've lined up 'Irish' Jack Dolan. He's one of the top boys in this game—heads his own agency, and he's president of a statewide association of detectives. Warwick Hotel on Fifty-fourth. Now get over there and get the goddamn story—*in-depth!*"

Right. Well, Jack Dolan proved to be a prince of a fellow. Thirty-four or -five, lean and broad shouldered, tough chiseled features, he appeared to be straight out of top-drawer private-eye Lit—a 'battlin' s.o.b.,' as we say, with plenty of savvy. Dolan, I learned, is head of the Dolan-Whitney Detective Service, whose principal office is in Springfield, Mass., but whose service is worldwide. He broke out a fifth of Jack Daniels. I switched on the old tape recorder, and we started leveling. 'Private Investigation and General Security' it had said on the card he showed me, so I decided to plunge right into some straight-dope coverage. "'General Security', eh?" I said. "Well, you probably have certain opinions about the security arrangements they had that bad Friday down in Big D—inadequate, I suppose."

"Yes," Dolan said, "speaking pragmatically, you would have to say that. On the other hand, you've got to realize that in protecting against assassination, or against any other form of *deliberated* violence, your principal factor—*exposure*—is contingent, in the most absolute manner, upon the *cooperation* of the person you're protecting. If the Secret Service had their way, that bubble-top would *always* be up. But Kennedy wasn't that sort of person. He would stop the car, get out and shake hands with the crowd. So all you can do is *anticipate*, and be prepared. And they always have it pretty well figured out . . . exactly what can happen and what they can do about it. But in the final analysis it's just *theoretical*—because you get one kamikaze type, and that's *it*, there's really no protection at all. If a man wants to run out into the parade carrying a hundred and thirty-five sticks of fused dynamite . . . well, he doesn't even have to get very close."

"Would you say then that there *is* no real protection?"

"Well, that bubble-top is pretty good protection against a sniper, because even if the bullet goes through—as it probably would from a very high velocity rifle with armor-piercing shells—it would still be deflected enough so that it wouldn't actually hit where it was aimed, and then the chances of it being a lethal wound would be quite remote—but you can't stay in that bubble forever. And you know, the situation there in Dallas—a 6.5-millimeter rifle, with a four-power scope, at seventy-five yards—doesn't begin to suggest the actual effectiveness of long-range shooting. I mean, there are some extremely accurate rifles, with 20-, 24-power scopes, and marksmen who hit woodchucks consistently at *six-hundred* yards. And then if you use a *big* rifle, like a .357 magnum, with a hollow-nose lead bullet, that mushrooms on impact to the diameter of a silver dollar . . . well, you don't have to shoot at a man's *head,* you can kill him by hitting him almost anywhere between the hips and the shoulders. And that's a pretty big target. So you see, there is no real protection—and of course, this is especially true if you come up against someone who's prepared to give his own life, on the spot so to speak, in exchange for yours."

"Did anything else impress you about the assassination—the investigation of it and so on?"

"Yes, two things in particular impressed me—again in connection with the mechanics of the shooting itself, when they were considering whether or not it could have been done by one person alone. There were two basic misapprehensions—one, that the Presidential car, the occupants of it, represented a 'moving target.' Well, you see, if a target is moving *directly away from you,* as was the case there, then the point of aim and the trajectory of the bullet remain the same as with a stationary target. The second thing was the business about 'three shots in five seconds.' They had some experts saying it was 'difficult to get off three shots in five seconds' and so on. Now the misapprehension there is this: in competition-shooting, where you have so many seconds to fire so many shots, it's *someone else* who designates when the timing starts—*here* it was a case where the first *shot,* already aimed, started the clock. In other words, the timing began *with* the first shot, not *before*—so it was, in fact, only *two* shots in five seconds, because the first shot was already fired, when the timing began."

I told Dolan about my two previous interviews, and asked if *he* would have taken the cases which I presented.

"No, I wouldn't. My experience has been that dealing with weirdos doesn't pay off in the end. Something usually happens—they get *attached* to you or something, like you were their psychiatrist. They want it to go on indefinitely. If I see that a guy has a straight persecution complex, is a compulsive liar, or some other kind of nut, I just have to tell him 'Later.'"

"But can you always *recognize* them?"

"Not always, no—I recently had a curious case of that nature . . . an elderly man came in, very sympathetic fellow, said he had been arrested and charged with molesting two young girls—eight or nine years old. He was out on bail, waiting for his trial. He told me—*quite convincingly*—that he was being *framed*, by the girls' father, who he had had a terrific argument with, and who was supposed to be kind of nutty. He wanted me to investigate this, get some evidence that there was no validity to the molesting charge. Well, as I say, he seemed all right to me—a little bit eccentric perhaps, but he had no police record of any kind, and usually someone his age accused of that sort of thing *does* have a record—so I took the case, and started to work. Well, the father of the two girls he was charged with molesting acted very strange about it, wouldn't discuss it at all, and he wouldn't let me talk to the girls. The more I looked into the matter, the more favorable it seemed to be for my client. Now the client had done this man, the father, a lot of favors, and he seemed to have a genuine interest in the welfare of these two children. I mean, he had some money, you see, and the other guy, the father, didn't—and I'm thinking maybe he's just a guy who likes *kids*, you know, likes to hug them and so on, and that it's as simple as that. Anyway, the investigation is going along okay—getting a lot of good solid endorsements of the client's character, and some negative stuff on the other guy—when one day he turns up at the office, the client does, and he's acting sort of shy or sheepish, which was a little out of character for him, and he finally says: 'Listen, there *was* an incident I think I should tell you about . . .' and he goes into this weird story about how he was at a party, out on Long Island, and he was in the garden, and he had to go to the bathroom. Then he gave an involved explanation of why he didn't go into the house—because one bathroom was occupied and he wasn't sure where the other one was, all quite plausible, so he took a leak right there where he was, in the garden. But there was this *little girl* there, in the garden, who ran inside and told her mother that he had *done* something to her. He said, 'Christ, I was only taking a leak!' Then he

said: 'This is going to look bad, on top of the other charge—it's going to preju-
dice the jury.' And *then* he said: "I want *you* to say that I *wasn't* on Long Island
at the time they claim, but that I was with *you*.' I mean, I could hardly believe
it—right out of left field, this strange request. I said, well, no, of course I couldn't
do that. And he got very excited, pacing the floor, talking about how 'this *new
development*' is going to 'complicate the case.' Meanwhile I'm sitting there
wondering: *is this just a coincidence?* Because, of course, it *could* be. And maybe
I'm overreacting to it, because he still hadn't said what happened. But then he
starts taking things out of his pockets and putting them on my desk. 'Listen,'
he said, 'I've got some things here I'd like you to keep for me, because it might
not look too good if I'm picked up with them on me.' And he's taking out all
kinds of pill bottles and I don't know what else. I didn't *want* to know. I said:
'All right, you can put them in this envelope, seal it, and put it in that safe.' And
while I'm opening the safe, I asked him exactly what it *was* that the little girl
had said he did. 'Oh, I don't know,' he said, 'she told her mother that I referred
to my penis and said: "*Look, you made my dolly cry!*"' I said: 'Well, *did* you
actually say that to her?' And he said: 'Oh, I was just fooling around. We were
just having some fun.' Well, you know he may have been very innocent in his
own way, but what the hell, you can't go around doing that sort of thing. I mean
it's very apt to be *misinterpreted*. Anyway, now he wants me to go out to Long
Island and investigate *that* incident. But before I could do it—in fact, the very
next day, he was busted, on a morals charge, caught really red-handed this time,
in a sort of total freak-out . . . exposing himself to a bunch of schoolgirls on a
crowded Fifth Avenue bus, and then trying to *urinate* on them—the whole bit.

"He got seven years—and, of course, I didn't get paid. But the point is,
you never know. I mean you *want* to give the client the benefit of the doubt,
but you can't always be certain that you don't have a nut on your hands. And,
as I say, it doesn't pay to take cases like that."

"Well, how about this—suppose someone comes to you and says he's
being *blackmailed*. The reason for the blackmail is that he escaped from prison
one time and since then he's led an ordinary respectable life, under a different
name, and so on—and now he's being blackmailed by someone who *knows* that
he's a fugitive. Naturally he can't go to the police with his problem, so he comes
to you and wants you to help him in some way. Would you take a case like that?"

"Well, it would depend on a number of things—primarily, on my
personal feelings about the particular case. I don't think you can generalize
about it."

"Well, suppose you *didn't* take the case—would you feel obliged to report it, the fact that you know of an escaped prisoner, to the authorities?"

"No, your first obligation, your first *allegiance*, is to the client. My obligation . . . of *confidence* is of paramount importance. I *must* preserve that. Of course if the man is *raving*—I mean, if he's an obvious danger to society, that's something else. It's simply a matter of common sense and personal judgment, within an ethical framework of *confidence*."

"Like stories heard by a psychiatrist?"

"Something like that, yes. In our society, private investigators have a definite function and a definite responsibility. I mean, suppose a man is charged with a crime; he's out on bail, waiting for his trial, or maybe he *isn't* out, but he wants someone to help him prepare his case, someone with investigative experience, to uncover certain information—well, he can't get help from the police, *they're* the ones responsible for the charge. He has *no one* to turn to except the private investigator."

"Have there been cases where your work has actually helped people in situations like that?"

"Many cases. One of the most interesting, and important, was a case involving Lenny Bruce."

On the Persecution of Lenny Bruce

"As you know, Lenny was found guilty on a narcotics-possession charge, by the Los Angeles County Court, in 1963 . . . May 16th, to be exact. The judge referred the disposition of the case to the Los Angeles County Psychiatric Court—which sentenced him to ten years '*rehabilitation*.' While waiting for his appeal hearing to come up, he engaged me to investigate various circumstances surrounding the trial—particularly the so-called expert testimony to the effect that he was an addict. The principal 'expert' in this instance was Dr. Thomas L. Gore. Dr. Gore was a psychiatrist regularly employed by the County of Los Angeles; his job was to testify as to whether or not the defendant in these cases was addicted to narcotics. Each year his testimony sent hundreds of people to these 'rehabilitation centers'—which is the State's euphemism for a prison-hospital. Early in the proceedings it became apparent that Dr. Gore had entered the case with an opinion of the defendant which had nothing to do with whether or not he was a narcotics addict—he simply *didn't like* Lenny Bruce . . . didn't like his *act*. His manner was surly, aggravating . . . insulting. His first question, for example, was: 'How long have you been smoking marijuana?' The second was: 'Have you ever taken a fix in the leg?' Now there's a narcotics-addiction test given by the State of California—the Nailline Test—and this is a test required by the State for anyone applying for a driver's license who has had any record of the use or possession of narcotics. Lenny Bruce *requested* that he be given the Nailline Test—because it isn't actually *required* of a person on trial— and he took the test and passed it. Dr. Gore, when asked by the defense to explain this, said: 'I think he was just trying to fool us.' Now Dr. Gerald Forte, a nationally prominent figure in psychiatric circles, who was a Special Advisor on Mental Health to President Kennedy, voluntarily came forward, asked permission to examine Bruce, and stated unequivocally that, in his opinion, Bruce 'could not possibly be a drug addict.' Dr. Thomas Curry, who originated the Nailline Test, made the same statement—both of which are on public record. And yet, on Dr. Gore's testimony, Lenny Bruce was sentenced to ten years compulsory rehabilitation. Now the obvious question, from Lenny Bruce's point of view, is: who *is* Dr. Gore, and how well *qualified* is he to be in a position of such power? Well, our investigation revealed some interesting information about Dr. Thomas L. Gore. We sent an agent to Tennessee, which was Dr. Gore's early stomping grounds, and we learned the following—all of which, by the way, is *thoroughly* documented—a matter of public record, official hospital record, or sworn and substantiated affidavit. In 1948, Dr. Gore was discharged from his position as Superintendent of the Davidson County Hospital, in Nashville, Tennessee, for the 'mishandling of funds' of that hospital. There was twenty-five thousand dollars missing when Dr. Gore left, and it is *still* missing to this day. He was tried in Nashville, found guilty, given a suspended sentence, and discharged from the hospital. Thereupon he moved to Albuquerque, New Mexico, where he opened—guess what—that's right, a *loan-company* . . . a loan and finance company, lending money to G.I.s. But to go back to the County Hospital story for a moment—during his two years' tenure there, 1947 and 1948, Dr. Gore did some fairly unusual things. I may as well tell you the most outlandish one first—he had the bars removed from some of the windows, whereupon several 'patients' escaped. When they were returned to the hospital, he had them *castrated*—and he did it personally. Two of them—Foster Regan and Lee Conchen—are still living, and are still in the hospital. Now these were *mental* patients, but there was nothing in their records to suggest that they were sex criminals, rapists, or anything of the kind . . . not that *that* would have given him the right, legal or otherwise, to do what he did, but . . . he *castrated* them. And this is the man who 'rehabilitates' people for the State of California. One year he had an immense *hole* dug on the grounds of the hospital, for no apparent reason—the hole is still there and has never been explained; on another occasion he had a vast quantity of *corn* transferred from one silo to another without explanation—these are affidavits given to us by the man who was farm-manager for the hospital during that time—and then, when the corn had all finally been moved, said: 'All right, move it back again.' They moved it back into the first silo. Dr. Gore carried a pistol, and he would fly into uncontrollable rages. We have affidavits from former employees of the hospital, to the effect that when they tried to quit, because of some outrage or other, he would threaten them with his pistol. On one occasion, he had the notion that people driving up to the hospital were approaching too fast—so he had the road narrowed and had deep trenches dug along each side of it; now a person had to drive very cautiously not to go into the ditch. Well, one night a State Police car pulled in and immediately crashed into this trench—so he had to have it filled in again. Now Dr. Gore had always represented himself— on documents, license applications, and so on—as having been not merely the Superintendent of the Davidson County Hospital, but as having also been the Chief of Staff. You see, the job of Superintendent is primarily administrative, and is subordinate to the Chief of Staff—which is a functional psychiatric job. We obtained an affidavit from the physician who *was*, in fact, the Chief of Staff during this time, an affidavit stating that in his opinion Dr. Gore was a paranoiac. Now this is strong stuff, because, you know, doctors will almost *never* be openly critical of one another, unless there is damn good reason for it. However, back to the story. When Dr. Gore moved to New Mexico and opened his loan company, he also opened a private mental institution, called 'The Lodge on the Chartreuse Trail.' Consider the mentality behind a sign like that. Anyway, one of his early patients was a young newspaperman, and by all accounts a very promising one—except that his father said he had a 'drinking problem.' Well, it seems that Gore persuaded the old man to send the boy to him, all the way from Tennessee to New Mexico, to 'The Lodge on the Chartreuse Trail,' to be cured of his drinking problem. And the boy died there. According to Dr. Gore, he committed suicide. There was a brief flurry of investigation, which soon subsided—but the circumstances surrounding his death gave, and continue to give, rise to conjecture for a number of people.

"So there you have a sketchy portrait—by no means complete—of the man primarily responsible for sentencing Lenny Bruce—and countless others—to ten years in prison-rehabilitation. Now when the appeal was heard, all this was used to discredit Dr. Gore's previous testimony. And the point is, going back to your question, that these are things which could *not* have been uncovered, and fully documented to stand in court, by the ordinary citizen—but only by an experienced investigator."

Then I thought of something else that might ring a bell with big Jack Dolan: "You know, what I find to be one of the most interesting aspects of your work—is this whole idea of *knowing* something about someone that isn't *supposed* to be known and, presumably, *isn't* known except to you and the client—and of course to the person himself. Now when you have information like this, and you and the client prepare to use it—to settle 'out of court' so to speak—how do you keep it from becoming a form of *blackmail?*"

"Well, blackmail . . . blackmail is a very negative oversimplification. 'Dark persuasion' might be a better term. Now, for example, I had a case recently . . . a man came to me, middle-aged businessman, wealthy, solid-citizen type, family man, with a highly respected position in his community—a position which would not allow for any scandal—and he laid the following on me—he said that while his wife and children were visiting her parents, he had been invited to dinner, at the home of one of his closest friends . . . a couple whom he and his wife had known for many years, and that his wife—he made a point of this—that his wife and the friend's wife were 'extremely close.' Well, when he got there, it turned out that the husband had been suddenly called away, called out of town on business. But she had the dinner all ready, so he stayed. They had drinks and so on, one thing leading to another, and before the evening was through, they had gone to bed together. Well, the next day it seems the wife had an attack of remorse, and when her husband came home she told him what had happened—apparently telling it in such a way that the guy, my client, emerged as pretty definitely the aggressor. So the husband goes after him, hopping mad: 'Ed, how could you *do* this to me?!? Your best friend!' and so on, you know, the whole bit. And now, of course, the *client* was feeling pretty remorseful too. 'Charlie, I don't know how it could have happened! God, if I could only undo it! If there was only some way I could make it up to you!' Well, it turned out there *was* a way he could make it up. Charlie—that wasn't his name, of course, but let's call him 'Charlie'—Charlie needed *money*. Certain investments hadn't panned out, certain obligations had to be met, that sort of thing.

Well, Ed *had* money, so he started laying it on Charlie—five thousand, ten thousand, another five . . . when he finally came to me he had paid out about twenty-five thousand dollars within three years. He was beginning to feel the bite—but he was afraid to stop paying because Charlie seemed on the verge of blowing his stack and telling the world how his best friend had laid his wife. And it was beginning to look like this might go on indefinitely. I said to him: 'Tell me, Ed, did *you* do it to her? Or did *she* do it to you? Or did you just *both* do it together?' Well, he was very honest about it, he admitted that it was probably his fault, he'd had a few drinks, he got carried away, didn't realize what he was doing, and all that. I said: 'Well, you know sometimes they do it to *you*, Ed, but still make you think you're doing it to *them*.' But he was so torn up about it, I mean he felt so guilty—as I say, he was a very straight, decent, sort of Andy Gump type, led a pretty sheltered life—and he simply felt so bad about the whole business that he couldn't even try to reconstruct how it had actually happened. But to me, being of a more cynical turn of mind I suppose, the thing smacked of collusion in front. I mean that they, the husband and wife, had set him up . . . and knocked him over. Anyway, that turned out to be irrelevant, because my investigation of Charlie—who was also supposed to be the solid-citizen type— revealed an unsavory police record in a couple of other states, along with an actual two-year stretch he had done for fraud and embezzlement. So now we were in a pretty good bargaining position—either he takes the heat off my client, or I turn this information over to the local Chamber of Commerce, the Better Business Bureau, et cetera, et cetera. We even managed to get back part of the money—about ten thousand anyway—but I consider these to be methods of *persuasion*, not blackmail."

As I sat there, getting all this fab coverage from Dolan, I began to regret having laid out the fifty on the cracker-discrimination case. That big five-o would have pretty well covered a high-stepping evening on the town with the nifty Mike Hammer secretary. I determined not to part with the second fifty, though I did intend to 'follow up' on the case, by phone . . . but then I thought, what the hell, the Big J. had said it was crackpot stuff anyway—so I decided to call the cracker-dick and tell him to forget the whole thing. I used Dolan's phone, and when the guy answered, I told him that I had decided to drop the case. He became abruptly and furiously excited, reverting to his most basic Brooklynese as he started shouting about having "done incurred heretofore unforeseen expenses in connection wid dis case"—namely, fifteen dollars for a parking ticket. I suggested that was something that was hardly my responsibility, but he insisted that it was because it had happened "*due to the nature of dis case.*" When I pressed him for details, he exploded in a feverish outburst: "I was in a *school-yard,* fer chrissake, maybe five, ten minutes, when these two cops from the 86th precinct *bum*-rap me! Can you imagine? Two dumb *harness*-bulls run *me* in for 'loitering with sexual intent'." When I offered my commiserations, he snarled: "Those guys are gonna be walkin' a beat in Flatbush before I'm through with 'em!"

Apparently he had gone out without his private-dick license, assuming he had one, and had looked so suspicious hanging around the schoolyard that a passing prowl car had grabbed him and hustled him down to the station. By the time he could straighten the matter out and get back to his car, he had gotten a parking ticket. I solemnly promised to send him the fifteen and hung up.

When I recounted the incident to Dolan, he poured out a couple of tall ones, chuckled, affected a cracker drawl, and said: "Wal now, Ter, there's bound to be one or two in ever dang barrel. But I don't think you should condemn the whole goddamn profession because of a couple of crackpot weirdos!"

I raised my glass. "I'll drink to that, Jack Dolan!" I said, and we lifted a toast to the truth of it.

—1970s

The Beautiful-Ugly Art of Lotte Lenya

For some time, now, there has been the faint stirring and just-discernible heart-beat of a strange new life in the off-Broadway wings of the American musical theater. The strongest evidence to date has been the seven-year run, completed last winter at New York's Theatre de Lys, of the Kurt Weill and Bertolt Brecht *The Threepenny Opera*—an English version featuring the composer's craggy-faced, throaty-voiced, passionately dedicated widow, Lotte Lenya, in the role she immortalized 30 years ago in Berlin. It has been confirmed by the current musical evening, *Brecht on Brecht*, also at the Theatre de Lys, also starring Lotte Lenya, for which tickets are increasingly difficult to come by; by the sale of Lenya's records; by plans in New York, Chicago and Philadelphia for more Brecht, more Weill; by the extraordinary popularity of *The Threepenny Opera*'s opening song, "Moritat," known more familiarly as "Mack the Knife." Something in this German theater of the twenties and early thirties—in the words of its great playright, Brecht, the songs of its great composer, Kurt Weill, the voice of its great star, Lotte Lenya—speaks hauntingly, and directly, to Americans in the sixties. Brecht and Weill are dead, but Lenya, working quietly off-Broadway, is probably the most alive talent in the American theater today.

What the work of Brecht and Weill, and its interpretation by Lenya, offer the audience of today, particularly the young audience, is the chance for a genuine emotional experience, in contrast to the ordinary, purely cerebral, experience—in contrast, that is, to the experience which, instead of *being*, merely *represents*. The genuine emotional experience, though it may sometimes be recaptured, cannot be consciously sought out for the first time, nor can it be otherwise anticipated; a great effort should be made, however, to recognize such experiences when they do occur, and, above all, freely to accredit them. Serious care is necessary in this because our conditioning is strongly against it—if there is one monumental tragedy of our era, it is that so many people pass their entire lives in a wasteland of cold symbols.

Consider, for example, how persons who habitually attend the musical theater will come away from a modestly staged show in Greenwich Village such as, say, *The Threepenny Opera*, with certain dominant impressions—impressions almost invariably tempered by the qualification, "off-Broadway." (All over the country, this phrase has come to stand for the offbeat, the experimental, the small scale, the surprise.) Then, the following evening, they attend a big Broadway opening near Times Square. An exciting first night! Dressed to the teeth! Blazing lights, lavish surroundings, fame and fortune on every side. Curtain up! Colossal sets, magnificent costumes, huge orchestra, a mammoth production. Marvelous! All this *equates* to marvelous . . . and yet, somewhere dimly heard, as though from a farther room, what endures is the haunting melody of the "Moritat," and the strange, warm lilt of an incredibly human voice. No memory of set, or costume, no memory perhaps of anything tangible—only the persistence of a genuine experience.

When I asked Lotte Lenya recently what single thought might best characterize the spirit of the whole Brecht-Weill body of work, she replied with a line from the song "As You Make Your Bed": "Ein mensch ist kein tier . . . man is not an animal." This sentiment is not only in sharp contrast to certain current Broadway values (see man the animal, man the automaton, immortalized at a performance of this year's smash success, *How to Succeed in Business Without Really Trying*) but also to the shuffling and self-conscious negativism of much of the current *off*-Broadway "theater of the absurd" experiments. At its best, this theater, epitomized by Beckett and Ionesco, and by the amazing work of Jack Gelber (*The Connection*), has much to give. But at its most common, or derivative, it offers little more than a turgid and effete narcissism. It reduces man even beyond the status of animal, to that of vegetable—in antithesis not merely of Broadway, but indeed, of life itself.

Standing apart from the spirit of both "off" and "on," *The Threepenny Opera*, which brought Lotte Lenya out of a fifteen-year retirement, was sustained, not by the wholesale support of theater parties, tourist tickets, or massive advertising (or—at the opposite extreme—by an urge to be avant-garde), but by a devoted following who returned time and again for this phenomenal experience. As the New York *Herald Tribune* critic wrote: "When she [Lenya] stepped to the front of the stage in the second act to sing 'Pirate Jenny,' the miniature confines of the theater stretched and were replaced by a broad and sweeping arena of genuine sentiment. For that's what art can do, and that's what the artist does." And now, with *Brecht on Brecht* (which has just been recorded by Columbia) the phenomenon continues. And what is quite remarkable is the observable manner in which the appeal of this music and theater cuts across lines of background and normal differences in taste. Persons who seldom, if ever, go to the theater, even those who ordinarily care little for music, are invariably charmed, saddened, or in some way genuinely moved by her songs. This appears to be true whether the songs are sung in German or in translation, and it is especially noticeable in playing Lenya's records, such as the *Berlin Theatre Songs* for a group of guests who, one is persuaded, are of severely diverse and conflicting judgments. Only a few vocal artists of recent times—most notable, Billie Holiday, Edith Piaf, and Judy Garland—have achieved this state approaching universal faultlessness.

The American popularity of this German music of the twenties may be partly explained by the increased meaning of the word *disillusion* to a widening U.S. audience. The cynicism—or disillusionment—of continental Europe has long been well in advance of any Anglo-American counterpart, because Europeans have been more inescapably confronted with the dramatic contrasts of the human condition. Overt class distinction, wars and travel all go to account for this. On a trip, say, from Geneva to Seville, one sees vicissitudes of life in a diversity which could not possibly be encountered elsewhere within a comparable radius of travel. Frequent crossing of frontiers will shake one's beliefs to their very foundations. Now, with the gradual, but very real, breakdown of the isolationist syndrome in America, established values of the past have been brought into question in this country too, and many of them have failed to survive. It is in this sense that the word "disillusion" is used, and in its application to the American mind, it is by no means to be considered a negative factor. For if the loss of innocence brings sadness, it also brings wisdom.

Lenya herself sees an analogy between aspects of present-day America and the uncertain days of the Weimar Republic—". . . those nervous days when the Strauss waltz was still played to people who were listening for something else." Lenya's artistic inheritance was the heart of the *Bauhaus*—the creative movement which, from 1920 to 1933, relentlessly discarded old forms and meanings on almost every level. Its Berlin theater was a theater of disillusionment, and *The Threepenny Opera*, first presented in 1928, was an immediate success. It is a tale of sordid setting, with a killer as hero, prostitute as heroine. Yet the audience was able to make the leap in the unconscious and identify with these characters through some profound and ineffable correspondence with conditions their own lives. Brecht is saying "*Look, this is you! How ugly!*" And the audience is touched, because it does, indeed, recognize itself, and more—for beneath the terrible cynicism is a suppressed tenderness that can bring tears from the stone.

In our own culture, musical poetics have played a rather ethereal role, bearing no actual relationship to life itself. The lyrics of a musical, such as, say, *Oklahoma*, while pleasing enough to their purpose, do not pretend to any basis in reality—they represent a kind of stylized *ideal*, most suitable, really, to the imagination of children. Our cultural exception to this more or less fairy-tale approach has been in the realm of the *folk song*—songs which were not contrived, but which grew out of imminent real-life considerations and experience; but these, other than on the collector's level, have seldom gotten outside their place of origin intact. By the time they reach the general public, they have been so "cleaned up" and commercialized as to be devoid of real emotional content. They again merely *represent* the original.

The lyrics of Brecht, on the other hand, have precisely this folk-song quality of honest relevance. They do not project an idealized picture of life; they proclaim that ours is by no means the best of all possible worlds, and in doing so, seem to portray a world with which the listening audience can identify; and thus the people in that world become credible, and their songs have meaning. In short, the characters are not completely *literary*, drawn as good or bad, but as in life contain a multitude of qualities and contradictions. Literary characters cannot be forgiven their faults, because the audience knows that these faults were assigned for the very purpose of delineating the good characters from the bad ones. This is not the case in life. One often forgives, overlooks, or understands negative qualities in a person—qualities which, on the stage, could only be interpreted as villainous.

Lenya, like the other great singers referred to, is a classic example of the *natural*. She had no formal training in voice and does not read music—yet she has a perfect ear for the most complex musical patterns and a better sense of time-phrasing than might ever be acquired through study. But it is, of course, the confluence of many factors which gives her work its singular purity. For one, it is certainly true that she has never even considered performing work which she cannot treat seriously. In consequence, her repertory has been devoted exclusively to work of an extremely high caliber—principally the lyrics of Brecht, and of another major German poet-dramatist, Georg Kaiser . . . and, of course, to the great music of her husband, Kurt Weill.

The quality possessed by Lenya, and by all singers of extraordinary talent, or perhaps more exactly, the ability, is that of taking a song at its utmost seriousness. They sense its ultimate scope, and they yield to it wholly and un-guardedly, and with the effect, finally, of bringing something new to the song itself. It is scarcely an exaggeration to say that each song ever sung by these performers becomes her own—her rendition is definitive, and all previous versions merely its framework, and all subsequent ones its reminiscence. For, as the critic said, "That's what an artist does."

And yet there is always the requisite of public inclination to be considered—the *national mood,* as it is sometimes called—and this most certainly pertains in the case of highly individualistic styles. It was not conceivable, for instance, that songs in German, or otherwise readily identified with the German language, could have met popular American response during World War II. This is obvious enough, but it conceals a more subtle principle which holds true, by degree, throughout the entire range of an artist's style or its content. On the surface there would seem to be very little in our own musical heritage or tradition which would lend itself to an appreciation of the kind of song Lotte Lenya has popularized—as, for example, in this stanza from "Ballad of a Drowned Girl," described as her body is carried slowly downstream:

> *The evening sky was the color of smoke*
> *And it lifted the cold starlight*
> *But the early sky was gold and fair*
> *So for her there would still be morning and night.*

While translations cannot but do injustice to an original, we are nonetheless struck by the strange abstract character of the images presented here and by the complex irony they contain—a far cry, certainly, from the moon-June simplicity of our own perennial favorites.

And yet it is surely the ultimate *simplicity,* or directness of these pieces which is behind their appeal. One can hardly imagine a more straightforward sentiment, for instance, than the refrain from "As You Make Your Bed":

> *If somebody's to do the stepping, it'll be me*
> *If somebody's to be stepped on, it'll be you.*

There is every indication that the Brecht-Weill renaissance will continue; productions are being planned of *Mother Courage, Rise and Fall of the City of Mahagonny, The Seven Deadly Sins.* Columbia recordings of these scores, with

Lenya singing, have already been issued, as have the albums *September Song and Other American Theatre Songs,* and, of course, as previously mentioned, the excellent *Berlin Theatre Songs,* and the complete *The Threepenny Opera* and *Brecht on Brecht.*

This theater of Brecht and Weill is filled with disillusion, but disillusion carries its own seed of hope—life is ever changing, and one senses that the change must be, as the lyrics so often proclaim, "towards the light." And here, with the notion of light and darkness, we reach the fascinating recurrent image in Brecht, the heart and keystone of his work: paradox. That which is ugly becomes in some strange way beautiful; that which is harsh, bitter, cynical, becomes painfully tender. This is true of the whole and true of the parts. Consider the forceful, staccato ugliness of the following stanza, again from "Ballad of a Drowned Girl":

> *When her pale body had decayed in the water*
> *It happened, very slowly, that God gradually forgot her*
> *First her face, then her hands, and at the very last, her hair*
> *Then in the rivers she was carrion with other carrion.*

Weill's music is harsh, defiant, dissonant, *ugly*—and yet, paradoxically, like the lyrics, it is compelling, insistently haunting, and in the end overwhelms with a single sustaining line of melodic tenderness. And the personages of the play: ugly. Lotte Lenya, with her angular-boned face and body, presents an archetypal ugliness. It is a vibrant, sensual, magnificent ugliness—which transcends itself and becomes absolute beauty. Alongside her, the ordinarily pretty stage actress can only appear to be wearing a colorless mask—a mask, one might almost say, of death. What we have here, in Brecht, Weill, and Lenya, is *life* in its bedrock essence, and art at its very peak.

—September 1962
Glamour

Riding the Lapping Tongue

Terry was invited by the Rolling Stones to cover their 1973 tour—which he wrote up for the Saturday Review.

Whether it's New York or Tuscaloosa, Norfolk or L.A., one factor is constant: The dressing room of the Rolling Stones is always Groove City—the juice flows, smoke rises, crystals crumble, poppers pop, teenies hang in, and Mick knifes through like a ballet-dancing matador . . . all to the funky wail of Keith's guitar tuning up, and sometimes the honking sax of a solid, downhome pickup sideman, like Texas Bobby Keys. And in Buddha repose, Charlie sits twirling his sticks Sid Catlett-style. Scene of good karma.

SLOW ZOOM IN ON MIRRORED FACE OF FALLEN ANGEL as Mick sits down at the lighted glass, and the makeup man leans in intensely to begin his magic ritual—transfiguration toward sympathy for the devil. I watch cautiously. It's a heavy number, a lot of head-stuff coming down.

Outside in the Washington, D.C., stadium, fifty thousand fans are stomping it up to the screams of Stevie Wonder . . . while they wait it out. Like the teenies, they've been hanging in—since two o'clock this afternoon, many since the night before. Now it's 10:30; they'll soon be impatient.

Just beyond the dressing-room entrance I squeeze through the gauntlet of cops, and one of them asks for my pass. I flash it: a small, white silk banner, lettered in red, glued to my sleeve:

ROLLING STONES ACCESS GUEST
Washington, D.C. July 4, 1972

It occurs to me he should be checking sleeves in the other direction. Without the pass, would I be forced to stay in the dressing room indefinitely?

But now I'm a part of the milling crowd, and almost at once a curious man lays a hand on my sleeve, his face like that of a red fox.

"I'd read this if I were you," he says in a voice with neither warmth nor accent, and he hands me the following mimeographed sheet:

THE STONES AND COCK ROCK

If you are male, this concert is yours. The music you will hear tonight is written for your head. It will talk to you about *your* woman, how good it is to have her under your thumb, so that she talks when she's spoken to. Men will play hard, driving music for you that will turn you on, hype you up get you ready for action . . . like the action at Altamont, San Diego, Vancouver. This is your night, if you are male. . . .

The Stones are tough men—hard and powerful. They're the kind of men we're supposed to imitate, never crying, always strong, keeping women in their place (under our thumbs). In Vietnam, to save honor (which means preserving our manhood), our brothers have killed and raped millions of people in the name of this ideal: the masculine man. Is this the kind of person you want to be? . . .

We resent the image the Stones present to males as examples we should imitate. . . .

If you are female, you don't need this leaflet to tell you where to fit in. You will get enough of that tonight. If you choose to be angry, to fight, to unite with other women to smash the sexist society that has been constructed to oppress you, tonight, here—and every day, throughout America—we the men who wrote this leaflet, will attempt, to the extent we can successfully attack our own sexism, to support your struggle.

—Men Struggling to Smash Sexism

Later on the plane, I show this bit of weirdness to Keith. "'Cock rock,'" he muses with a wan smile. "So that's it. Right then, we'll use it," and he begins to beat out an eccentric tattoo on the glass holding his Tequila Sunrise, chanting Leadbelly style:

Ah'm a cock-rockin' daddy,
an' you oughtta see me bla-bla-bla . . .

But the smile reflects the weariness of one too long and too profoundly misunderstood, and it doesn't sustain. "It's a drag, man, the way people dig evil—

not evil itself, but the *idea* of it . . . grooving on the vicarious notion of it . . . it's *their* fascination with evil that locks us into this projection of it."

The Tequila Sunrise is a drink of exceptional excellence in every regard: two parts tequila, three parts orange juice, one part gin, dash of grenadine.

Thus, your basic Tequila Sunrise is not merely one of those chic, absurdly yin, innocuously thirst-quenching drinks (so prized by dehydrated athletes, entertainers, and heavily Dexed writers working against viciously unfair deadlines), it is also Bombsville-oh-roonie. Moreover (and here's another definite plus), the scariest dash of grenadine into the orange, unstirred and allowed to seek its own cloudlike definition, lends the whole (in certain half-lights) an effect of advanced psychedelia.

In fact, some of our finest moments were aboard this plane, Sunrise in hand, hopping from one gig to the next—Fort Worth to Houston, Houston to Nashville, Nashville to New Orleans—short flights, and, like the dressing rooms, a boss groove and comfort to us all. The craft itself was a regular four-engine passenger plane, refurbished somewhat toward the concept of comfort and groove. A few seats had been replaced with a large buffet, always laden with endsville goodies, mostly to eat. The fuselage was emblazoned with the Stones' symbol, fashioned by Warhol, a giant, red extended tongue, not outthrust so much as lolling or lapping. Hence the craft's name, unofficially, *The Lapping Tongue* . . . or, more familiarly, *Tongue*.

The stewardesses—two fabulous teenies nicknamed Ruby T. and Brown Sugar—would begin mixing the Tequila Sunrises as soon as we started up the ramp. On most planes, of course, you can't get a drink until you're in the air—aboard *The Lapping Tongue* you usually had a drink in hand before reaching your seat.

By way of indicating the scope of the operation, the roster of Tour Personnel as it appeared on the cockpit door of the *Tongue* numbered forty-nine, though only about half this number were actually on the plane—the logistics of tour travel (advance PR men, security arrangements, property trucks, etc.) requiring otherwise—so that at any given moment the plane was no more than a quarter full . . . leaving ample room for "dancing in the aisles," so to speak.

The fantastic T. Capote joined the tour in New Orleans, and together we were soon contriving a few chuckles by way of fantasizing a nifty sky-jack action and subsequent media coverage:

CAPOTE SKYJACKS ROLLING STONES
Writer's Demands for Return of Group
Described as "Extremely Bizarre"

NEW ORLEANS (AP) June 30—Well-known author Truman
Capote, in what authorities termed "a curiously worded document,"
made known today the "conditions" under which he will release the
English rock group, "The Rolling Stones," after having comman-
deered their private DC-7 by claiming to have "a laser beam concealed
on my person." His first demand was that the plane and its passengers
("kit and caboodle") be flown at once to Peking "for immediate acu-
puncture treatment of the eardrums." Subsequent demands were of a
more complex nature, though often quite general. "Grotesquerie in
high places," stated one such condition, "to cease *tout de suite*." Another demand concerned "authors Vidal and Mailer" and referred to
"an unnatural act," though it was not specific, saying merely "as shall
become them." . . .

et cetera, et cetera, building, gathering momentum, reaching out, even into areas
of possibly questionable taste—certainly beyond the purview of a quality-lit
mag of *SR* stamp and kidney. Suffice to say we grooved in this odd manner
until the real thing came along—namely, the fabulous Brennen's restaurant
where the great Tru used to dwell, and it was red-carpet time for the prodigal's
return. *Gumboville!* Louisiana gumbo. Surely the supreme funkiness of *haute
cuisine* the world over. HOLD ON GUMBO, SHIMMERING DISC OF AROMATIC DELIGHT,
MOVE IN ON SLOW WAVERING DISSOLVE, back through time and space to the Coliseum in Vancouver, on Saturday, June 3, where the tour began, as the announcer
says to a hushed and darkened house: "Ladies and gentlemen, the greatest rock-
and-roll band in the world—The Rolling Stones," while from the top balcony
someone drops a long string of exploding firecrackers, and Mick leaps into the
purple pool of light. *"Dig It!"* he screams, and Jumping Jack Flash is on.

With the American tour completed, it has become apparent to certain persons
who did not previously recognize it—critics and the like—that Mick Jagger
has perhaps the single greatest talent for "putting a song across" of anyone in
the history of the performing arts. In his movements he has somehow combined
the most dramatic qualities of James Brown, Rudolf Nureyev, and Marcel
Marceau. He makes all previous "movers"—Elvis, Sammy Davis, Janis Joplin,

and even (saints protect me from sacrilege) the great James B. himself—
appear to be waist deep in the grimpenmire. This tradition (of movin' and
groovin') had its modest beginning with Cab Calloway at the Cotton Club in
Harlem where he would occasionally strut or slink about in front of the bandstand by way of "illustrating" a number. After each he would take his bow,
mopping his forehead, beaming up his gratitude for the applause as he reverted
to his "normal" self for the next downbeat (and invariably a change of pace).
This tradition, where the performer presents a series of alternating masks—
each separated by a glimpse of (presumably) his own actual face (smiling while
he readjusts the mike, wipes his brow, waits for the applause to die, etc.)—has
been sustained right up through the present, with Elvis and Sammy Davis
being its ultimate personifications. The phenomenal thing Jagger has accom-
plished is to have projected an image so overwhelmingly intense and so incredibly comprehensive that it embraces the totality of his work—so that there is
virtually no distinction between the person and the song. This is all the more
remarkable when it is realized that there is also virtually *no connection* between
the public midnight-rambler image of Jagger and the man himself. On the contrary, he is its antithesis—quiet, generous, and sensitive. What this suggests,
then, is an extraordinary potential for *acting*; and this is, in fact, his future—a
future that began with his superb characterization in *Performance*, and that
would have included the role of Alex in *A Clockwork Orange*, for which he was
ideal, had it not been for Kubrick's aversion to big guns.

While his movements are the synthesis and distillation of all that has gone
before or all that appears to be possible in and around a song on a stage, his
sound is uniquely his own, its roots, of course, are in the music of the black
South—and, with the exception of Elvis Presley, he has done more than anyone else to liberate it from the "race record" category of limited pressings on
obscure labels distributed solely in the black ghettos of America.

Slow pull back revealing Mick not alone on stage but with several
others. Pan left, in on Keith. Keith creates the music to which Mick moves,
and while the heaviest impact of the group is undeniably audiovisual, the sound
alone has made the Stones the only white band played on a number of otherwise exclusively "black music" disc-jockey programs around the country. "I
usually do it," says Keith, "with the idea of its being moved to." Yet when you
hear the sheer, drifting lyricism of things like "Ruby Tuesday," "Dandelion,"
"She's a Rainbow," or the intricately haunting beauty of "2,000 Light Years"
and "Paint It Black," one is amazed that Keith's body of work hasn't received

more considered critical attention. It is certainly as deserving of such as Paul McCartney's or that of any other contemporary composer.

QUICK SLAM CUT to backstage in the heart of Dixie. A short, fat man in a business suit, face perspiring, big white handkerchief in hand, trying to get into the dressing-room area and being circumvented, in a coolly muscular way, by our two black security chiefs, Stan (The Man) Moore and Big Leroy Leonard. Ever ready, I switch on my Sony cassette and move right in.

> STAN (to Leroy): "Well now, he *say* he the *mayor.*"
> LEROY: "Shee-it."
> STAN: "He *say* he want to present them the *keys* to the *city.*"
> LEROY: "Shee-it."

Turns out it *is* the mayor. So the lads dutifully assemble, and somehow (*noblesse oblige*) manage to keep a straight face while he addresses them (verbatim transcript):

> Wal, ah tell you *one* thing—them boys you got there (referring to Stan and Leroy) sho do look after you, and that's a fact . . . [winks] . . . wouldn't mind havin' a few like that mahself, hee-hee . . . wal, now then, ah got to tell you all when it comes to *music,* Law'ance Welk is moah to *mah* taste, not to say *undahstandin'* hee hee . . . but mah daughtah, Thelma Jean, says you awright, an' ah reckon anything good enuf foah Thelma Jean, wal now, er, uh, is good enuf foah me . . . so ah want to present you boys with the *keys to this heah city!!* Now y'all enjoy yourselves, ya' heah?

CLOSE UP MAYOR'S GRINNING FACE, CURIOUSLY MALEVOLENT. DISSOLVE THROUGH TO MATCH WITH SIMILAR PERSPIRING ROUND WHITE FACE, GRIM: This time it's a policeman. He's got an armlock on a young man, hustling him up the exit ramp with what appears to be undue urgency. It put me in mind of a Perelman satire on Kipling, and I wondered what the cop would think if I began jumping with glee and yelling: "Frog's march him! For God's sake, frog's march him!"

Stan looked on sadly. "Man," he sighed, "that's the hardest part of my job—trying to cool out the cops."

"Overreacting?"

"I used to call it that, but that doesn't tell the story. You see, if a man is *aware* that he's overreacting but he does it anyway, then you're into something else. The other day a police chief told me he wanted to have fifteen officers, in riot helmets, standing shoulder to shoulder in front of the stage facing the audience. Can you dig it? *They* become part of the spectacle, like if you're playing inside a prison, or at a Hitler rally. I ask him: 'Will they have their guns drawn?' I don't think he knew I was kidding. 'They get 'em out quick enough,' he said. You see, he was probably hoping they'd *charge the bandstand.* I mean, why should the Hell's Angels get all the publicity? That's where he was at."

MONTAGE, SERIES OF QUICK CUTS: TOP SHOT, 2,600 screamers storming the backstage area (Vancouver) after being told the concert is sold out, sending thirty-one police to the hospital. Crowd and fighting dissolve when opening chords of "Brown Sugar" are heard. CLOSE UP, Botticelli face upturned at the edge of the stage (Seattle), radiantly ecstatic as she screams at Bill Wyman: "Bill, Bill! Oh my God, you are so *stone beautiful* I can't believe it!" MEDIUM SHOT, sea of astonishment as audience stares up in narcissistic enchantment (San Francisco) at Chip Monck's fantastic forty-foot mirror slowly turning above the stage, affirming existence and placing them for a fleeting moment at least, in the same glittering picture as the Stones. LONG SHOT from top balcony (Los Angeles) Mick Jagger quells fifth-row disturbance by taking a drink from his water jug, then dispensing contents, benediction-style, over the fray, calming them wondrously. CLOSE UP, face in twisted anguish (San Diego), screaming like a character out of Burroughs: *"I got the fear!"* while being forcibly subdued by three big cops. A red-haired girl tries to help him, is dragged away by the hair. Others join in: fighting begins. LONG SHOT, Keith swooping in and out of purple-haze spot (Tucson) with extraordinary birdlike movements. MEDIUM SHOT, young man clutching harmonica hurls himself on stage (Albuquerque) and practically into the arms of Stan the Man. The young man's eyes are wildly alight. "I gotta blow with Mick," he's yelling. "You gotta let me do the gig with Mick!" Stan firmly escorts him away, murmuring, "Hey, baby, this isn't cool—let the cat do his thing, you do yours." A giant harness bull rushes over, truncheon at the ready and eager to use it. "No, it's cool, it's cool," says Stan and leads the boy off the stage. EXTREME CLOSE UP, slender fingers racing back and forth, Paderewski-style, on edge of stage (Denver), belonging to young mystery man who follows Stones everywhere, manages to get practically *under* Nicky Hopkins's piano at each concert. Has never tried to meet him. MATCH CUT to other fingers, dealing . . . bad scorpio vibes from out of place (Minneapolis); tripping hustler tries to rip off locals with weirdly cut coke, New Jersey grass, and other indigestibles. MEDIUM SHOT, young girl crying uncontrollably as her boyfriend holds her hands and keeps saying, "You mustn't rub it in," and the tear gas continues to slowly filter in from the outside, where they decided to lob a few canisters (better safe than sorry, eh?) into the crowd, just to show they meant business. MEDIUM SHOT, Mick burying his face in an urn of rose petals, then flinging them over the crowd (Kansas City), floating down through the blue smoke slow-motion time, and the darling frenzied teenies, leaping gazellelike, grasping at each tiny dream. LONG SHOT AND SLOW ZOOM IN TO CLOSE on the great Charlie Watts (Fort Worth), arms rising alternately, slowly, but in each upraised hand sticks twirling with strobe-effect speed over his head. CLOSE UP, heeled boot rapping out crack-crack-crack flamenco tempo, as Keith surges into "Midnight Rambler" (Nashville) and turns it every way but loose. MEDIUM GOING TO CLOSE, full-on weirdness (Washington, D.C.) as paraplegic is hoisted from band-side wheelchair and onto the shoulders of his buddy. Buñuel City. SLOW SWEEP PAN of four enchanted front-row (Norfolk, Va.) teenies in T-shirts (braless though pert) lettered:

Mick Taylor—We Love You!

And when he gave them his smile (boss charm, boss humility), they squirmed and squealed, and (or so it seemed) tingled all over. CLOSE UP, rich golden glow of the Selmer bell as Bobby Keys brings it all back home (Charlotte, N.C.) in an extended magic line of "Sweet Virginia." CLOSE UP, the groove and gas craglike features of the great Chip Monck—now in gnarled concern, as he points to a jagged opening in the concrete foundation of the bandstand, where a bomb had been planted earlier in the day and had gone off prematurely. Don't tell Mick. CLOSE UP, thermometer reading 115° (Toronto), heat prostration rampant, people falling like proverbial flies. Mick zooms in, does his fantastic thing, and off in the dressing room it was *exhaustionville extremis*, everyone falling down, apart, lying on the floor; forget it. Seemed impossible that anyone could do a second show, especially Mick. SLAM CUT to Mick leaping into "Jumping Jack Flash"—a satyr possessed, mad dervish, speed beyond the point of no return. . . .

"One thing about Mick," someone muttered, "he goes all out—every time."

That seemed to say exactly where it was at. None of the grand old clichés, like "great showmanship" . . . "kid's gotta lotta heart" . . . "the show must go on" . . . nothing like that, just a straightforward *"he goes all out . . .* [and the pause was like *bop-bop-bop*] . . . *every time."*

Later, over a big Teq Sun on the *Tongue*, in the extreme rear of the plane (banquetted for boss comf and conviv), I gave it certain thought. True enough, I decided, there's not been one like him, nor is there apt to be. I was quaffing off the last of the T.S. in a silent toast, one hand raised toward our fabulous nifties for the old refill, when who should fall by but the great Keith himself— snarling he was, and out of sorts by bloody weirdo half.

"Have a look at this then, mate," he said, affecting a curious accent, and tossed a copy of a pop-Sun-mag-sup (*NYTimes Mag.* July 16). It was one of those stories written by someone so far removed from the scene as to be re-markable for *any* truth at all. The author was described in the square below as "the rock-music critic for the *Times.*"

"What's that then, 'rock-music critic for the *Times*'?"

"Well, that's pretty heavy," I said. "It's something like being football critic for *Women's Wear Daily.*"

Then I read with some amazement that the Stones (especially as repre-sented by Mick) have copped out, have joined the genteel elite, indeed *"have used their radicalism to gain admittance to the easy good life of wealthy members of the entertainment world's establishment."*

I laid the rag aside and went for another Teq Sun. While standing there at the bar, I became aware of a foot-tapping melody nearby.

"What's that then?" I asked.

"Oh well, that's the Mick's new thing," was the answer. "You know, like the successful young poet asked the old poet, 'What shall I do now? And the old poet said, *'Etonnes-moi!'"*

I listened more carefully. It was a full-on studio-type recording, quite impressive—as indeed were the lyrics. It was the title song of an album in progress, to be called *The _____ Blues.* For those readers who are into literary anagrams and the like, the omitted is a ten-letter word beginning with a "c" and ending with an "r." And it isn't *"contractor."*

—1972
Saturday Review

The Quality Lit Game

Placing an MS. with New Yorker Mag?

In the late 1950s Terry had a strong distaste for the literary establishment of New York, which had rejected all of his novels (and most short stories) until after they were successfully published in Britain and France. Terry's hipster sensibility, and his capacity to shock and outrage, were antithetical to The New Yorker *zeitgeist of the time.*

Being in the neighborhood the other day, and with nothing particular to do, I decided to call round to *The New Yorker* offices and see if anything was up.

Actually, I had never put foot inside these offices before, but the ambience was at once so strikingly casual that it set me all a-pique and impulsive. I stopped the first person who sauntered by. "You, there," I said, "have the writer White fetched out." Except that I spoke in English, I did this more or less the way Kafka himself would have done it, in a dream, leaning lightly forward on a Malacca cane, pointing at things with my chin.

The person I had addressed—a sort of egghead man wearing a loose-fitting sweater—was genuinely taken aback. For an instant he seemed on the verge of saying something obscene, but then he turned with a shrug and shuffled away toward the back of *The New Yorker* offices.

Now, I don't say this would happen as a rule—it may have been that by intruding a note of classic austerity into the sans souci *New Yorker* ambience (which I *think* we can agree is simply part of a rather elaborate defensive mechanism) I pricked their conscious guilt—but, sure enough, in a few minutes old White himself was to be seen, pretending at first that he didn't notice me, as he walked up from the back of the offices, stopping to speak to people here and there, trying to remain cool, though, of course, this was a completely unprecedented situation.

When he reached where I was standing, he merely nodded. In my turn, I leaned forward on the cane. "You are the writer White?" I asked evenly. He nodded, perfunctorily, without deference or presumption. "*J'accuse!*" I said narrowly, leveling a finger at him, then turned abruptly and left the building.

Later during the day I stopped 'round at the bar below *The New Yorker*. White goes there often. He was there, of course, lushing it up (White won't experiment with drugs, but he says, 'What's wrong with a drink or two?'). He was standing at the bar alone. I wondered how best to approach him. It's no secret, of course, that White has plenty of influence in an editorial capacity at *New Yorker* mag. Whenever there's a question about a story at the mag, they shoot the ms. over to White. None of these have ever been accepted—White shoots them right out to the sender. Some of these mss., however, have been completely rewritten by White, and appear, under various names, in *New Yorker* mag.

On the other hand, they say White is incorruptible, that he won't give a friend a break, and so on. Well, no matter, I thought, if one can gain White's friendship and confidence, the least that can come of it would be the advantage of borrowing books. (*New Yorker* mag receives seven or eight hundred books a month from publishers who hope to get a decent review from White) and I was thinking to myself: Now, I warrant White cops a handsome share of those books! Meanwhile, I tried to frame an opening remark—something unique, of course, and incisive. Then I had it. I stepped up, put my hand on his shoulder, saying briskly, "Well, White, I just called 'round your publisher's. He says this last book of yours may very well outstrip *Silver Chalice!*" White, in the middle of a deep draught when I stepped up, was seized with a fit of coughing. I was quick to follow up the advantage:

"*Looks* like you've got another runaway best-seller on your hands, White."

White doesn't go for this sort of talk. "Go to hell," he said. You see, White prides himself on the subtle incisiveness of his work, the elusive image, the haunting multisense of a single phrase, certain delicate innovations in syntax, and metaphors couched in parable, or vice versa—all of which makes it a little embarrassing for him to be on the runaway best-seller list, along with a lot of trash. My job—to reassure him.

"Now listen, White," I took it up, "you've the idea a best-seller is immediately suspect—trash, in fact. Am I right? Well, you're wrong on that count, Mr. E. B. White! Now then, take the Bible—"

White started to speak, but I was too quick for hint, "Nathanael West," I sighed. "I know, White, I *know*! But you've got to forgot Nat West. He just wasn't—well, wasn't *realistic*! Am I right?"

White started to soften. Probably be was beginning to feel the big hot fire that is Truth in what I was saying.

"What do you want?" he demanded.

White is not a large man, but he is wiry and fast; a cynic's cynic, he has the heart of gold; urban nigh unto decadence, he loves the first green, the morning wind, the falling leaf, the newborn creatures, the steady squish of the cider press; a recluse's recluse, he is *completement engagé,* the first to fight the good fight wherever the front lines lead.

"It's a question of style, White," I said. "I mean, why the '*we*' in your writings? Admittedly schizoid?"

"Blatantly!" snarled White, without hesitation.

"*Touché,* White," I said. "So far, so good. Now, then: why the extensive use of parentheses? Fancy yourself another Jim Joyce? Another Billy-Bob Faulkner?"

"*Billy-Bob?*" said White incredulously. "You must be insane!"

White takes a back seat to no one, you see, *and* rightly so.

Just then, however, as I was about to ask if I could borrow *Cress Delahanty,* White was joined by several others—people from the offices of *New Yorker* mag, I gathered, by their stamp and kidney—who elbowed me aside and surrounded White, getting his opinion on this and that, trying to ingratiate themselves with really painfully awkward remarks about baby chicks and new-mown hay. I can tell you, it was enough to set old Nat West spinning in his gravey-wavey.

—1950s

Flashing on Gid

Maurice Girodias ran the Olympia Press in Paris, publishing erotic literature in English—ostensibly for men embarking on long lonely voyages. The high quality of the writing he published (such as Nabokov's Lolita*) made it a lucrative export for America, where such books were largely unknown. Terry's project with Girodias was* Candy, *written with poet Mason Hoffenberg. Published in 1958,* Candy *was banned by the French government for obscenity. The wiley Girodias exported it illegally by physically changing the cover and title (to* Lollipop*).* Candy, *first published in America by Putnam's—while also appearing in myriad paperback pirated editions—went on to become one of the biggest selling books in American publishing history.*

The exquisitely urbane Monsieur Maurice Kahane, aka Gid Girodias, was introduced to me in Paris, about 1950, by Alex Trocchi, editor of *Merlin*, the elitist literary mag that was archrival of our own *Paris Review*. With his typical aristo presumption, Girodias had been trying to seduce the former Ludgate Scholar into joining his Olympia Press stable of pornographers—"*mes écrivains méchants,*" as he chose to call them.

"I gave him short shrift and no mistake," Trocchi said, in his grandest manner, and in what may have been the very first of the countless lies and exaggerations I was to hear about (and from) Gid Girodias over the next forty years.

"Short shrift" indeed. In less than a month after his lofty pronouncement, Trocchi had made his debut as the soon-to-be-notorious Frances Lengle, author of *Helen and Desire;* within a year he was the brightest jewel in Olympia's crown, and indeed was giving instruction in the art of erotica to aspiring scribes.

Like everyone else, I found Girodias irresistible—boss charm and what at first appeared to be an extraordinary generosity. He seemed to fancy himself one of the last of the *grands seigneurs* and tried to act like one. Our first meeting was a casual happenstance. Gid was screening some porn footage that featured a dead ringer for the young Simone Signoret, whom, indeed, he claimed it to be (I was later assured by Roger Vadim that it was not she but a saucy doppelgänger), and insisted afterward on taking me to lunch "at an amusing little hole-in-the-wall I've just discovered."

The hole proved to be one of those bastions of bourgeois respectability, the absurd kind of French restaurant that has a prix-fixe lunch—a kind of boul' Mich mom-and-pop operation. It was certainly not a restaurant where you would send back the wine—or so I presumed until he did it, twice, each time with a show of annoyance charmingly tempered with a saintly forbearance. Noblesse oblige personified. "It is only when I have to deal with French waiters," he said, half closing his eyes with his eternal ultra-ennui, "that I begin to understand the phrase 'white man's burden.'" And, having said that, he ordered absinthe—somewhat to my surprise, since it had been outlawed in France for about two decades. "I like to keep a cache at different restaurants," he explained. "Our poets love it so."

In print his conversation appears absurdly supercilious, but as speech, delivered with the faintest quasi-lisp and eyes half closed, he managed to bring it off, and sounded not so much fruity as disarmingly effete. This tone was not merely in his manner but also in his attitudes. On that very first day of our acquaintance, for example, as we left the restaurant on the rue de la Harpe and started walking toward boulevard Saint-Michel, a friend of mine, H. L. "Doc" Humes, one of the founders of *The Paris Review* and a grand eccentric in his own right, pulled up alongside us, riding a Vespa. After a brief exchange he went on his way.

"*Moi, je n'aime pas le vélo,*" said Gid in a tone of absolute disdain. "I would not wish to be seen on one. Your friend just now, is he a student?"

"No," I explained, "he's a grand eccentric."

Gid shook his head gravely. "He will not be taken seriously if he rides a *vélo.*" His own tastes ran more toward the Maserati and the Lamborghini—between which, he claimed, he could not decide, hinting that it was merely his ambivalence that prevented him from owning one or the other instead of his rather mainstream Citroën. "Françoise Sagan," he told me, "is trying desper-

ately to decide between the two. I can't help her. We were on the phone for
two hours this morning."

It was not always possible to know if he was exaggerating or lying out-
right. If money was concerned, you could be fairly sure it was the latter. His
most severe critic in that regard appeared to be Samuel Beckett: "The man is a
menace," he was fond of saying. "I have seen him take the pennies from a dead
man's eyes," he would add with mock gravity, to which Trocchi would respond
by crossing himself and murmuring something in Latin.

Trocchi was Beckett's number-one protégé, and sometimes we would
have lunch with him in the kitchen of his walk-up off the boulevard Raspail.
Beckett's great dish was a straightforward *rognons sautés*, with a splash of (if
memory serves) Madeira at the finish. Trocchi and I would usually pick them
up at Les Halles (after scoring smoke at the Soleil du Maroc) and take them
along to Sam's. Also the occasional *riz de veau* or, again, something that Trocchi
would prepare, the damnable "bangers and mash"—an infantile indulgence on
both their parts, in my view.

Very early in our relationship, I detected in Girodias a marked disapproval
of the style of dress of Alex and myself—a style that might best have been described as modest, if not indeed occasionally threadbare.

"In France," he said, "literary men dress correctly. Look at Camus and
Sartre. You won't see them without a necktie or a proper shirt."

"Beckett and Genet don't wear ties," I reminded him. "And neither does
the great Hank Miller."

He half closed his eyes and wearily tilted his head. "My dear boy," he
lisped, "you have just named three of the most ne'er-do-well *non gratas* in all
Paris."

Although he admired and envied people as famous as those three, it suited
his curious vanity to pretend that they were scruffy wastrels.

Something in a similar vein occurred later on when he could not quite forgive or fathom my own slight acquaintance with Jean Cocteau. Girodias was a
sort of *arriviste extraordinaire*, and Cocteau, that paragon of ancient grace and
decadence, was not really aware of his existence, except perhaps in the most
peripheral sense. One of my best friends at this time was a young man named Jean-
François Bergery. He worked as a reporter for *Paris-Match*, and he was the son
of a French diplomat and a Russian countess who was a niece of Diaghilev; he
was also a godson of Jean Cocteau, and he would occasionally take Trocchi and
myself to the latter's sumptuous Trocadero town house, where we would smoke

opium and dream to the strains of the Cocteau faves, Bartók and Stravinsky (*The Miraculous Mandarin* and *L'Histoire du soldat*, if memory serves).

Trocchi, with his storm-tossed leonine drop-dead good looks and his Nietzschean slant on things, was OK; but to Jean-François, one of the great snobs of the Western world, Gid was not acceptable. *'Ça ne marche pas,"* Jean-François would say.

I didn't get around to asking him why not.

It was during the Cocteau/opium period that I wrote a short story called "Candy Christian," about a fabulous, blue-eyed, pink-nippled, pert-derriered darling who was compassion incarnate, living in the West Village, so filled with universal love that she gave herself—fully, joyfully—to Derek, a demented hunchback. Of course, that was merely the surface, the flimsy trappings, as it were; the meat and potatoes of the piece lay elsewhere. Suffice it to say I showed the story to Trocchi. He wanted to publish it in *Merlin*—for nil recompense. I told him no thanks; I had just had something published under a similar arrangement in an ultra-obscure mag called *The Paris News Post*, H. L. Humes editor in chief (before he met up with Plimpton, Peter Matthiessen, and *The Paris Review*).

"Well, in any case," said Trocchi, "this spunky heroine of yours should have more adventures! I would like very much," he went on, "to see her involved with the Roman Catholic Church."

I asked him if he would like to write such an episode himself, since he had an absolutely Joycean love/hate in that regard. And he might have done so, had not another great friend of mine, Mason Hoffenberg, poet and hemp-maven extraordinaire, surfaced at almost the same moment and been doubly keen for the opportunity. Just as well, I decided, because Trocchi was now tokus-over-teakettle into the writing of *The Wisdom of the Lash* or some equally racy volume for Olympia's "Traveller's Companion" series.

"Alex tells me," said Gid slyly over our next aperitif at the Flore, "that you and your friend Mason have embarked on a rather picaresque saga. May I show a few pages to one of my senior editors?"

The book we were writing—an extension of Candy's West Village adventure—was humorous, which could hardly be said of any of Olympia's books, with the notable exception of *Lolita*.

"Not suitable for your list, I'm afraid," was my reply.

But he was determined to see it, and with characteristic gall and cunning he persuaded Trocchi to make a copy of our ms. and let him read it—or scan it. I don't think he was much into actual reading. In any case, he must have thought it suited his purpose, because he made us the grand-sounding offer of ten thousand francs a month, for four months or until we finished the book, whichever happened first. Grand-sounding, yes, unless one considered that the exchange rate then was one hundred francs to the dollar. I complained to Trocchi about it. But he was jubilant.

"That's four hundred dollars, man," he exclaimed. "Nabokov only got two-fifty. You're getting top dollar! Break out the bubbly! Light up the wog-hemp! Let's get it on with a right rave-up!"

Our most frequented café in those days was the Café Saint-Germain des Près, opposite the Flore. It was there one winter's morn, while Mason and I were having our customary *grande tasse*, that a certain Greg E. Corso, author of the epic poems "Bomb" and "Gasoline" and the novel *American Express*, presented himself at the table. He plopped a manuscript down and said in his usual gross manner, "Now dig this . . ."

It turned out that the ms. was, of all things, *Naked Lunch*. It seems that Burroughs had given it to Allen Ginsberg and he had given it to Gregory. Mason and I set out to convince Gid that it was worthy of his distinguished imprimatur.

His first response was to leaf through it impatiently. "There is no fucking in the book," he said. "No sex at all in the book."

We pointed out something on page seventeen.

"Ah, yes!" he said triumphantly. "All the way to page seventeen! And still it's only a blow job!"

He got up from his desk and turned to an old wooden filing cabinet. His offices had a Dickensian mustiness and clutter, which he seemed to believe lent his operation a degree of respectability. He took out a couple of letters.

"Let me show you what our readership requires," he said, bringing them over. If memory serves, they were from a couple of Indians in the British Army, and they pleaded for books that were "brutally frank" and "frankly explicit," phrases they had picked up from porn advertisements.

"Could we truly recommend such a work as this to these readers? And the title is no good. What does it mean, this 'Naked Lunch'?"

I told him that Jack Kerouac had suggested the title, hoping that might impress him. But Mason had the right idea: he said that it was American slang for sex in the afternoon.

Gid brightened somewhat. "*Ah, comme notre cinq-à-sept!*" he declared, referring to the cherished French tradition of having sex (with a mistress, of course) every day from five to seven P.M.

"No, this is more like an *orgy*," he was told.

And eventually he came around.

I have read, God (certainly) knows, other accounts of how this great milestone book came into print, but the actual facts are those above. The scary thing about it is that Girodias could have as easily remained adamant, as indeed he did in another celebrated case, when a certain C. Ames Plimpton decided to break his dear mom's heart for good by writing a dirty book for the infamous Olympia Press, and to this end submitted a four- or five-page proposal outlining the work—a spin-off, I believe, of the grand old R. L. Stevenson classic, *The Suicide Club*. The outline seemed to me very promising indeed, but Girodias was livid. He simply could not believe that "anything worthwhile" could come from someone as upstanding as George Plimpton.

"He was born with a silver spoon," he said, "and he has put it in his mouth! His parents pay for that so-called magazine of his!"

"Perhaps you think he's too grand for the rest of us," I suggested, "and that's why you're against his work. Am I right?"

This set him off, and no mistake. "Grand?" he fairly shouted. *"Grand manqué! Grand manqué!"*

He was still ranting when Mason and I headed down the steps and off to the Flore.

Perhaps my most outlandish experience with Gid Girodias occurred when he was trying to dupe J. P. Donleavy out of absolutely everything pertaining to *The Ginger Man*.

I had made the mistake of mentioning to Gid an experience I had shared with George Plimpton and *The Paris Review*'s number-one patron, Sadruddin Khan, younger brother of Aly and son of the big Aga—namely, a visit to the fabulous Maison de la Langue, surely Paris's most exclusive and opulent whorehouse at that point in time. I had described to Gid how the patron was undressed and secured to a hospital gurney, whereupon three angelic preteenies carefully anointed him from head to toe with banana oil and then proceeded, with small darting pink tongues, assiduously to lick it off. Years later, in a published interview, Girodias insinuated that I had gone into "lascivious detail" regarding the procedure, but like so many of his utterances it was simply untrue—I had, in fact, merely *alluded* to the highlights of the episode.

"Donleavy is coming over from Dublin," he told me. "I'm hosting a *grande soirée* for him, and as part of his entertainment I'd like you to take him to that fancy bordello you and Plimpton go to. How much does it cost?" I told him I had no idea of the cost, since I had been a guest. "Perhaps he has an account there," I suggested. I was referring, of course, to Sadri Khan, but Girodias thought I meant Plimpton, and it set him hopping.

"*Mais ça ne m'étonne pas du tout!*" he shouted. "And do his parents know that all the money they give him for the magazine is going to a French whorehouse?"

The soirée itself proved to be quite a gala affair—thanks mainly to the attendance of one particular acquaintance of Mason's and mine, Mohammed Hadj (to whom, incidentally, *Candy* is dedicated), proprietor of the Café Soleil du Maroc and ofttimes purveyor of what Girodias rather affectedly called "the damnable wog-hemp."

On this occasion, however, Girodias's generally low opinion of Monsieur Hadj (and, indeed, of Arabs by any other name) seemed much ameliorated, perhaps because his M.O. for the evening, I soon began to discern, was to get Donleavy so totally blotto that he could have his way with him, in terms of contracts, royalties, or whatever else might relate to *The Ginger Man*. And in that regard it was apparent that a bit of hashish would be a welcome addition to his arsenal of derangements. "Baudelaire," I heard him confide to our hapless guest of honor, "used to have it in his confiture."

At one point in the evening I fell into consort with Trocchi and the English publisher John Calder—a deadly combo, derangement-wise—and so failed to follow the complete dismantling of J. P. Donleavy; suffice it to say I recall him being bundled out the door and into the Paris night by Gid and his brother Eric. I later heard that he returned to Dublin the very next clay, back to the snug comfort of hearth and home.

Gid's great love, as is generally known, was the fabulous Iris Owens, brilliant Junoesque authoress of the two excellent novels *After Claude* and *Hope Diamond Refuses*. Under the pen name "Harriet Daimler," she also wrote several of Olympia Press's top-of-the-line titles, including *The Woman Thing, Innocence,* and *The Pleasure Thieves* (with "Henry Crannach," who was, in fact, her best friend, the ultra-cutie-pie Marilyn Kanterman). Aside from her Junoesque beauty, Gid was smitten by her rapier wit and devastating logic. She was a pre-Sontag Sontag, and he was determined to get the best of her. He had a typical Frenchman's attitude toward women—i.e., that they were all bimbos— so Iris Owens, with a chess-playing poet's head on her, was an infuriating enigma and challenge. At first he was prepared (in self-defense, of course) to write her off as a "dyke mathematician," until he got a glimpse of her very endearing feminine charms. Then he was hooked. I got the impression that she was fond of him, but she certainly never reciprocated the total adulation he obviously had for her. Indeed, it was at those moments when he exhibited his vulnerability and his despondency over this great unrequited love that he was most sympathetic, and then I would begin to regret not having insisted that Gid share our pipe at the home of the great J. Cocteau.

—1991
Grand Street
Reprinted by permission of Jean Stein and *Grand Street*.

Rolling Over Our Nerve Endings

In the early '60s, Terry wrote passionately about authors whose work was unavailable in the United States, especially Henry Miller and William Burroughs. This piece was perhaps the earliest mainstream review of Burroughs's work.

In life there are things which are funny, and then there are things which are merely presumed to be funny. Literature, out of a misguided appeal to an imaginary popular taste and in the caution of self-distrust, generally follows the latter course, so that the humor found in books is almost always vicarious—meeting certain "traditional" requirements and producing the kind of laughter one might expect: rather strained. The work of William Burroughs is an all-stops-out departure from this practice, and when he writes at the top of his ability, there is nothing to match it.

The element of humor in *Nova Express*, as in *Naked Lunch* and his two other novels, has moral strength of historic proportions, whereby the existentialist sense of the *absurd* is taken to an informal conclusion. It is an absolutely devastating ridicule of all that is false, primitive, and vicious in current American life: the abuses of power, hero worship, aimless violence, materialistic obsession, intolerance, and every form of hypocrisy.

No one, for example, has written with such eloquent disgust about capital punishment; throughout his work recur sequences to portray the unfathomable barbarity of a "civilization" that can countenance this ritual. There is only one way, of course, to ridicule capital punishment—and that is by exaggerating its circumstances, increasing its horror, accentuating the animal irresponsibility of those involved, insisting that the monstrous deed be witnessed (and in Technicolor, so to speak) by all concerned. Burroughs is perhaps the first modern writer to seriously attempt this; he is certainly the first to have done so with such startling effectiveness.

Social analogy and parallels of this sort abound in his work, though one must never mistake it for political comment—which, as in all art worth the name, is more instinctive than deliberate—for Burroughs is first and foremost a poet. His attunement to contemporary language is probably unequalled in American writing. Any one with a feeling for English phrase at its most balanced, concise, and arresting cannot fail to see this excellence. In *Naked Lunch*, for example, in describing the difficulty of obtaining narcotics prescriptions from wary doctors in the southwestern United States, he writes:

"Itinerant short con and carny hyp men have burned down the croakers of Texas . . ."

None of these words is unusual, but the sudden freshness of using "burned down" (to mean "having exploited beyond further possibility") in this prosaic context indicates his remarkable power of giving life to a dead vernacular.

Or again, where the metaphysical finds expression in slang:

"One day Little Boy Blue starts to slip, and what crawls out would make an ambulance attendant puke . . ."

And, psychological:

"The Mark Inside was coming up on him and that's a rumble nobody can cool . . ."

Imagery of this calibre puts the use of argot on a level considerably beyond merely "having a good ear for the spoken word." Compared to Burroughs's grasp of modern idiom in almost every form of English—and his ability at distillation and ellipsis—the similar efforts of Ring Lardner and of Hemingway must be seen as amateurish and groping.

The role of drugs is of singular importance in Burroughs's work, as it is, indeed, in American life. In no other culture in the history of the world has the use of narcotics, both legal and illicit, become so strange and integral a part of the overall scene. And reviviscent addiction has reached such prevalence and intensity that, in the larger view, it can no longer matter whether it be considered a "crime" or a "sickness"—it is a cultural phenomenon with far more profound implications than either of these diagnoses would suggest.

Burroughs's treatment of narcotics, like his treatment of homosexuality, ranges from that of personal psychology, through the sociological, and finally into pure metaphor. And he is perhaps the first writer to treat drug addiction and homosexuality with both humor and humility.

The Burroughs-Gysin theory of "Cut-Ups"—whereby manuscript pages are cut lengthwise in half (or any other way) and then pieced together "at hazard"—has been attacked by those who believe in a Divine Order of Art Past. This school acknowledges no possible greatness beyond that of Shakespeare, Proust, Joyce, Kafka and Faulkner. They are the same people, of course, who at first thought Jackson Pollock was a fake, Picasso a fraud, Frank Lloyd Wright and Bertrand Russell fools. What they overlook, because of their own obsession with *censorship*, is the very quality of extreme *self-censorship* which is foremost in the minds of those they condemn—or, as the Man said: "Any fool can drip paint, but how many have the when/where to stop it?" If Burroughs were cutting up *Saturday Evening Post* stories, it would still come out all right, because he would cut them down to the letter; using his own writing (because there is never even a two-word cliché—except for the freshly obscene—in his text), he can work with half pages.

The debt of young writers to these novels (which include *The Soft Machine* and *The Ticket That Exploded*) is incalculable. No one writing in English, with the exception of Henry Miller, has done as much towards freeing the writer (and tomorrow the reader) of the superstitions surrounding the use of certain words and certain attitudes. It is probably true to say that what Burroughs has done is to up-date Joyce, in American idiom; and, if so, *Nova Express* is to *Naked Lunch* as *Finnegans Wake* is to *Ulysses*. It is poetry of the most consummate control:

"Muttering in the dogs of unfamiliar score—Cross the wounded galaxies we intersect—Poison of dead sun in your brain slowly fading—Migrants of age in gasoline crack of history—Explosive bio advance out of space to neon . . . the important thing is always courage to let go—in the dark."

For those who fail to see "form" in this, and are disturbed because of it, one may conclude only that they see in life itself a "form" which has eluded philosophy from the beginning of time.

—1964
New York Herald Tribune

Writers at Work: Henry Green

Terry's admiration for Green's novels, which were mostly written in dialogue and had surreal touches, led to Green becoming a friend and mentor. Terry was a contributing editor to The Paris Review *in the '50s, having published a few short stories there. Terry suggested Green as a subject for the journal's* Art of Fiction *series.*

Henry Green is the pseudonym of H. V. Yorke, the London-Birmingham industrialist whom W. H. Auden has said to be the best English novelist alive.

Mr. Green wrote his first novel, *Blindness*, while still a schoolboy at Eton, and this has been followed by nine more. Of his life otherwise, he has noted:

> I was born in 1905 in a large house by the banks of the river Severn, in England, and within the sound of the bells from the Abbey Church at Tewkesbury. Some children are sent away to school; I went at six and three-quarters and did not stop till I was twenty-two, by which time I was at Oxford, but the holidays were all fishing. And then there was billiards.
>
> I was sent at twelve and a half to Eton and almost at once became what was then called an aesthete, that is a boy who consciously dressed to shock. I stayed that way at Oxford. From Oxford I went into the family business, an engineering works in the Midlands, with its iron and brass foundries and machine shops. After working through from the bottom I eventually came to the top where for the time being I remain, married, living in London, with one son.

Mr. Green is a tall, gracious, and imposingly handsome man, with a warm strong voice and very quick eyes. In speech he displays on occasion that hallmark of English public school, the slight tilt of the head and closing of eyes when pronouncing the first few words of some sentences—a manner most often in contrast to what he is saying, for his expressions tend toward parable and his wit may move from cozy to scorpion-dry in less than a twinkle. Many have remarked that his celebrated deafness will roar or falter according to his spirit and situation; at any rate he will not use a hearing aid, for reasons of his own, though no doubt discernable to some.

Mr. Green writes at night and in many longhand drafts.

His novels, by date of publication, are: *Blindness* (1926), *Living* (1929), *Party-Going* (1939), *Pack My Bag* (1940), *Caught* (1943), *Loving* (1945), *Back* (1946), *Concluding* (1948), *Nothing* (1950), and *Doting* (1952).

In his autobiographical novel, *Pack My Bag*, he has described prose in this way: "Prose is not to be read aloud but to oneself at night, and it is not quick as poetry, but rather a gathering web of insinuations which go further than names however shared can ever go. Prose should be a long intimacy between strangers with no direct appeal to what both may have known. It should slowly appeal to feelings unexpressed, it should in the end draw tears out of the stone."

An ancient trade-compliment, to an author whose technique is highly developed, has been to call him a "writer's writer"; Henry Green has been referred to as a "writer's-writer's writer," though practitioners of the craft have had only to talk with him momentarily on the subject to know that his methods were not likely to be revealed to them, either then or at any other time. It is for this reason—attempting to delve past his steely reticence—that some of the questions in the interview would seem unduly long or presumptious.

Mr. Green lives in London, in a house in Knightsbridge, with a beautiful and charming wife named Dig. The following conversation was recorded there, one winter night, in the author's fire-lit study.

T.S.: Now you have a body of work, ten novels, which many critics consider the most elusive and enigmatic in contemporary literature—and yourself professionally, or as a personality, nonetheless so. I'm wondering if these two mysteries are merely coincidental?

MR. GREEN: What's that? I'm a trifle hard of hearing.

T.S.: Well, I'm referring to such things as your use of a pseudonym, your refusal to be photographed, and so on. May I ask the reason for it?

MR. GREEN: I didn't want my business associates to know I wrote novels. Most of them do now though . . . *know* I mean, not write, thank goodness.

T.S.: And has this affected your relationships with them?

MR. GREEN: Yes, yes, oh yes—why some years ago a group at our Birmingham works put in a penny each and bought a copy of a book of mine—*Living*. And as I was going round the iron foundry one day, a loam-moulder said to me: "I read your book, Henry." "And did you like it?" I asked, rightly apprehensive. He replied: "I didn't think much of it, Henry." Too awful.

Then you know, with a customer, at the end of a settlement which has deteriorated into a compromise painful to both sides, he may say: "I suppose you are going to put this in a novel." Very awkward.

T.S.: I see.

MR. GREEN: Yes, it's best they shouldn't know about one. And one should never be known by sight.

T.S.: You have however been photographed from the rear.

MR. GREEN: And a wag said: "I'd know that back anywhere."

T.S.: I've heard it remarked that your work is "too sophisticated" for American readers, in that it offers no scenes of violence—and "too subtle," in that its message is somewhat veiled. What do you say?

MR. GREEN: Unlike the wilds of Texas, there is very little violence over here. A bit of child-killing of course, but no straight-shootin'. After fifty, one ceases to digest; as someone once said: "I just ferment my food now." Most of us walk crabwise to meals and everything else. The oblique approach in middle age is the safest thing. The unusual at this period is to get anywhere at all—God damn!

T.S.: And how about "subtle"?

MR. GREEN: I don't follow. *Suttee*, as I understand it, is the suicide—now forbidden—of a Hindu wife on her husband's flaming bier. I don't want my wife to do that when my time comes—and with great respect, as I know her, she won't . . .

T.S.: I'm sorry, you misheard me; I said, "subtle"—that the message was too subtle.

MR. GREEN: Oh, *subtle*. How dull!

T.S.: . . . yes, well now I believe that two of your novels, *Blindness* and *Pack My Bag*, are said to be "autobiographical," isn't that so?

MR. GREEN: Yes, those two are mostly autobiographical. But where they are about myself, they are not necessarily accurate as a portrait; they aren't photographs. After all, no one knows what he is like, he just tries to give some sort of picture of his time. Not like a cat to fight its image in the mirror.

T.S.: The critic Alan Pryce-Jones has compared you to Jouhandeau and called you an "odd, haunted, ambiguous writer." Did you know that?

MR. GREEN: I was in the same house with him at Eton. He was younger than me, so he saw through me perhaps.

T.S.: Do you find critical opinion expressed about your work useful or interesting?

MR. GREEN: Invariably useless and uninteresting—when it is of daily papers or weeklies which give so little space nowadays. But there is a man called Edward Stokes who has written a book about me and who knows all too much. I believe the Hogarth Press is going to publish it. And then the French translator of *Loving*, he wrote two articles in some French monthly. Both of these are valuable to me.

T.S.: I'd like to ask you some questions now about the work itself. You've described your novels as *"non-representational."* I wonder if you'd mind defining that term?

MR. GREEN: *"Non-representational"* was meant to represent a picture which was not a photograph, nor a painting *on a photograph*, nor, in dialogue, a tape recording. For instance the very deaf, as I am, hear the most astounding things all round them, which have not, in fact, been said. This enlivens my replies until, through mishearing, a new level of communication is reached. My characters misunderstand each other more than people do in real life, yet they do so less than I. Thus when writing, I "represent" very closely what I see (and I'm not seeing so well now) and what I hear (which is little) but I say it is "non-representational" because it is not necessarily what others see and hear.

T.S.: And yet, as I understand this theory, its success does not depend upon any actual sensory differences between people talking, but rather upon psychological or emotional differences between them as readers, isn't that so? I'm referring to the serious use of this theory in communicative writing.

MR. GREEN: People strike sparks off each other, that is what I try to note down. But mark well, they only do this when they are talking together. After all we don't write letters now, we telephone. And one of these days we are going to have TV sets which lonely people can talk to and get answers back. Then no one will read anymore.

T.S.: And that is your crabwise approach.

MR. GREEN: To your question, yes. And to stop one's asking why I don't write *plays*, my answer is I'd rather have these sparks in black and white than liable to interpretation by actors and the producer of a piece.

T.S.: Do you consider that all your novels have been done as "non-representational"?

MR. GREEN: Yes, they all of course represent a *selection* of material. The Chinese classical painters used to leave out the middle distance. Until *Nothing* and *Doting* I tried to establish the mood of any scene by a few but highly pointed descriptions. Since then I've tried to keep everything down to bare dialogue and found it very difficult. You see, to get back to what you asked a moment ago, when you referred to the emotional differences between readers—what one writes has to be all things to all men. If one isn't enough to enough readers they stop reading and the publishers won't publish any more. To disprove my own rule I've done a very funny three-act play and no one will put it on.

T.S.: I'm sorry to hear that, but now what about the role of *humor* in the novel?

MR. GREEN: Just the old nursery rhyme—"Something and spice makes all things nice," is it? Surely the artist must entertain. And one's in a very bad way indeed if one can't laugh. Laughter relaxes the characters in a novel. And if you *can* make the reader laugh he is apt to get careless and go on reading. So you as the writer get a chance to get something into him.

T.S.: I see, and what might that something be?

MR. GREEN: Here we approach the crux of the matter which, like all hilarious things, is almost indescribable. To me the purpose of art is to produce something alive; in my case, in print, but with a separate, and of course one hopes, with an everlasting life on its own.

T.S.: And the qualities then of a work-of-art . . .

MR. GREEN: To be alive. To have a real life of its own. The miracle is that it should live in the person who reads it. And if it *is* real and true it does, for five hundred years, for generation after generation. It's like having a baby, but in print. If it's really good, you can't stop its living. Indeed once the thing is printed, you simply cannot strangle it, as you could a child, by putting your hands round its little wet neck.

T.S.: What would you say goes into creating this life, into making this thing real and true?

MR. GREEN: Getting oneself straight. To get what one produces to have a real life of its own.

T.S.: Now this page of manuscript you were good enough to show me—what stage of the finished work does this represent?

MR. GREEN: Probably a very early draft.

T.S.: In this draft I see that the dialogue has been left untouched, whereas every line in the scene otherwise has been completely rewritten.

MR. GREEN: I think if you checked with other fragments of this draft you would find as many the other way around, the dialogue corrected and the rest left untouched.

T.S.: Here the rewriting has been done in entire sentences, rather than in words or phrases—is that generally the way you work?

MR. GREEN: Yes, because I copy everything out afresh. I make alterations in the manuscript and then copy them out. And in copying out, I make further alterations.

T.S.: How much do you usually write before you begin rewriting?

MR. GREEN: The first twenty pages over and over again—because in my idea you have to get everything into them. So as I go along and the book develops, I have to go back to that beginning again and again. Otherwise I rewrite only when I read where I've got to in the book and I find something so bad I can't go on till I've put it right.

T.S.: When you begin to write something, do you begin with a certain *character* in mind, or rather with a certain *situation* in mind?

MR. GREEN: Situation every time.

T.S.: Is that necessarily the *opening* situation—or perhaps you could give me an example; what was the basic situation, as it occurred to you, for *Loving?*

MR. GREEN: I got the idea of *Loving* from a manservant in the Fire Service during the war. He was serving with me in the ranks and he told me he had once asked the elderly butler who was over him what the old boy most liked in the world. The reply was: "Lying in bed on a summer morning, with the window open, listening to the church bells, eating buttered toast with cunty fingers." I saw the book in a flash.

T.S.: Well, now after getting your initial situation in mind, then what thought do you give to plot beyond it?

MR. GREEN: It's all a question of length; that is, of proportion. How much you allow to this or that is what makes a book now. It was not so in the days of the old three-decker novel. As to plotting or thinking ahead, I don't in a novel. I let it come page by page, one a day, and carry it in my head. When I say carry I mean the *proportions*—that is, the length. This is the exhaustion of creating. Towards the end of the book your head is literally bursting. But try and write out a scheme or plan and you will only depart from it. My way you have a chance to set something living.

T.S.: No one, it seems, has been able to satisfactorily relate your work to any source of influence. I recall that Mr. Pritchett has tried to place it in the tradition of Sterne, Carroll, Firbank, and Virginia Woolf—whereas Mr. Toynbee wished to relate it to Joyce, Thomas Wolfe, and Henry Miller. Now, *are* there styles or works that you feel have influenced yours?

MR. GREEN: I really don't know. As far as I'm consciously aware I forget everything I read at once including my own stuff. But I have a tremendous admiration for Céline.

T.S.: I feel there are certain aspects of your work, the mechanics of which aren't easily drawn into question—because I don't find terms to cover them. I would like to try to state one however and see if you feel it is correct or can be clarified. It's something Mr. Pritchett seems to hint at when he describes you as "a psychologist poet making people out of blots," and it has to do with the degree to which you've developed the "non-existence-of-author" principle. The reader does not simply forget that there is an author behind the words, but because of some annoyance over a seeming "discrepancy" in the story must, in fact, *remind* himself that there is one. This reminding is accompanied by an irritation with the author because of these apparent oversights on his part, and his "failings" to see the particular *significance* of certain happenings. The irritation gives way then to a feeling of pleasure and superiority in that he, the reader, sees *more* in the situation than the author does—so that all of this now belongs to *him*. And the author is dismissed, even perhaps with a slight contempt—and only the *work* remains, alone now with this reader who has had to take over. Thus, in the spell of his own imagination the characters and story *come alive* in an almost incredible way, quite beyond anything achieved by conventional methods of writing. Now this is a principle that occurs in Kafka's work, in an undeveloped way, but is obscured because the situations are so strongly fantasy. It occurs in a very pure form however in Kafka's *Journals*—if one assumes that they were, despite all said to the contrary, *written to be read*, then it is quite apparent, and, of course, very funny and engaging indeed. I'm wondering if that is the source of this principle for you, or if, in fact, you agree with what I say about it?

MR. GREEN: I don't agree about Kafka's *Journals*, which I have by my bed and still don't or can't follow.

But if you are trying to write something which has a life of its own, which is alive, of course the author must keep completely out of the picture. I hate the portraits of donors in medieval triptyches. And if the novel *is* alive of course the reader will be irritated by discrepancies—life, after all, is one discrepancy after another.

T.S.: Do you believe that a writer should work toward the development of a particular *style*?

MR. GREEN: He can't do anything else. His style is himself, and we are all of us changing every day—developing, we hope! We leave our marks behind us like a snail.

T.S.: So the writer's style develops with him.

MR. GREEN: Surely. But he must take care not to let it go too far—like the later Henry James or James Joyce. Because it then becomes a private communication with himself, like a man making cat's cradles with spider's webs, a sort of Melanesian gambit.

T.S.: Concerning your own style and the changes it has undergone, I'd like to read a sample paragraph—from *Living*, written in 1928—and ask you something about it. This paragraph occurs, you may perhaps recall, as the description of a girl's dream—a working-class girl who wants more than anything else a home, and above all, a child . . .

"Then clocks in that town all over town struck 3 and bells in churches there ringing started rushing sound of bells like wings tearing under roof of sky, so these bells rang. But women stood, reached up children drooping to sky, sharp boned, these women wailed and their noise rose and ate the noise of bells ringing."

I'd like to ask about the style here, about the absence of common articles—*a, an,* and *the*—there being but one in the whole paragraph, which is fairly representative of the book. Was this omission of articles throughout *Living* based on any particular theory?

MR. GREEN: I wanted to make that book as taut and spare as possible, to fit the proletarian life I was then leading. So I hit on leaving out the articles. I still think it effective, but would not do it again. It may now seem, I'm afraid, affected.

T.S.: Do you think that an elliptical method like that has a function other than, as you say, suggesting the tautness and spareness of a particular situation?

MR. GREEN: I don't know, I suppose the more you leave out, the more you highlight what you leave in—not true of taking the filling out of a sandwich, of course—but if one kept a diary, one wouldn't want a minute-to-minute catalogue of one's dreadful day.

T.S.: Well, that was written in 1928—were you influenced toward that style by *Ulysses*?

MR. GREEN: No. There's no "stream of consciousness" in any of my books that I can remember—I did not read *Ulysses* until *Living* was finished.

T.S.: That was your second novel, and that novel seems quite apart stylistically from the first and from those that followed—almost all of which, while "inimitably your own," so to speak, are of striking diversity in tone and style. Of them though, I think *Back* and *Pack My Bag* have a certain similarity, as have *Loving* and *Concluding*. Then again, *Nothing* and *Doting* might be said to be similiar in that, for one thing at least, they're both composed of . . . what would you say, *ninety-five* percent? . . . ninety-five percent *dialogue*.

MR. GREEN: *Nothing* and *Doting* are about the upper classes—and so is *Pack My Bag*, but it is nostalgia in this one, and too, in *Back*, which is about the middle class. Nostalgia has to have its own style. *Nothing* and *Doting* are hard and sharp; *Back* and *Pack My Bag*, soft.

T.S.: You speak of "classes" now, and I recall that *Living* has been described as the "best proletarian novel ever written." Is there to your mind then a social-awareness responsibility for the writer or artist?

MR. GREEN: No, no. The writer must be disengaged or else he is writing politics. Look at the Soviet writers.

I just wrote what I heard and saw, and, as I've told you, the workers in my factory thought it rotten. It was my very good friend Christopher Isherwood used that phrase you've just quoted and I don't know that he ever worked in a factory.

T.S.: Concerning the future of the novel, what do you think is the outlook for the Joycean-type introspective style, and, on the other hand, for the Kafka school?

MR. GREEN: I think Joyce and Kafka have said the last word on each of the two forms they developed. There's no one to follow them. They're like cats which have licked the plate clean. You've got to dream up another dish if you're to be a writer.

T.S.: Do you believe that films and television will radically alter the format of the novel?

MR. GREEN: It might be better to ask if novels will continue to be written. It's impossible for a novelist not to look out for other media nowadays. It isn't that everything has been done in fiction—truly nothing has been done as yet, save Fielding, and he only started it all. It is simply that the novelist is a communicator and must therefore be interested in any form of communication. You don't dictate to a girl now, you use a recording apparatus; no one faints anymore, they have blackouts; in Geneva you don't kill someone by cutting his throat, you blow a poisoned dart through a tube and *zing* you've got him. Media change. We don't have to paint chapels like Cocteau, but at the same time we must all be ever on the lookout for the new ways.

T.S.: What do you say about the use of symbolism?

MR. GREEN: You can't escape it can you? What after all is one to do with one-self in print? Does the reader feel a dread of anything? Do they all feel a dread for different things? Do they all love differently? Surely the only way to cover all these readers is to use what is called symbolism.

T.S.: It seems that you've used the principle of "non-existent author" in conjunction with another—that since identified with Camus, and called the *absurd*. For a situation to be, in this literary sense, genuinely *absurd*, it must be convincingly arrived at, and should not be noticed by readers as being at all out of the ordinary. Thus it would seem *normal* for a young man, upon the death of his father, to go down and take over the family's iron foundry, as in *Living;* or to join the service in wartime, as in *Caught;* or to return from the war, as in *Back*—and yet, in abrupt transitions like these, the situations and relationships which result are almost sure to be, despite any dramatic or beautiful moments, fundamentally *absurd*. In your work I believe this reached such a high point of refinement in *Loving* as to be indiscernible—for, with all the critical analyses that book received, no one called attention to the absurdity of one of the basic situations: that of *English* servants in an *Irish* household. Now isn't that fundamental situation, and the absence of any reference to it throughout the book, intended to be purely *absurd*?

MR. GREEN: The British servants in Eire while England is at war is Raunce's conflict and one meant to be satirically funny. It is a crack at the absurd Southern Irish and at the same time a swipe at the British servants, who yet remain human beings. But it is meant to torpedo that woman and her daughter-in-law, the employers.

As to the rest, the whole of life now is of course absurd—hilarious sometimes, as I told you earlier, but basically absurd.

T.S.: And have you ever heard of an actual case of an Irish household being staffed with English servants?

MR. GREEN: Not that comes quickly to mind, no.

T.S.: Well, now what is it that you're writing on at present?

MR. GREEN: I've been asked to do a book about London during the blitz, and I'm into that now.

T.S.: I believe you're considered an authority on that—and, having read *Caught,* I can understand that you would be. What's this book to be called?

MR. GREEN: *London and Fire, 1940.*

T.S.: And it is not fiction?

MR. GREEN: No, it's an historical account of that period.

T.S.: Then this will be your first full-length work of nonfiction?

MR. GREEN: Yes, quite.

T.S.: I see. *London and Fire, 1940*—a commissioned historical work. Well, well; I dare say you'll have to give up the crabwise approach for this one. What's the first sentence?

MR. GREEN: "My 'London of 1940' . . . opens in Cork, 1938."

T.S.: . . . I see.

—1958
The Paris Review
Reprinted by permission of *The Paris Review.*

King Weirdo

Terry had a long-standing interest in Poe. At age twelve, he rewrote The Narrative of A. Gordon Pym, *transposing his classmates and teachers into the often grotesque roles. This outraged his classmates to such an extent that while Terry discovered the visceral power of satire, it was clear that Texas would not be the best place to develop his newfound sensibility. Throughout his life, Terry practiced Poe's technique of combining outrageousness and credibility through invented first-person narratives.*

Knocking around in the quality lit game you're bound to meet a wiseacre or two who will express surprise to learn that Ed Poe wrote a novel—and indeed, beyond surprise (almost chagrin), that they, with all their crypto heavy-Lit backgrounds, were quite unaware of it. These so-called 'quality lit cowboys' (or 'butterflies' as they're known around Longhorn Cafeteria down at the big U. of T.) should not be taxed too severely in this particular, for here is a work which does not appear on any reading list at any school in the country—by virtue of its extreme weirdness. "Too hot to handle!" seems to be the cry of dons and department heads alike. "Christ, he must have been absolutely *bonkers* when he wrote *that* piece of swill!" *Officially,* of course, an effort is made to present a somewhat lower-key, more commonsense-type profile when confronted, claiming the work to be of 'inadequate format.' "Too darn short for a novel," snaps Jack Hollander of New Haven's Yale U., *par exemple*—but I'm afraid this won't wash since wordwise it comes in at a strong seventy-seven thou, making it longer than *Madame Bovary* (42 thou) and *Miss Lonelyhearts* (27 thou) put together—though not, natch, necessarily in that order. Thus one is forced to the sad conclusion that such a blatantly absurd 'reason' for the systematic exclusion of this longest and very ambitious work of the most celebrated author in the history of the country smacks a little too strongly of the old *papiers pentagoni* gestalt—if you follow my drift. It is a heinous conspiracy, in short, to suppress public knowledge of that with which they are unprepared to cope . . . preferring instead that the image of 'the devine Edgar' remain essentially that laid down by the late great Chuck Baudelaire, and the rest of the *soi-disant* 'frog elite' (specifically Rimbaud, Mallarmé, and Valéry . . . with the incredible Verlaine abstaining—though *not,* scholars please note, through gayness alone). It is an image, that is to say, of Poe as 'master craftsman' and 'prince of supernatch'—instead of 'King Weirdo, *not for the squeamish.*'

In my own case, it was by dint of sheerest chance that I escaped the ignorance which befell my callow peers without exception. The circumstances, briefly, were these: Miss Dinsmore, our seventh-grade English teacher (now this was at Winnetka elementary in your basic Big D. Dal Tex) announced one day we were going to read a story or two by "one of the country's greatest authuhs—a southernah like Mistah Clemens." She went on to a brief account of the "tragic, tragic life of this brilliant man," touching on his "alcoholic problem" and his "spiritual disso-*loot*ion," elaborately avoiding any mention of his teeny-bop bedmate—doubtless because that was precisely the age (13) of about half the girls in the class. She then proceeded to read aloud one of the stories— "The Purloined Letter," if memory serves, or, in any case, an equally dumbbell selection, meant to quell rather than catapult the fantasies of the young. So that my intro to Poe was a little bit south of Nowhere City. It wasn't until the following day, at Big D. Public Library, that it all came together. Miss Dinsmore, a very down-home opportunistic type ("two buhds with one numbah-six shot," she used to say, ". . . twelve-gauge, that is"), had contrived to combine the Poe assignment with another sustaining (and apparently endless) bit of horror-show wretchedness called "Getting to Know Your Public Library"—Card Cat, Dewey Des, Reader's Guide to Bla-bla-bla, the whole store—a real nightmare, so that this particular trip (shaping up as a bummer in front) involved (1) legging it over to Big D Pub (a drag in itself), (2) locating and reading another story by E. A. Poe (cinch), and (3) finding, reading and summarizing the "most recent article on Poe to appear in *SRL*" (*forget it*). Anyway, when I got the old Poe down from the shelf and back to the library table, I started to scan—a phrase here, an image there—hoping perhaps for a glint, a taste of the now fabled and fantastic "spiritual disso-*loot*ion" of a certain Mr. E. A. Poe, and when my eye hit the following, I was pretty sure I'd found it:

It was not until some time after dark that we took courage to get up and throw the body overboard. It was then loathsome beyond expression, and so far decayed that, as Peters attempted to lift it, an entire leg came off in his grasp, as the mass of putrefaction slipped over the vessel's side into the water . . .

Holy Mack! What manner of weirdness was here. The idea of hassling a corpse overboard is perhaps commonplace enough, but to have an *"entire leg"* come off in your grasp . . . far out. But what really nailed it down for me was the imagery, ". . . *the mass of putrefaction* SLIPPED *over the side"*! Christ, you could practically *taste* it! UGH! ACCHH! Who did this happen to? I had another look. *Peters.* Then I caught a description:

The mouth extended nearly from ear to ear; his lips were thin, and seemed, like some other portions of his frame, to be devoid of natural pliancy, so that the ruling expression never varied under the influence of any emotion whatever. This ruling expression may be conceived when it is considered that the teeth were exceedingly long and protruding, and never even partially covered, in any instance, by the lips. To pass this man with a casual glance, one might imagine him to be convulsed with laughter; but a second look would induce a shuddering acknowledgment, that if such an expression were indicative of merriment, the merriment must be that of a demon.

An arresting countenance, no mistake, and I immediately flashed on his standing at the side, an 'entire leg' still in his hand, peering down, as the 'mass of putrefaction' *slipped* over and hit the water—accompanied by, as Poe went on to say, *"the glare of phosphoric light with which it was surrounded discovered to us seven or eight large sharks, the clashing of whose horrible teeth as their prey was torn to pieces among them . . ."* failing to mention that *also* illuminated by that phosphoric glare was the visage and horror-show grin of one Dirk Peters.

I checked the title, *The Narrative of A. Gordon Pym.* I thumbed it through. Holy Mack, this wasn't a *story,* it was a *book.* But having had a taste, I had another, in at the beginning this time, and when I saw that it wasn't something someone *had made up,* but something that had actually *happened* . . . well, it was Hook City for yours truly. Because that's what it appeared to be—a genuine documentation; following the title was an 'Introductory Note,' by A. G.

Pym, which explained how an earlier portion of the work had been published in the *Southern Literary Messenger* (issues of January and February 1837) 'under the garb of fiction.' The reason for this was that the magazine's editor, Mr. E. A. Poe, had at first been unable to persuade Mr. Pym to relate the events in any detail—so grotesque and implausible they were, and so uncertain of his own literary ability was Mr. Pym. In consequence, Mr. Poe himself had 'fictionalized' a portion of the adventure—and it was for this reason alone (Poe's authorship of a small part of it) that it was being included in the present anthology of Mr. Poe's work. He ended the introduction by expressing his gratitude to Mr. Poe for having convinced him to set down the account in his own words and without misgivings in regard to style, insisting, as he did, that *"its very uncouthness, if there were any, would give it all the better chance of being received as truth."*

Such trappings, of course, are a well-worn ploy with the great Ed Poe, to render as real the most weird, all unbeknownst to me at the time, and so it came down, impressionable lad that I was, as straight gospel. The fact is that on this one he went to really extraordinary lengths, even for him, to give the thing an aura of *fact*—including those ace hallmarks of the factual account, *vagueness* and *uncertainty*: *"His father was a fur-trader, I believe, or at least connected in some manner with the Indian trading-posts on Lewis River"* is typical; but the following is undoubtedly one of the best ever concocted: *"The stowage on board the Grampus was most clumsily done, if stowage that could be called which was little better than a promiscuous huddling together of oil-casks . . ."* with the footnote *"Whaling vessels are usually fitted with iron oil-tanks—why the Grampus was not I have never been able to ascertain."* This is the sort of totally irrelevant and gratuitous bit of 'ignorance' which gives an account verisimilitude.

—1970s

The Scandal Continues

Senior editor at Random House Joe Fox was a good friend who edited Terry's first collection, Red Dirt Marijuana. *Terry was doing book reviews at* The Nation *around the time he sent this mock review to Joe as "yet another joke at his expense."*

When Boy Likes Girl. Stories For The Teens, Selected by Aurelia Stowe. 239 pp. Random House. $2.95.

It's gas-mask time, folks—the Random House garbage truck is here again. Shoveling the filth this trip is none other than Miss Aurelia Stowe, a name which should ring a bell with readers of *Confidential,* since not too many issues ago she was featured therein (in an article called "Aurelia Stowe's It, But Good!") as the only *woman* in the criminal history of New York State ever tried and convicted of sodomy. Nice choice for editing a children's book? Sure it is, *nice and typical,* considering its imprint.

Her first selection is a dandy, entitled "The Slip-over Sweater," by Jesse Stuart—the single writer in this anthology, incidentally, not presently serving a long-term prison sentence—whose style obviously derives much from an overreading of the late Sherwood Anderson. His story concerns a small-town "eccentric" and cashmere fetishist who regularly uses a "slip-over sweater" as a condom. After forcing himself (and his "eccentricity") upon a six-year-old basket case (a victim of pregnancy tranquillizers) he is found out, his house besieged by townspeople, and he eats the sweater, choking to death in a grotesque manner, while the townspeople (and the author) cackle. Mr. Stuart would do well to leave writing alone and get back into a mental hospital where he belongs.

"My Theory About Girls" by Leslie Weiner is the next entry. If this story is any indication, Miss Weiner's theory about girls evidently is that they are all stark raving sex maniacs. There is not *one single word* in this story that is not sheer filth (and by an author who in taking on a pen name simply could not resist a touch of obscenity even there—could not even wait until the story was under way!).

The only redeeming quality about "The Perfect Date" by Dania Ann Whiteley is a certain literary irony (I am speaking quite *relatively*, of course) in the title itself, it ("Date") being singular, when, in fact, this author's notion of the "perfect date" turns out to be intimacy with not one but half a dozen (or as many as she can get, actually) full-grown gorillas.

"Mask of Fear" by Ruth Sterling (Ha!) is another piece of sick fetishist trash, having to do with pig masks, steel wool, scorpions, etc., ad nauseam, and par for the course. "Double Date," "Too Slow for the Crowd," "Plenty of Other Girls," and "*Detour* in Summer" are rather obvious from their titles, considering the source.

In "Muscle Man" by Janet Roberts we are exposed to some colorful up-to-the-minute teen jargon. According to Miss Roberts, the word "muscle" is used by teen girls to designate the male sex organ ("Let me feel your *muscle*," "Say, dig his *muscle*," "Give me some *muscle*," etc.), and Miss Roberts gets plenty of mileage (and plenty of "muscle" too, no doubt) out of this—20 pages worth to be exact.

In short, *When Boy Likes Girl* is not a book to buy, but rather to spit on. Unless, of course, you happen to own a vomitorium.

—1961
The Nation

When Film Gets Good . . .

Terry wrote many book and theater reviews in the early '60s, sometimes taking a "round-up" approach to the state of the novel, as in the following piece written for The Nation.

[in this review:]
James Baldwin, *Another Country*, Dial
David Benedictus, *The Fourth of June*, Dutton
William Golding, *The Inheritors*, Harcourt, Brace & World
Robert Gover, *One Hundred Dollar Misunderstanding*, Grove
Graham Greene, *It's a Battlefield*, Viking
James Jones, *The Thin Red Line*, Scribners
Peter Mattheissen, *Under the Mountain Wall*, Viking
Henry Miller, *Tropic of Capricorn*, Grove
Adrian Mitchell, *If You See Me Comin'*, Macmillan
Vladimir Nabokov, *Pale Fire*, Putnam
Flannery O'Connor, *Wise Blood*, Farrar, Straus & Cudahy
Katherine Ann Porter, *Ship of Fools*, Little, Brown
Igor Sentjurc, *The Torrents of War*, McKay
Ignazio Silone, *Bread and Wine*, Atheneum
John Wain, *Strike the Father Dead*, St. Martin's
John A. Williams, *Night Song*, Farrar, Straus & Cudahy

The quality of fiction seems much improved over that of recent years—that is to say, more fully exploits the known, or at least presently accepted, potentials of the medium. From another point of view, however, there is scarcely a handful, or let us say armload, of these books that is worth a single reel of *L'Avventura*, *Jules and Jim*, or a number of other recent films.

It used to be that books were to be more highly regarded than plays, and that plays, in turn, were better than movies. It was not the advent of television itself that rattled this hierarchy, but the fact that, seven or eight years ago, all the major film studios, to improve poor balance sheets, began unloading their entire back catalogs of films onto the TV networks. It was then possible to see, free and in the comfort of home, the *exact type* of film which was being shown outside; and people in the millions started kicking the movie habit—lending breakneck acceleration to the decline in movie attendance—until, in 1959, it was 50 percent of what it had been before TV, and still dropping. It was recognized that a "different" type of general film than was being seen at home would have to be created to bring people back into the theaters. And here a felicitous occurrence: while the old guard of the American film industry pondered on how to create a film which was different and yet still lousy, other interested persons noted that a number of "cheap foreign films" were filling the theaters. And these films *were* different, categorically different—the difference, one must say, between good and bad. At last it had been proved that it was economically feasible to make and distribute good movies instead of bad ones. This led to the wholesale importation of films from cultures which had known this for a long time, and it also gave rise to "independent production" in America. Now, when Film gets good, Book is in trouble. Theoretically, it is not possible for a book to compete, aesthetically, psychologically, or in any other way, with a film. Of sensory perceptions it is well established that the most empathetic are *sight and sound*. It is for this reason that to *see* someone badly hurt, for example, hit by a car, bleeding, crying with pain, is a totally different experience from reading about it in the paper. In short, next to having been the victim oneself, the most meaningful thing would be to have witnessed it firsthand. "Seeing," as they say, "is believing." Film, by its very nature, more closely approximates firsthand experience than does print. And there, of course, the advantage only begins.

What these new developments mean in terms of the novel is something which seems so far to have been ignored in literary criticism and, at least consciously, by authors themselves. It has become evident that it is wasteful, pointless, and in terms of art, inexcusable, to write a novel which could, or in fact should, have been a film. This ought to be a first principle of creative literature and of its critical evaluation; without it the novel, in the present circumstances, has only a secondary function as art. The recent improvement in the quality of fiction is not due to the sudden excellence of films (and to the necessity for the novel to keep ahead of them), but to the fact that with the publication of *Lady*

Chatterley's Lover and Henry Miller's *Tropic of Cancer*—along with the favorable court decisions about their legality—the publishing field is now wide open, and both publishers and authors have become bolder.

Unfortunately, though, most novels continue to be written as though they were supposed to be nothing more nor less than good movies—or rather what *would* have been a good movie by the old standards, but is now Class B. A primary example from recent fiction of this sort is *Ship of Fools*. There is probably not a line, an image, scene, or technique in this large book which could not have been done, with infinitely more grace and drama, by a filmmaker using *methods now in practice* (emphasis is there because, although the film medium itself is capable of anything, even introspective narration, it would be irrelevant to compare a novel to cinematic techniques not already in use). *Ship of Fools* is to be considered a good novel, but only by persons unaware of present possibilities or new demands—that is to say, it has that sort of existential maturity of outlook and conclusion on life and relationships requisite to so-called serious fiction, it does not lapse too often into sentimentality, avoids seeming foolishly romantic; it is even, one might say, cynical: the "Ship" is Life, and we are the "Fools." This, however, is not enough; it has been done before, so what is the point? It could be a good, entertaining movie; but it is not a good book, almost for that reason.

Another case in point, though to a different end, is James Jones's *The Thin Red Line*. This book has the surface appearance of the cinematic-novel, but it is so far in advance of any film treatment of war that it is overwhelmingly successful. If nothing else, the preponderance of four-letter words, not merely in dialogue, but in the text itself—and which are vital to the tone of the work— would put it beyond the present cinematic pale. Moreover, such images as: "Through the glasses Stein could see the blue-veined loops of intestines bulging between the bloodstained fingers . . ." are not apt to be done in the required Technicolor for a very long time to come. This is surely one of the strongest and most effective war novels ever written; even its immense length and Jones's habit, or method, if it is that, of redundance ("Some were simply watchers, standing and looking.") work to advantage, suggesting the insane confusion, tedium and endlessness of war. And there is behind the work a new kind of narrative; it is the "omniscient author" taken toward a logical extreme, where the narration itself, although faceless, without personality, expresses feelings, both of individuals and collectively, in their own terms. For a mild, printable, example, the narration will not say "Welsh was still angry about it" but "Welsh

was still pissed-off about it." Narration which uses four-letter idiom traditionally requires that the narrator emerge as a personality. Jones has ignored this
requirement and has given the purely textual part of his work a tone which is in
perfect harmony with each incident and character it describes.

War novels present a curious creative problem, for no matter how "anti-
war" they ostensibly are, they never wholly convey their positions. The reason for this is that the worst aspect of war cannot be treated dramatically—the
worst aspect being those moments when men are reduced, by pain, fear, shock,
hunger, to a level of mere survival-reflex. At these moments, men cease to
exist as personalities—they are no longer distinguishable, one from another.
Without personality, or human behavior, you cannot have drama—you have
only identical ciphers, or animals. So that while a novel, as an antidote to chau-
vinistic myths of glory and adventure, may attempt to portray war truthfully,
showing its horror, degradation, brutality, filth and privation, it can never quite
reach full strength, because there is always that one area which is beyond dramatic treatment, and which is the worst of all. Given that inherent limitation,
Jones's achievement is most certainly a remarkable one; if *The Thin Red Line*
does not wholly de-glamorize war, it probably comes as near doing so as is
possible.

Another recent major war novel, though in completely traditional format, is *The Torrents of War*, by Igor Sentjurc. War seen through the eyes of
the German Army—as represented here by a naive young doctor and a sadistic infantry sergeant. It treats the involvement of the healer and the killer, during
the battle of Stalingrad, and like Jones's novel it is unsparing in its disenchant-
ment. The thesis of both these strong novels would seem to be that the means of
war vitiate the ends. This represents a significant departure from the Hemingway
attitude, which, with the notable exception of *The Naked and the Dead*, has so
long dominated our war fiction.

As for recently published novels which more clearly distinguish themselves as non-cinematic, *Pale Fire, Tropic of Capricorn* and *One Hundred Dollar Misunderstanding* are perhaps foremost. *Pale Fire* is an extremely complex
novel, and an uproariously funny one. It concerns the line-by-line interpretation of a 999-line poem, by a scholar who is gradually revealed in his journal
("an awkward moment at the pool today," "unfortunate incident in the locker
room," etc.) to be, among other things, a raving faggot. A waspish and self-
centered man, his homosexuality is, of course, but symptomatic of the general
neurosis (in the end, absolute lunacy) which so strongly shapes his interpreta-

tions of the poem, as does his highly personal attitude toward the poet himself. It is a devastating ridicule of literary criticism, or any likely "objectivity" of it. This is, however, but a single deceptive surface of this extraordinary novel. There is a brilliant twenty-page analysis of *Pale Fire*, in the October *Encounter*, by Mary McCarthy, which should enhance anyone's appreciation of what is surely one of Nabokov's finest novels.

Tropic of Capricorn is Henry Miller's internationally famous book about growing up absurd in America, now issued here for the first time, 23 years after it was written. Except for *Tropic of Cancer*, it is unlike anything that has ever been published in America. In many respects it is even more impressive than the earlier volume, because of the intensity with which Miller explores the sources of his life and his relentless efforts to formulate a rational attitude toward his country. Like *Tropic of Cancer*, it is hilariously Rabelaisian, but its essential qualities remain, as in the earlier volume, its adult honesty and straightforwardness. The publication of the *Tropics,* and the imminent publication of Burroughs's *Naked Lunch,* do a great deal toward raising creative expression to a new level; and their public acceptance serves to emancipate publishers from chronic fear of whatever is new, or "formless." Such books are of real value in the scheme of things; because they are still in advance of cinematic methods, they make literature purposeful. The same may be said of *Pale Fire* and *One Hundred Dollar Misunderstanding;* generally it requires a book which may at least be *suspected* of "obscenity" to make an appreciable splash.

One Hundred Dollar Misunderstanding is a novel by Robert Gover, a new writer of obviously great talent. It gives us the thoughts of James Cartwright Holland, a very dumb American college boy, who seems too typical for comfort, and alternatively the thoughts of Kitten, a fourteen-year-old Negro prostitute, who is probably as refreshing a mixture of innocence and wisdom as has been concocted since Salinger's Teddy. The "misunderstanding" develops when James C. Holland, having been badgered into it by some of his frat brothers, goes to "this Negro ill-repute house." After demonstrating his virility, he suggests that he and the girl, Kitten, spend the weekend together, which they do. She assumes that it is either an ordinary business proposition, in which case it will be one hundred dollars, or else that James C. will become a kind of sugar-daddy "invessment"; he, in turn, assumes that she is emotionally involved with him. She is completely illiterate and speaks in an outlandish Negro jazz argot, and he like an amateur Senator Dirksen. Neither can understand a word the other is saying, and they simply marvel at each other's stupidity. This gives rise to fantastic private speculations on the part of each, especially the girl, whose insights and comments on white-man civilization are scathing.

As to scathing comment, James Baldwin has finally written his own "protest novel," *Another Country*, and it is a lulu. Many people are going to be put off, right and left, by the sheer audacity of it. It is not an *ideal* truth, but is definitely one man's truth, and the suggestion that it may be a general truth is forcefully put. In essence, it is this: that if a person, or a group of them, has been severely mistreated, there is no immediate redress—that even when mistreatment ends, hatred for the oppressor remains, as does the oppressor's sense of guilt; it is, then, unrealistic to expect anything short of hatred from Negroes toward whites— not as a matter of volition, or principle, but as a fundamental of psychology. It would be *nice* if one could forgive, Mr. Baldwin is saying, and it would be nice if one could fly. This is hardly the most popular viewpoint; it does not, how- ever, seem to have been expressed in anger, but in reflection—and its validity lies simply in the fact of its understandable existence. The author does not preclude relationships of unlimited warmth, rapport—"love," if you like— between colored and white, but makes clear that no such thing is to be ex- pected, and is, in fact, the exception that proves the rule. The designation "Another Country" (as in the exasperated phrase "That's *something else!*") refers to America, and the novel deals with a year in the lives of seven or eight principal characters, the central one of whom is a jazz musician. There is prob- ably enough sex in this novel for every taste, and some of it not too tasteful at that —as is, one may suppose, the case in life. Although of rather ordinary cinematic format, *Another Country*, by virtue of its introspection, its sexual denial, its real- istic dialogue, and its unpopular truths, falls outside the current limitations of film.

A second novel with a colored jazz musician as its central figure—and one of the best treatments of this milieu yet written—is John Williams's *Night Song*. The hero is a saxophonist named Richie Stokes and directly parallels the life and character of the late Charlie Parker. As with Parker, everything Richie (whose nickname is "Eagle") does, whether with drugs or musical conceptions, is on a monumental scale. Williams has succeeded in several difficult areas, including the rendition of jazz argot without seeming to parody it. While on the road, for example, the band manager has assigned a young tenor man to look after Richie, to make sure he shows up for the concert that night. The young man stops by the Eagle's room:

"You almost ready?" he asks.
"I stay ready, baby. Anybody readier got to go by me."
"I'm hip they do, Richie."

In this brief exchange Mr. Williams captures not merely the adulation of the young man for the master, but the fact that he is wistfully humoring him, even sadly foreseeing his doom. This is in sharp contrast to the abuse of this same argot as it occurs in another recent jazz novel, *If You See Me Comin'*, by the English writer Adrian Mitchell, which purports to be a week in the life of a blues singer:

"Who would you like to see as Prime Minister?"
"Johnny Dankworth," I said, "Or Fidel Castro, with Michael Foot blowing Foreign Secretary."

If Williams's novel is one of the best on the subject, *If You See Me Comin'* is probably the worst. English writers should, on no account, write about jazz. Even that intrepid and mellowing old pro, John Wain, botches that aspect in his latest, *Strike the Father Dead*—a calm and all too likely tale of the son who runs away to become a jazz pianist, and takes as mentor (and father substitute) a gently philosophic American Negro jazz musician. In putting aside his angry youth, Mr. Wain has also disposed of his power to surprise. But, of course, there'll always be an English Angry, and young David Benedictus has come through now in admirable fashion with his first novel, *The Fourth of June*, a sort of Fellini version of *Tom Brown's School Days*. The cruelty and snobbism of Eton provide the backdrop for this extremely funny and superbly written book. Mr. Benedictus's style is almost as deft as was the young Evelyn Waugh's, and his anger is as real—but unlike Waugh's it seems neither bitter not brittle. At times, in fact, there is that remarkable infusion of strange soft-focused warmth reminiscent of scenes (on the library steps at night) in *Portrait of the Artist*. Along with other gifts, Mr. Benedictus has the rare ability to make the unknown seem familiar.

If England has become notorious for Young Angries, it has always been so for Old Eccentrics. Mr. William Golding belongs to the latter. No one could have written four more odd or outlandishly creative books than he has. He has told us how it feels to go insane, to drown, to commit suicide, to be dead, to be a child—all in an uncannily convincing manner. He is certainly one of the most original writers of the day. But in his new book, *The Inheritors*, he tells us how it feels to be a Neanderthal man, and here he has perhaps gone a bit too far. This is so nearly anthropomorphic that it can only remind one of the well-known story about the Hollywood producer who, having heard that Maeterlinck's "*Life*" (as it was popularly called) had sold eight million copies, bought the film rights, then, upon reading it, went into a towering rage. "This is impossible," he kept shouting, "the hero's a goddamn *bug!*"

Fictional heroes with names like Lok, Oa and Fa somehow already suggest a questionable scope of dramatic action, allegorical or otherwise, and when each is saddled with an I.Q. of about 8, things are bound to be slow. The big question is: can the reader identify with a Neanderthal man? There *is* such a thing as "writing down" to an audience, granted—but *this* is nothing short of insulting.

A more plausible (nonfiction) treatment of this kind of thing would seem to be suggested by Peter Matthiessen's *Under the Mountain Wall*, a highly creative portrayal of the Kurelu natives of New Guinea—a tribe which still lives in the Stone Age, and very much in the purity and innocence which Mr. Golding attributes to his own imaginary characters. They inhabit a remote landlocked valley beneath the Snow Mountains in an unmapped section of western New Guinea, and they are believed to be the most primitive culture in existence. Mr. Matthiessen lived with the tribe during the spring and summer of 1961, "because the Kurelu offered a unique chance, perhaps the last, to describe a lost culture in the terrible beauty of its pure estate." He has managed this description in a most extraordinary and successful way, by giving us the story of a warrior named Weaklekek, and a swineherd, Tukum, through their own eyes. The events of the story are totally absorbing, including as they do the ritualistic, but very real, tribal war which is fought each year. (When a warrior is killed in battle, the burial ceremony includes cutting off a finger of a young girl in sacrifice.) The implements and weapons of the Kurelu are made of wood and stone, and the monetary unit is the conch. Through the use of a prose which is structured in folktale cadence, the author has conveyed the strange existence of a Stone Age people in a beautifully poetic way.

Finally now, there have been at least three cases of late of the reissuance of good books which were out of print in their hardcover editions: Flannery O'Connor's *Wise Blood*, Silone's *Bread and Wine*, and Graham Greene's *It's a Battlefield.* Surely this is more to the point than the publication of new books which are patently worthless. The latter two, interestingly enough, are described as "revised editions," but these revisions—the picayune and idiosyncratic notions of their authors—have not blighted their original quality, nor do they obscure the very encouraging sign which their being reissued (just as they were) really is.

—November 17, 1962
The Nation
Reprinted by permission of *The Nation.*

Drugs and the Writer

Terry kept company with some of the most notorious "heads" of the twentieth century: John Lennon, Harry Nilsson, Timothy Leary, William Burroughs; and he was often asked by journalists about the role of drugs in literature.

I think Big Chuck Bukowski (if, indeed, that is his name) is probably right that drink brings good luck to writers. God (certainly) knows it brings warmth and companionship—to an otherwise absurdly forlorn situation. Faulkner always liked to say: "A writer without a bottle of whiskey is like a chicken without a goddamn head." And Hemingway, of course, enjoyed nothing more than eulogizing the "Godly Brothers Gordon" for hours on end. Joyce would "knock back a whopper" at every opportunity. In fact, one would be hard-pressed to name more than five writers of first account who were not drinkers. For whatever reason, this does not appear to be the case with women. Indeed, there is (almost) nothing worse than a drunken woman writer. Exceptions abound, up to a point. Simone de Beauvoir, whom I knew during her Nelson Algren period, worked very well behind absinthe, or its substitute, Pernod, sipping it for hours at the Flore and turning out her typical top-of-the-shelf stuff. But whenever Nels got her on to Boiler Makers she would soon be totally wrecked, and start singing Piaf. This was not bad in itself but she would apply her creative gifts towards 'improving' on these grand old *La Vie En Rose*–type favorites, and would end up rendering some kind of grotesque distortion. Nels had to give her a snappy "*Tais-toi,* cherie!" on more than one terse occasion.

Dot Parker was no stranger to the grape, nor indeed to the double belt by all accounts. But she could handle it, according to Benchley ("She may have stumbled, but she never fell"), and there's every reason to believe she did some of her best work under the steadying influence of a certain *Monsieur Courvoisier,* V.S.O.P.

This is not to suggest that any of these writers were alcoholics. I don't believe that a serious writer is in danger of becoming an alcoholic, because, after a certain point, one would not be working *behind* it, but directly in front of it, at peril of getting wiped out blotto, thereby defeating its purpose—which is, after all, motivational and as a hedge against the desolation of such a lonely endeavor. Good writers have so much (dare one say 'beauty and excitement'?) to come back to that they are not likely to go very far afield for any great length of time. It may be that addiction to alcohol exists among writers only as a psychological painkiller for the '*manqués,*' who had set great store by the potential ID value of it.

I think this may be said for other recreational drugs as well—with the notable exception of heroin, the effect of which is to reduce everything to a single glow, where it is no longer a question of doing or becoming—one is. A difficult package for anyone to resist. Almost no one kicks a major junk habit; only super-artists, whose work is even stronger than the drug itself: Burroughs and Miles Davis are rather obvious examples. Mere mortals, however, beware.

But, as Dr. Leary advises, "Don't just say 'No,' say 'No thanks.'"

—1990s

Strolls Down
Memory Lane

Strange Sex We Have Known

My first encounter with "Dr. Benway" (whom I was later to know as the master scribe and film buff extraordinaire, William S. Burroughs) was on the sleepy sands of St. Tropez in the south of France in the summer of '47. I had been suffering from—or rather, *complaining of*—a certain lesion, a rather persistent lesion, on the hinder fleshy part of my left calf, just below the knee. It wasn't *painful*, but it was irritating in a *psychological way*, and I was keen to deal and have done with it. An acquaintance of mine, Allen Ginsberg—who later achieved international poetic renown (*Howl, Kaddish*, etc.)—was staying at the same hotel, and when I showed him the lesion, he said: "Doc Benway will put that to rights in double quick order!" (little did I realize at this point in time that it was simply another joke at my expense by the mischievous Al Ginsberg) and he set up a meet at Benway's beach house.

Dr. Benway was (and *is* to this very day) a most remarkable personage.

"Your lesion," he observed in his dry and singular tone, "has the mark of *genitalia*," and he poised a finger near it, just so, not quite touching. I glanced down and noted, with some surprise, that it did indeed resemble a tiny vage, with its puckered pouting lips, half-parted and moistly glistening— but I was reluctant to admit as much to the formidable Benway. "You must be mad," I exclaimed instead with a show of indignation, and instinctively drew back; but the fantastic Benway continued as though not having heard: "Naturally it would follow that the treatment of choice would be to . . . *fuck it away*." And before I could protest, he raised a finger of caution: "*But* an extremely *small sexual member* would be required—perhaps that of a *gerbil*— and by damnable good fortune, hee-hee, I happen to have just such a specimen here in this very lab. . . ." He gestured towards a shoddy complex of small cages nearby, and continued: "You entertain no superstitious qualms, I take it, towards *bestiality*?"

I informed this "Doctor Benway" in no uncertain terms that I did indeed entertain such qualms, and would *not* consider being "fucked in the lesion" by a gerbil, *nor* any other member of his devilish menagerie! I had failed, however, to reckon on the man's powers of persuasion, which border on the veritably hypnotic.

"Similar case a few years back," he went on, unperturbed, "man-of-the cloth developed stigmata in both hands and both feet, each of the blessed wounds being in the shape of a female cunt, not unlike your own, only larger—so that when the populace filed by in holy reverence to view the miraculous visitation, they found his worship—his coarse mandrill-root pulsating in gross distention—going at it into both hand-wounds like a maddened warthog. They could not restrain him—he finally broke his own back trying to fuck the lesion in his left metatarsus. . . ."

I must admit to being somewhat taken aback by the sheer grossness of this account, but it did put me in mind, a few years later, of a story so bandied about that I dare say it carries no "kiss-and-tell" onus at this late point in time— namely, that curious tale of how LBJ was "caught in the act" (if one may coin) on the Kennedy death-plane from Dallas, trying to force his rude animal-member into the mortal wound of the young President. I recounted the bizarre incident to Benway, but it was apparently old hat to him.

"Hee-hee," he chuckled, nodding sagely, though more through *politesse*, if my guess is any good, than through your true humorous enjoyment, "yes, a classic case of . . . *neck-ro-philia*, was it not?"

I'm not too keen on *puns* myself, but I let it pass; after all, a man of Benway's stature (Ginsberg had shown me a lot of weird microfilmed diplomas, citations, credentials, depositions, endorsements, etc.) was not to be challenged unduly.

"Very well, Benway," I said, "if that is your view—"

"It is not only my *view*," he quipped in his inimitable fashion (cross between Ben Johnson and W. C. Fields), "it is also my gol-dang *pur-view*! Hee-hee-hee. . . ."

Needless to say, Benway's "treatment of choice" proved to be less than useless—and, in fact, I very nearly succumbed to a damnable case of the pesky "gerbil-clap."

I was intrigued, however, by the emphasis he placed on what was later to become his infamous "view-syndrome," and when I pointed this out he was good enough to address himself to that very issue.

—1974
National Lampoon
Reprinted by permission of *National Lampoon*.

Frank's Humor

The poet Frank O'Hara was tragically run over in 1966 while sleeping on a beach in Long Island. The Festschrift *which had already been in preparation for him became a bittersweet homage.*

I don't recall spending a dull moment with Frank. He could change the most grotesque vernissage, or sleep-city cocktail party into a veritable romp—mysteriously, as if by magic, almost as if he could do it with his *attitude* alone—a sudden shriek of delight, or a Madison high-kick.

His sense of humor was one of the keenest I have ever encountered. We would carry on elaborate charades, just the two of us, and never crack. When Frank was working at the Museum [of Modern Art], for example, we would occasionally have lunch, and he would tell me all about a new acquisition, somehow conveying the excitement of the work by his own extraordinary perception and his remarkable gift for expressing it—as though he himself had shared in the experience of its creation. He would end up exhausted by the time we finished eating. "My God," he would sigh, perhaps thinking he might have seemed overly dramatic, "now then, Terry, *you* say something! What shall we do next? 'What shall we *ever* do.'"

"Well . . ." I would venture tentatively, "we *could* go back to your office and make an obscene phone call to Patsy Southgate."

"What a marvelous idea!" Frank would exclaim. "Did that just occur to you? Is that what you were thinking of all the time I was talking about the Rauschenberg?"

"No, no, long before that. I've been thinking about it for years."

"Oh she'll *love* it! What shall we say?"

"We'll think of *something*," I assured him.

"Good!"

On the walk back to the office, Frank would pursue it gleefully.

"And who else? Who else shall we call?"

"How about Maxine?"

He would stop in the middle of Fifth Avenue, the traffic bearing down on us, and throw back his head with a great whoop.

"Maxine! Oh dear Mary, how can we *ever* think of anything to shock Maxine?!?"

"I did not suggest," I would remind him primly—at the same time trying to get us safely across the street—"that the project was without certain challenge."

He would abruptly remove his arm from mine and look at me with haughty disdain. "And *why*," he would demand icily, "are *all* of these calls to *girls*? Don't you think it's *possible* to shock a *fellow*? What are you anyway, some kind of weirdie *hetero-nut*?"

Back at the office, I would surreptitiously slip an envelope (previously prepared) onto his desk. It would be addressed:

F. O'HARA
Personal

"Well, now," he would exclaim, snatching it up. "What's *this* all about?!? And '*personal*'! Good grief, shut the door!"

"My lovers," he would say, with a closed-eye imperious toss of his head, "know far far better than to write me on a *typewriter*! They all write in marvelous . . . *beautiful* . . . *script!*"

"Well, maybe it's from a *new suitor*—who doesn't yet know how demanding you are."

A new suitor . . ." he would reflect, "yes, that's quite possible, isn't it? I wonder . . ." He would strike a pensive pose, tapping the letter thoughtfully, delicately, on the desk, "there *was* that young lacrosse player at the Coast Guard Beach last weekend. He seemed awfully keen . . . now what *was* his name? Bruce? Dirk? Don't you *just* love people named 'Dirk'? *Guys*, I mean, of course. Ha, ha. Yes, it could possibly be from *Dirk*, but that possibility seems fairly remote—"

"Maybe," I interrupted, ". . . maybe it's from somebody you met at one of those spade bars in Riverhead—you know, *The Bluebird*, or that one across the street."

He would throw his head back and grimace in a gesture of distaste and exasperation.

"*The Bluebird!* Oh my God! *How* did you know about that?!?"

"Larry Rivers told me," I would say. "Lar said you insisted on stopping at Riverhead and cruising *The Bluebird* . . . 'for heavy dork' is the way he put it, while he waited in the car."

"Ah, but *did* he tell you the *real* reason? The reason *behind* the *reason*? Namely, that *he* was looking for a new 'assistant'—if one may employ a euphemism for the *slave labor* he uses—and was hoping that I might recruit— dare I say 'shanghai'—one of those poor potato-pickers from Mississippi for his own vile purposes of commerce?"

"I'll check it out with Lar," I said loyally, as one not to be easily duped.

"Oh well," Frank would counter in mock annoyance, "if you don't *believe* me!" Now what was that about 'dork'?"

"'Cruising for dork' is what Lar said, *dark* dork," and I'd spell it out.

"Oh?" Frank would lift a brow, he said that, did he? '*Dark dork*'?" And he would begin to sing spiritedly: "Oh there's no dark dork like my Dirk's dark dork!"

"You're making that up," I'd say, accusingly.

"No, no, it's from an early work." And then in great agitation: "Where *is* that letter opener?!?"

"Why don't you just tear it open?" I'd ask.

"Oh?" would be the raised-eyebrow reply, "with my *teeth* I suppose?!? No, you see, Terry, *that* is the difference between us. *I* do things properly, or not at all, whereas *you*—and some others I could name—behave in an animal fashion . . . Ah, here it is!" And finding the opener, he would slit the envelope in a grand manner, and take out the paper, which might read:

"F. O'Hara, attention!
All sexual excess in and
about your offices to
stop at once."
        signed
        A. Wallingford
        Chief Curator

Frank would feign outraged indignation. "*What!?!* Why that old *queen!* Ha! Methinks the lady doth protest too much!"

"Perhaps it's simply another case," I would venture, "of *unrequited love* . . . Berkson told me that old Wallingford was *plenty hot* for your heavenly bod and gross dork."

"Precisely!"

"Hell hath no fury, eh Frank?'"

"Right, Ter!" and he would shake the paper in a show of annoyance. "And I don't have to take this . . . this *hypocritical innuendo!*" He would reach for the phone. "I think I'll give him a piece of my . . . ha-ha, *mind* right now!"

"Wait," I cautioned, "why not just a simple '*J'accuse!*,' and then hang up—I dare say he'll get the message."

"*No,*" Frank would insist, "no, I shall require more satisfaction than *that!* Besides I don't think he speaks French—the great clod! Ha, ha, ha!"

One time Frank took me to a swanky East Hampton lawn party, given by a grand old dowager patron of the Museum. We were immediately separated as Frank was swept up into the swirl of the excitement his arrival always generated. A little later our paths crossed again. "Oh *there* you are!" he exclaimed. "Come, I want to introduce you to our hostess, Mrs. Henrietta Tiffendale! You'll simply *adore* her!" He led the way.

"Oh pardon me, Mrs. Tiffendale," he said in his most courtly manner, "allow me to present one of my dearest friends, the very distinguished American writer . . . Mr. *James Baldwin!*"

"Oh how delightful!" the dowager would cry, beaming idiotically, "I am *such* an avid reader of yours, and needless to say, a great admirer! You have no idea!"

"Well . . ." I managed, "thank you very much."

"Oh!" exclaimed Frank, peering over our heads, pretending to recognize someone across the room, "please excuse me, someone's just arrived whom I *must* see!" And he would hurry away, barely managing not to break up before abandoning me.

"Who is it?" I might shout after him, somewhat irate at my predicament, "*Franz Kafka?*"

I countered Mrs. Tiffendale's small talk with a bit of my own, and was on the verge of a graceful withdrawal when several other guests strolled over.

"It is such a pleasure," she said to them, "to introduce you to the distinguished American writer, Mr. James Baldwin."

There were cordial handshakes all around—while in the distance, at the bar, I could see Frank doubled with laughter as he recounted the 'bit of mischief' to Mike Goldberg and Joe LeSueur—who, to be sure, were not long in joining in his show of mirth at my expense—heightened, no doubt, by the fact that one of the guests I was being introduced to was Alfred Kazin, or it may have been Dwight Macdonald—in any case, someone fairly knowledgeable re the quality lit crowd.

"Well," said our hostess, "I suppose *you* two have quite a bit to talk about," referring to Kazin/Macdonald and me/Baldwin.

"Yes," said the former, in what must have appeared to the others as a cryptically terse manner, "we certainly do—but I think *not just now*." And he brusquely escorted his wife away.

About an hour later I was standing at the bar and heard a familiar hiss in my ear. "Be careful! I'm afraid the hostess knows you're a *fraud*!" I turned to see Frank scurrying away in one direction, and the hostess approaching from another.

"Young man," she said sternly (this was about 20 years ago, of course). "I now happen to know that you are *not* James Baldwin."

Meanwhile Frank was unable to resist returning to witness my chagrin (and perhaps compound it). She turned to him sympathetically: "I am very much afraid you have been deceived, Frank—this is *not* James Baldwin."

Frank, munching a canape, regarded me in thoughtful silence, then sighed and shook his head as though with sadness at having been thus betrayed. I decided, however, to take it a step further. "Well," I began, "I didn't mean to say that I was *the* James Baldwin—merely that my *name* was James Baldwin. A coincidence."

"No, no," she countered, "you distinctly said 'the very distinguished writer, James Baldwin.'"

"No," I reminded her, pointing at Frank, "*he* is the one who said that."

"But you must have given him that impression," she insisted, but I remained adamant. "No," I said firmly, "and moreover I don't know why he insists on calling me 'James'—everyone else calls me 'Jim.'" Then someone like J. J. Mitchell or Arnold Weinstein would come over. "Oh," Frank would say, "have you met Jim Baldwin?" and quickly explain, "not *the* James Baldwin, of course, but just plain 'Jim Baldwin.' *Poetry*—isn't that basically your field, Jim?"

"Yes, poetry is my basic field."

"Yes, he was telling me something about an 'Ode to Dirk'—was that it, Jim?"

"Ode to *dork,*" I reminded him. And so it would go, until one of us could no longer keep a straight face, and hurry away leaving another Hampton dowager hostess hurt and confused . . . or at least confused.

One remarkable quality of Frank's was his consummate sense of *fairness*—his willingness, or ability, to see the other side of things. If someone were putting down the work of another artist, and it all got to be a little too unanimous, or strident, Frank would find something good to say about it—or, again, whenever the praise was relentless and overwhelming, Frank might nail it with a zinger: "Yes, but I suppose it does get to be a bit, uh, *predictable,* doesn't it?" Or he might turn to you, beaming, and say: "Aren't sycophants just *too* marvelous!"

This kind of thing, this ambidextrous percipience (he'd like that), was nowhere more apparent than in his humor. I remember, for instance, one summer Sunday when we were lolling about at someone's house in Southampton— the Oppenheims, if memory serves—and I said to Frank: "Now then, let me ask you this, Frank—do you think, do you honestly think that it's possible to tell, simply from someone's appearance, whether or not he is *completely gay?*"

"'Completely gay'?" He seemed intrigued by the phrasing, and considered it for a moment—before speaking firmly and with great authority: "No, you certainly cannot." Then, five minutes later, he was leafing through the Sunday *Times Men's Fashion Supplement,* pointing out the different male models. "Now this one is *completely gay,*" he would say, "you can tell by his *stance,*" or "Here's one who is *partially* gay now, but will probably be *completely gay* within 6 or 7 months . . ." and "Now here's someone who is *completely gay,* but doesn't know he's gay at all!"

One of our great mutual friends was the fabulous Patsy Southgate, and we would often tell her outrageous lies about each other. Despite her breathtaking Miss America plus–type beauty, she was very perceptive, with a keen sense of mischief, and would always go along with the deception, feigning annoyance, indignation, anguish, or whatever the ruse might warrant.

"Do you know what your so-called friend, Frank O'Hara, did the other night?" I recall asking her on more than one occasion, in a tone of sharp rebuke.

"Now what?!?" she would demand in feigned exasperation, all wide-eyed astonishment, and, of course, doubly fab because of it.

"Well!" I'd explain, "there was this ultra posh soiree at Plimpton's—a super-smart gathering of quality lit heavies—Burroughs, Capote, Corso, Gelber, Genet, Ginsberg, Heller, Mailer, Roth, Styron, et cetera, et cetera—not to mention certain personal, and *very straight,* friends of mine—Marquand, Matthiessen, and of course, the venerable host himself."

"But what happened?" Patsy would demand, in breathless (and, as previously noted, breath*taking*) anticipation.

"What happened," I would begin, in a most effectively pained, and martyrized, tone, "was the arrival of a certain Frank O'Hara."

"Frank *crashed* the party?!?"

"No, no, no—he was invited, of course, and not without good reason . . . *but,* what happened was that when *we* met—*very center stage,* if I may say so— he *embraced* me, which in itself was no surprise, and which I took, in the first flush of my naivete—to be in a manly European fashion . . . just as he had done with Genet and Ionesco . . . you know, the perfunctory hug and the perfunctory 'kiss' on the cheek. Quite acceptable, I think you'll agree."

"But of course!"

"Imagine then, *if you can,* my devastating *malaise* when, during what I had anticipated as a classic, indeed prosaic, embrace of friendship, Frank should . . . *try for tongue!*"

"What!"

"Yes," I said grimly, "a French kiss, he tried for French."

"Oh no!" She would stamp her foot in a show of pique, and would rush to the phone. Frank would sheepishly admit to the incident, claiming he had "been overcome with feeling and desire" and then go on to invent some fantastic story about "Terry's warm—shall I say 'passionate'—response," leaving the fab Pat, of course, in a state of most artfully contrived bewilderment.

We managed to get quite a bit of mileage out of this over the years.

"Ran into your friend, Frank, the other night," I would say to Patsy.

"Gosh, I hope he didn't . . ." she would hesitate, but I would force her to say it.

"Didn't *what?*"

"Well, you know," demurely averting her eyes, "try for French . . ."

"No, thankfully he did not," I would reply. "Norman was there, and you know how he feels about that sort of thing—and, in fact, Norman Bluhm was also there, and *he* feels even stronger."

"Well thank goodness!" Patsy would say.

"But," I would caution her, "I am now *fairly certain* there's something *going on* . . . between Frank and Ruth Kligman."

"Frank and Ruth?!? Something hetro?!?"

"No, this is *beyond hetro*, because Lar (Rivers) is somehow involved—a three-way thing, with Frank, Ruth and Lar—so its got to be *heavy* and *extremely weird*."

Patsy would get right on it, phoning Frank, demanding an 'explanation.' Frank would play it to the fullest, hinting at all manner of unspeakable curioso.

Once I asked Larry Rivers about Frank's closest friends, who did he think was Frank's *best* friend, and so on.

"Oh my God," he said, "there were so many people who thought they were his best friend. I mean, he had this thing about making each person feel he was his best friend. I guess it was because he *cared* so much, about everybody."

Yes, I guess it was. Anyway, I know there are people who were better acquainted with Frank than I, but I'm certain there are none who enjoyed him more fully, think of him more often, or more fondly.

—1978
Homage to Frank O'Hara; Big Sky
Bill Berkson and Joseph LeSueur, editors.
Reprinted by permission of Bill Berkson and Joseph LeSueur.

Memories of Michael

Michael Cooper was an adviser to Robert Fraser—the renowned '60s London scene-maker whose art gallery was a great favorite of the Beatles and Stones. Cooper killed himself in 1972 at age thirty. Terry helped prepare a limited-edition tribute for him many years later.

Summer of '66 at the top of Duke Street, in the heart of Old Smoke, I turned the corner and was taken by surprise by the wailing strains of James Brown's "Papa's Got a Brand New Bag" and, almost simultaneously, had my first larger-than-life living-color confrontation with a certain Michael Cooper, Esquire. His Edwardian outfit was opulent in the extreme—lavender velour with great flounces of lace at cuffs and collar. He was standing in the middle of the street, and he had a soccer ball which he was bouncing from one foot to the other, Pelé style, quite impressively adroit. The music, I now noted, was coming from a tape recorder which dangled from one shoulder. I moved on a couple of doors along Duke Street to the Robert Fraser Gallery and Grill, as we were later wont to call it. I tried the door and found it locked up tighter than Dick's hatband.

"Looking for Robert, are you?" asked the young dandy, and when I turned I saw something I was to come to love—his extraordinary smile, piercing; and somehow both shy and knowing, almost conspiratorial. It reminded me of the lyric "I know you, you know me, one thing I can tell you is you've got to be free." His smile was absolutely enchanting.

"Yes," I said. "I'm supposed to meet him here at four." It was almost five now.

Michael laughed. "Oh, I expect he's hopped it," he said, affecting a slightly Cockney accent. "Off to *Meerakesh*, if my guess is any good. Having a right rave-up with Bill Willis and Chris Gibbs about now, I shouldn't wonder, ho-ho!"

I peered through the gallery window; in the shadows I could see the great B-52 sculpture by Colin Self, which he had said was inspired by *Doc Strangelove*. Michael tried for a flash finish with the soccer bail, à la Georgie Best, kicking the ball behind his back, and trying to return it, à la Georgie Best, over the shoulder with a kick of his heel, but botched the effort.

"Hold on," he said. "Is this a bloody Thursday?" I replied that it was indeed Thursday.

"Then Bob's having tea at his mum's."

"And not the right rave-up you had imagined."

"Yes, he has tea with his mum every Thursday, rain or shine." He considered it. "I should very much like to know what they talk about." He laughed. "Robert's poor taste in choosing his friends, most likely. Although she's a very nice woman. Actually quite charming."

"So he won't be coming back here to the gallery."

"No, we'll have to catch him at Mount Street. Have you been to his flat in Mount Street?"

I said that indeed I had, and in fact had only the previous evening made the acquaintance there of the ultra-fab Anita Pallenberg and her newly acquired paramour, the outlandish rocker, Brian Jones.

"Quite so," said Michael, "and a ruddy fine pair they are, too. Brian has just scored some rather spectacular hash. 'Nepalese Temple Bells,' they're called. Look a bit like American hand grenades. We're in for a proper treat if they're on the scene tonight."

So we went along to 20 Mount Street and the first evening of what was to be several years of camaraderie and high adventure.

It was a magical era, an era of change and astonishment; an era of new concepts in art, in music, in fashion. Michael was on the cutting edge of all of it. The longer I knew him, the more I saw what an extraordinary influence he was in every area. Photography, of course, was his major preoccupation, and his work was outstanding. He was considered, by persons who knew about such things, to be the best photographer in London; it was generally recognized that it was Michael (rather than David Bailey) on whom the character in the film *Blow-up* was based.

Many of my memories of Michael involve Robert Fraser. They were ideally suited for the remarkable friendship they enjoyed. Each regarded the other as a grand eccentric, with Robert playing a sort of older brother of more con-servative stamp. He had a rather protective attitude towards Michael, although it was Michael who was dominant in terms of influence; it was he who always managed to get copies of the latest Otis Redding or Sam Cooke, or to know about a private screening of a Bruce Conner film; and whenever he made a trip to New York, he would invariably return full of enthusiasm for the work of some new artist he had met through Larry Rivers, Andy Warhol or Den Hop-per. He once persuaded Robert to install a 45rpm record player under the dash-board of his car—a remarkable Italian device that would absorb the bumps and cobbles of Old Smoke without skipping a note. With Michael as DJ and 'Straw-berry Bob' at the wheel, driving like a demon, eyeglasses glinting in the chang-ing traffic lights, mouth fixed in a smile of stone manic hilarity, we would tool about the city, blasting with our rock'n'roll. A memorable period.

Michael must have been one of the very few people to have both a social and professional relationship with the Stones and the Beatles at the same time. With Peter Blake he created the historic *Sgt. Pepper's* album cover, and later worked on the Stones' award-winning *Satanic Majesties* cover as well.

I suppose he knew Brian Jones first; but of that group, it was Keith who became his great friend. Michael and Keith were very much alike in their gen-erosity and sense of fun. Keith was a young man of heroic (indeed, Homeric) appetites, whether it involved Jack Daniels or things of a less traditional na-ture (nudge, nudge), and Michael admired him tremendously. They would hang out, 'grooving on the moors,' as Michael sometimes referred to their sojourns.

I once heard him defending Keith in an amusing exchange with Robert. It was during an evening at Mount Street.

"Well, young sir," said Robert, waxing indignant, "buzz along the rialto has it that those two esteemed cronies of yours—Squire Richards and Anita Pallenberg—have shown some rather bad form, rather bad form indeed."

Michael brightened. "Oh? How's that, then?"

Robert took great glee (while feigning high seriousness) in recounting how Keith and Anita had run away together, into the North African night, leav-ing Brian to his own devices.

"'Spanish Tony' brought the news," he said in solemn conclusion and waited for Michael's response. It appeared, however, that Michael had already heard about it, from Christopher Gibbs, and in more detail.

"They left Brian half of the hash and half of the albums," he said in loyal defense.

Robert seemed to weigh the matter anew for a moment, but he remained skeptical. "Including the Little Richard?" he demanded. "I would wager my life they did not leave the Little Richard!"

Michael should have been born a grand seignior of great wealth and power; he had a taste for elegance in all things. He enjoyed nothing more than persuading Robert that we should go to one of the Scott's restaurants, where the waiters were dressed in formal attire, and were all at least seventy years old.

On one such evening, I remember, we were waiting at Mount Street for Brian to join us. Michael, not to be outdone by Brian's habitual finery, had somewhere come up with a long piece of ermine which he was fashioning into a collar, while Bob looked on with bemused ambivalence. "Going the extra mile, eh?" he said, with a rueful smile.

"Just a bit of swank," Michael explained. "It'll set Brian Jones hopping with envy."

"You know," said Bob, with a patient sigh, "Scott's *does* have certain standards. We may be turned away."

Michael loved getting a rise out of him. "Mick is joining us," he said. "He's bringing a big black hooker."

"Good Lord."

This was during Mick's obsessive 'hot black mamma' period, so the notion was quite conceivable; although in this case it proved to be just another bit of the old Michael mischief.

As it turned out, we were joined not by Mick but by Squire Richards himself. Robert's apprehension, however, regarding our reception at the ultra-sedate Scott's restaurant was not assuaged by Keith's extraordinary attire: a flamboyant combination of Kit Carson and a nightclub Apache dancer—lots of fringed leather and flowing silk scarves.

Then Brian arrived, his hair coiffed so as to resemble a large golden helmet and wearing the wide-brimmed and plumed hat of the Cavalier.

"Perhaps," said Robert drily, "I should call the restaurant and say we're coming from a costume ball."

But Michael was quick to reassure him. "It's cool," he said. "Scott's is unflappable."

And so it proved to be. The ancient men in livery bowed us in without a blink. It was apparent they had a discerning eye for persons of great quality.

Girls adored Michael; they trusted him; and he made them laugh. As in most things, his taste in women was exquisite. One of them was Felicity Meredith-

Owens, a beautiful redhead with very white skin and haunting gray-green eyes. Ethereal, but plucky enough to be called 'Ginger,' she was the daughter of some rather posh ex-Colonial parents, landed gentry living in the storybook setting of Banbury in Oxfordshire. Banbury is a 16th-century walled village of thatched cottages, dominated by a grand manor house, rising out of the wall itself; so one could see how, in the beginning, the wall was intended to protect both lord and peasant.

Robert, whose parents were socially acquainted with the Meredith-Owenses, was amused but with reservations at Michael's relationship with Felicity. He brought out his best upper-class stammer, and assumed a mock housemaster tone: "Do you think it's wise . . . spending so much time at that place in the country? It could get a bit dicey, you know."

Michael waved off the warning. "It's a *walled city*, Robert. There's everything but a *moat*. There'll be no busts at Banbury Cross!"

Robert frowned. "That is hardly what I meant, dear boy," he said. "Are you aware that her father is an *old-school Colonial?* Who served his queen in India? And one who does not, I dare say, look too favorably upon the sort of sense-derangement which you, and," here he gave us all a pseudo 'sharp look,' "others in this flat I could name, find so voguish."

"No, it's quite cool," Michael tried to assure him. "We were smoking some hash in the library the other day—it was *her* hash, mind you—and her father came in, afterwards, of course. 'What's that smell?' he wanted to know. 'It's incense, Daddy,' she said. 'Do you like the scent?'

"'No, I do not,' he said. 'It reminds me of the damnable wog-hemp.'

"'I won't use it again, Daddy,' she said. And off he went, none the wiser."

Actually her parents were gracious and sympathetic, and gave no indication that they were aware of Michael's involvement with heroin, even when he went there once to kick, with Felicity looking after him. She explained his prolonged solitude in his room by saying he had 'a touch of malaria.' Her parents suggested the family doctor look in on him, but Felicity said if he didn't improve soon his 'specialist' would come down from London—which did, in fact, prove to be the case . . . a specialist with the colorful sobriquet of 'Spanish Tony' and his speciality, of course, was *cannabis,* the damnable hemp. However, it did allow Michael to continue his withdrawal and go into a period of relatively straight and productive existence.

In August 1968 I was finishing work on a film in Los Angeles [Barbarella] and living at the Chateau Marmont. I had been there a couple of weeks, having an occasional meal at the Imperial Gardeno just below the hotel. The restaurant is renowned for its fast cheap cuisine—and its adjoining sushi bar was in those days affectionately known as the 'Crumpet Capital of the Western World' or, in different parlance, as 'Starlet-Quim City.' Small wonder that the establishment attracted a wide and varied crowd. There are few people in life who are almost immediately recognizable, at a distance, by what they are wearing. Chaplin comes to mind, and perhaps Quasimodo, and Michael Cooper most certainly. And there he was, hunched over the sushi bar, resplendent in silken pastels, only a shade more subdued than his London garb. He saw me at once, smiled his fabulous smile, raised his Nikon and snapped a couple even as I approached. It turned out that he had come over to see the opening of The Byrds, at the Crescendo or similar place on the Strip. I don't think anyone had put up money for him; I think he just believed it would be a good thing to do and somehow managed. He never seemed to let money (or the shocking lack of it) interfere with his travels—he would hit the road and trust for the best. And his trust was justified: his magnetic vibes, his magical smile, his karma, whatever, would watch over him. Right up to the end. In any case, he was also staying at the hotel, so we had another period of good times. If memory serves, we went to The Byrds' opening with Dennis Hopper, and I believe the event was a howling (grotesquely so) success.

One afternoon during that period I took Michael to an extraordinary bar which Burroughs and I had previously discovered called The Coyote. It was a gay bar with a cowboy motif, and its main feature was a competition one afternoon a week, during which the contestants would strip, and then, without touching themselves, would gyrate wildly to music of their choice, in the effort to achieve an erection and, ideally (unattained during our presence), have an orgasm. They were judged by audience applause and after everyone had performed, a winner was declared; but no prize was given. The owner, who called himself Mr. Trice, a grand queen of indeterminate age, was very protective of 'my boys,' as he referred to the contestants, and would not allow anyone to take photographs. Michael was naturally disappointed. We were also puzzled by the fact that although the performances were quite complex and the competition very keen, there were no prizes. Michael asked Mr. Trice why people would compete week after week, in a contest that offered no awards. He had a slight lisp and a tendency to close his eyes when he spoke, very much like Truman Capote. He said: "Well, my dear, I do believe it is simply for the exposure."

After another week or so I received a letter from *Esquire* magazine, inviting me to join a hard-hitting team of investigative journalists they were sending to cover the Democratic Convention in Chicago. The other members were William Burroughs, Jean Genet and Allen Ginsberg. This 'nightmare assemblage' brought a smile to Michael's lips, and he immediately began devising a means of coming along—which he managed to do in about a week. He arrived on the day of one of the big demonstrations, and just in time to join the front rank of the protest. We were marching from the center of Lincoln Park to the Convention Hall. Michael was next to my wife, Gail, and he would leave the rank every so often and take some shots of the group.

It was during that march and later the same evening that we got a glimpse of democracy-in-action, Machiavelli/Gestapo-style. In our own group of marchers were a couple of young men behaving in a rowdy and drunken manner, and looking very much out of place in these circumstances. They had crew cuts and were wearing T-shirts from the University of Notre Dame. In the row of marchers just behind us was an elderly silver-haired lady, a veteran of many such demonstrations. She also noticed the two rowdies and seemed to recognize them. She had a word with one of the 'marshals' who were there to maintain order. He also seemed to recognize the pair, and gestured them out. They left without a murmur, as though they were guilty of something and had been discovered—which was, in fact, the case; they were FBI agents, attempting to discredit the demonstration by their conduct. The elderly lady and the marshal had recognized them from previous encounters. Michael was visibly affected by the revelation of such 'official' chicanery. "Robert is going to be shocked," he said, and smiled before adding: "Perhaps we should spare him."

The second act of that particular drama occurred in the evening, in Lincoln Park, when the Chicago police ran amok. It was just getting dark when they begin clearing the park—prowl cars, paddy wagons, and cops on foot moving slowly, loudspeakers blaring: "*Everyone out of the park . . . last warning . . .*"

Michael and I were sitting under a tree with a group that included Burroughs, Ginsberg and Genet. Ginsberg was doing his 'om' incantations in a curiously effective effort to calm the people around us, as the prowl cars closed in. It was about this time that the first tear-gas canister hissed over our heads and landed not far away. The fumes drifted in our direction and people immediately began to cough and wipe their eyes. One particular prowl car was about to pass very close to where we were sitting when an outlandish thing occurred: a young man stepped out from behind a nearby tree and threw a rock the size of a brick through the windshield of the car. That was, of course, the signal for the police to go berserk. They piled out of the cars and paddy wagons, nightsticks swinging, as the tear-gas cartridges now fell in abundance. And what Michael and I had clearly seen (and to which I would testify in court at the 'Chicago Conspiracy Trial') was that the young man who hurled the brick through the cop car windshield was one of the two crew-cut young men wearing Notre Dame T-shirts—in short, what we had observed was the FBI in the role of *provocateur*. The cops, in an action which was later branded by the entire media as a 'police riot,' rampaged through the park, the streets and even into hotel lobbies, trying to beat senseless everyone they overran.

Michael could not believe the rage and viciousness which consumed the Chicago police that evening. When we got back to the hotel, and saw it again on the eleven o'clock news, he was visibly shaken; and later, when someone told us how savagely Abbie Hoffman had been beaten, Michael was literally moved to tears. It was a measure of his extraordinary sensitivity. And it was, of course, a dire foreboding, which I failed to perceive at the time; a foreboding of his vulnerability, a foreboding of that day of dread, in 1972, when Michael could no longer 'hear the beat of the drum' to which we were marching.

He was a person of tremendous love and vision. I do not expect to see his like again . . .

—1989
Blinds & Shutters
Reprinted by permission of Genesis-Hedley Publishers, UK.

Remembering Abbie

Abbie Hoffman, the impresario of '60s counterculture, was once described as "a cross between Lenny Bruce, Che Guevara, and Robin Hood."

Most people will remember Abbie for his wit and wisdom, his creativeness, his classy and genuine bravura, and, of course, for his fabulous mischief. I'll remember him for these things, but also for his remarkable courage. Not just the moral and spiritual integrity that motivated his life, but a simple down-home fistfight kind of courage, which I saw on a number of occasions, and I am remembering one in particular. It was a night in Chicago, in 1968, during the Democratic Convention. I was there on journalistic assignment—part of a hard-hitting team of ace reporters fielded by *Esquire* mag; besides myself, there was the infamous Wm. S. "Doc Benway" Burroughs and the late great French poet, playwright, and saintly ex-con Jean Genet.

Two nights in particular were very bad, when the Chicago police were 'running amuck.' (If memory serves, the press spelled it 'amok' but I continue to favor the spelling from my Texas Childhood, '*amuck*'—suggesting, as it does, a veritable *quagmire* of disastrous events. I can hear the nasal twang: "Yep, he run amuck an' shot his whole dang family, includin' that good bird dog of his." "*Whut?* He shot ole Ring? Boy, he must of sure run amuck!" "Wal, ah RECK-TUM. Haw!")

Anyway, back to the reminiscence. The Chicago Police, on orders of Mayor Boss Daley to suppress all demonstrations, were rampaging through the park, the streets, and even into hotel lobbies, trying to beat senseless everyone they overran. It was a pure My Lai blood lust freak-out, rather politely described by the media as a "police riot," which lasted for two days and nights. The incident I'm recalling happened on the second, and worst, night. Abbie, Burroughs, Genet, Allen Ginsberg, and I were together in a crowd of about 20 during the general and urgent exodus of Lincoln Park after the police swept through with prowl cars, tear gas and clubs. We were running along a side street, cops in furious pursuit. Halfway down the block, a paddy wagon appeared at the far end of the street and emptied about 50 more police, who charged towards us. As the first of the crowd encountered the approaching cops and were laid waste, panic ensued. Someone found an unlocked entrance to an apartment building, and a part of the crowd we were in began funneling away from the mainstream and through the door, and into the foyer of the apartment house—including Abbie, Genet and myself. Burroughs and Ginsberg were swept along the street behind us. I remember thinking 'Well they're fucked, and no mistake,' and that Allen's 'oms' would not get them out of it. He had been doing his *oms* in the park, in an effort to reassure the crowd as the police and the tear gas closed in, and, in fact, had continued until he was actually incapacitated by the fumes. A grand trooper, Al Ginsberg. My concern for Allen and Burroughs, however, was short-lived, as the cops were now storming through the entrance door and into the crowded foyer, where both staircases, up and down, were behind locked doors. We were trapped, and the police waded into the crowd, nightsticks swinging in rage, and cursing as if everyone there had been convicted of child molesting and treason. A scene of total chaos, people screaming and pounding on the locked doors of the two ground-floor apartments. I couldn't see Abbie and Genet, and for a moment I thought they must have stayed in the street. Then I caught a glimpse of Genet across the room; he was cornered by a huge cop, "harness bull" Burroughs called them, with all their leather straps and extra belts of tear-gas cartridges. His club was raised and wavering as if he was zeroing in on his target—i.e., Genet's bare noggin. Everyone had their arms crossed over their heads, but Genet was simply standing with his palms turned out.

"*Du calm, monsieur,*" he was saying softly to the cop, as one might to a misbehaving child, "*du calm . . .*"

A diminutive man and bald, he appeared exceptionally vulnerable, and the overhead light gave his pate a saintly glow. And then, an instant before the club came crashing down, Abbie was between them, yelling at the cop. "Don't hit *him*, man, he's a *poet!*" He literally put himself in Genet's place; he may well have saved his life.

Then one of the apartment doors opened, and about 15 people desperately surged through it, along with half a dozen police behind them—a veritable stampede, right through the center of what appeared to be a small, highly middle-class, living room. I got a glimpse of a coffee table being bowled over, along with a standing lamp, its shade still wrapped in cellophane strips, the light now angled crazily from the floor, lending the scene even more of a madhouse quality than already prevailed, as the cops kept on swinging their clubs, as far as the windows through which the escapees bolted onto the fire escape, into the alleyway and the night. By now, the front entrance was open again and people were making it out that way, as did I.

I ran into Abbie at the end of the block, standing under a streetlamp with several others. With only slightly veiled admiration, I told him how I had witnessed his heroic act in the foyer.

"Abs," I said, "that was great. You went the distance for the fab frog poet."

He tried to deprecate the incident by explaining it away.

"Man," he said, "didn't you see his *gourd*?" referring to Genet's bald head. "Nobody with a gourd like that can take the kind of whacks these guys are laying out." He flashed his extraordinary smile.

"Me?" and he touched his Afro-bouf. "I've got some *padding* for it. No problem."

But in the light from the streetlamp overhead, I could see where just above his left eye, from beneath the hairline, the blood still oozed and trickled. In the soft light it seemed to glitter, as bright as his smile.

—1989

Trib to Von

When a limited-edition tribute was organized for Kurt Vonnegut's sixtieth birth-day, Terry's solicited piece was deemed too outrageous for inclusion by the editor. It was later published in Evergreen Review.

I was genuinely flattered when asked to contribute to this birthday *festschrift* for the great Von, and I am delighted to do so—delighted to recount our evenings of mirth and enlightenment, and to elaborate on Kurt's varied attributes and qualities (monies lent, drugs preferred, services rendered, friendships bestowed or extended, etc.). One quandary: publisher has stipulated this be limited "to 2500 words or less"—whereas I find myself wondering if such a meager sum is sufficient—sufficient even indeed to *list* (at one word per) the mere number of the aforementioned. I can only try.

To begin then at the beginning. Our first meeting was in the early '50s, but my recollection is as vivid as if it were yesterday—or perhaps even this morning. While it is fairly amusing to look back on it now, the circumstances of that initial encounter were uncomfortably embarrassing at the time—indeed, almost 'compromising'—for both myself and the person I happened to be with at that moment, and I have always appreciated the fact that Kurt never humiliated me by referring to the incident, either in print or, so far as I know, in private.

Then, as today, the Von's appearance was quite striking. He was not so pulled together though in those days as he now seems to be; he was somehow more wild-eyed and hirsute, more mustachioed and unkempt. He had a kind of swarthy, ruffian look to him, collar half turned up, great slouch hat akimbo, like something out of an early Lautrec, what the French call *'un vrai costeau'* . . . which may well be the descriptive phrase of choice, since that first meeting did, in fact, occur in Paris—in Montmartre to be exact (*rue d'Argent*, I believe it was) where, at just about midnight, the literary scion, George Ames Plimpton, and a certain yours truly were emerging from a sensationally debilitating session at the famed *Maison de Langue*—or "House O'Tongue" as the ex-pats called it—generally acknowledged at the time to be the most expensive and opulently staffed whorehouse in Paris. There we had been guests of the very gracious Sadruddin Khan, the wealthiest patron of *The Paris Review,* of which Plimpton was and, in actual fact, is to this day, editor in chief, and quite a dandy in his own right. Indeed, there was hardly a more princely figure on either bank of the Seine than the Lincolnesque Plimpton, striding down the Boul'Mich, his black cape flaring about him like the plumage of some giant regal predator.

"You there," I cried out, when I was sure who it was, just crossing the street in front of us, "you Vonnegut!"

"What in great devil!" exclaimed the Plimp, startled into annoyance by the abruptness of my shout, imperious brows furrowing darkly, "who are you shouting at in the streets now?" he demanded, adding with a derisive chortle, "yet another of your wog-hemp *confrères?*"

"No, no," I was quick to assure, "that's *Vonnegut*—he's a real comer in the quality lit game, Plimp. You ought to get him for the mag."

Plimp scrutinized Kurt from afar with a formulative gaze, as the latter continued walking, apparently too preoccupied to respond.

"Don't care for the cut of his jib," murmured the Plimp, whacked out on hash, *"un peu trop du vrai costeau, n'est ce pas?"*

"No, no, I've read his stuff, Plimp, he's heavy duty. I think he's a *kraut.*"

Truth to tell, I hadn't really *met* Kurt as yet, just had him pointed out to me at the Café Flore—probably by Chris Logue or Alex Trocchi. I couldn't remember his first name, but I was sure it began with 'K.' *"Karl* Vonnegut, if memory serves. He's boss-scribe, Plimp. We're talking future Laureate, know what I'm saying? Nail him for the mag."

This seemed to kindle his interest somewhat, and set him musing aloud. "Hmm . . . *kraut,* is he?" and then went on, waxing somewhat expansive, "I came across a bit of early Hesse the other day—not previously published, of course—I'm thinking of running it in the next issue."

Ahead of us now, in the Montmartre night, Kurt started angling across the Boulevard Pigalle, making his way through the seething mélange of whores, beggars, and cripples—a Bosch / Bruegel quagmire, to be sure, eerily lit by stabs of red and blue neon—and I steered the Plimp hard after our quarry.

"I think you would be well advised, Mr. G. Ames Plimpton," I said then with genial authority, "if you devoted *less* time to the acquisition and use of the damnable hemp, and *more* to affairs of the *Review*. In short, you should get Vonnegut for the next issue."

Plimpton scowled fiercely. "Instead of *Hesse?*" he fairly shrieked. "You must be mad!"

"Not *instead* of Hesse," I explained, with such patience as I could muster for his derangement, "in *addition* to Hesse."

But the drug-induced pique of the Plimp was not assuaged. "Two translations in a single issue? Ho-ho! You've a great deal to learn about the quality lit game, my good man!"

Having had two stories accepted by the mag, I'd been made an "Advisory Editor" (in lieu of payment, natch), but now it appeared my lack of quality lit savvy had already put the post in jeopardy.

"Well, he doesn't actually *write* in German," I went on, hoping to soften the *faux-pas*, "he just has this German-sounding name."

Now the Plimp was definitely intrigued. "*Karl von Egut* . . ." he murmured, savoring the sound. "Yes, I like it . . . has *tone* . . . *class*. That's what we *need*! Too many *plain* names so far: 'Hill', 'Hall', 'Walter', 'Wilbur', 'Train', 'Frank', 'Fuller', 'Styron', 'Southern' . . . *Damnation*! Sounds more like a Presbyterian softball team than a proper quality lit lineup!"

The brief outburst seemed to afford him some relief, and he was soon ruminating again. "Hmm . . . *Karl von Egut* . . . do you know it has been virtually *donkey's years* since there was a 'von' in quality lit! The last was the vignettist, *von Steuben*—*Tales Of The Black Forest*, if memory serves—rather peripheral in my view. And now this '*von Egut*' surfaces . . . Well, I should very much like to know the *background* of our Herr von Egut! Could be a Hapsburg tie-in, of course . . . and, ho-ho, a tidy spot of patronage—touch wood!" And so saying, he lightly tapped me on the head—his idea of humor, the great deranged ninny. The notion of fresh patronage had set the Plimp alight with exuberance.

"Well, catch him up, man, catch him up!" he shouted, waving his arms in a grand manner, "we'll buy him a *schnapps*!"

So! Putting me on the send again, eh? I was beginning to have my fill with eternally playing batman for a certain 'Colonel' G. Ames Plimpton, but I managed to mask my vexation beneath a careless laugh. "Merely a *drink*?" I asked. "Why not take him back to the 'Maison'? Treat him to a tankard of hash oil and a spot of teeny-poon.

"*What?*"

"Yes," I said, and added in what I intended as a hiss of insinuation, "we'll just see if he chooses to go the *pre-knocker route* . . . like some we know, eh? Heh-heh-heh."

"Damnation!" Plimpton flared, somewhat as I'd expected, "can we not have done with that topic for tonight!?!"

He was referring to a rather obscure—though not wholly without interest—point of contention which had arisen earlier in the evening, at the *Maison de Langue,* when I remarked—in the most casual and conversational manner, *en passant,* as it were—that it seemed to me "somewhat unnatural" to have sex with a girl who had not yet reached adolescence—that is to say, a girl too young to have breasts—or rather any appreciable development thereof. The remark proved fairly injudicious, since it almost immediately transpired that our gracious host —the Sadruddin Khan—he who had brought us to this incredible "House of Tongue," had an avid predilection for girls of the 8 to 10 year bracket. "Bad form," Plimpton muttered concerning my remark, and "*Chaque à son goût, sir! Chaque à son goût! Damnation!*"

Plimpton himself, of course, was known to favor a more mature and full-breasted girl—'*amply endowed,*' as he used to express it, with a wise chuckle.

In any case, I now stepped up my pace and overtook the Von, as he paused at a kiosk to purchase a late-edition paper.

"Hey there, Vonnegut," I said, extending my hand. "*Player Piano*—am I right?" referring to a rather obscure novel of his I'd read. "You've got a winner-style, pal," and I turned, indicating the Plimp, who had just sauntered up. "Allow me to introduce my good friend, the celebrated *auteur,* James Baldwin."

Baldwin had just achieved local notoriety by publishing a scathing drug-crazed attack on saintly Richard Wright, calling him "Richard Wrongo— the Uncle Tombo" and blaming him for half the ills of the western world. Moreover, the article had appeared in the infamous *Zero,* one of our arch-rival mags—so that my barbed pleasantry was *double*-pronged—both fairly keen, if one may judge from the Plimp's quick grimace of ire. A look of *single-entendre,* one might say.

"Southern *will* have his occasional sordid attempt at the *bon mot,*" he observed grimly, extending his hand to Von. "George Plimpton," he said in his grandest manner, "of the *Paris Review* . . . at your service, Herr von Egut! *Bitte!*"

Kurt apparently (and mercifully) mistook 'Herr' for 'Harry', and gently (and, of course, with no trace of accent) corrected him. "*Kurt* is the name . . . Kurt Vonnegut."

The chagrined G. Ames, instead of responding directly, raised hand to mouth, stifling a sort of gagging cough, and leaving me to carry on the confab. "Yes, Kurt's the name," I said easily, "and quality lit's the game—how'd you like to write for *money*, pal?" again indicating the Plimp, in his affluent-looking cape.

"I *do* write for money," Kurt replied, with consummate dignity, "when conditions are . . . *optimum*."

Plimp cleared his throat and assumed full command. "I was wondering if you would care to join us in a nightcap . . ."

"And perhaps," I added genially, "a spot of teeny-bop frog hose-gobbling— or better yet, the eight-year-old '*specialité de la Maison*', eh Plimp?"

The Plimp cleared his throat noisely. "I rather doubt that Herr, er, uh, *Kurt* would be interested in hearing that sort of drivel," he said, and muttered yet another exasperated "Damnation!"

It was no secret, of course—at least not in our crowd—that the specialty of the *Maison* was oral sex in its myriad forms, but the *specialty* of *specialties*— the phenomonen, or "treat," if you will, that really set the *Maison* apart, made it unique among all the whorehouses of Paris, was its celebrated performance of *Le Cercle* or, in its full-blown title, *Le Cercle des Enfants du Paradis*. This remarkable "service" consisted of being strapped (wrists and ankles) on a sort of cushioned table—by an extraordinary Amazon-type beauty, clad in scant leathers, who called herself (*and* rather pointedly insisted upon so *being* called) "*La Maîtresse*"—who then "anointed one" (to use the Plimp's own phrase, and he seemed to derive a certain mischievous pleasure from cryptically referring to it in the presence of the uninitiated—elderly patrons of the mag, for example, gathered for a smart *soirée litéraire*, when great Plimp might casually glance at his watch and say to me with a wink: "Well, my dear fellow, the sun is over the yard-arm, and I shouldn't be at all surprised if we don't soon require a bit of '*anointing*,' eh? Ho-ho-ho.") His reference was to the highly refined *banana oil* which *La Maîtresse* sensually applied to the party in restraint, from head to toe, sparing only the genitalia. Application completed, she would rise to full height, and full hauteur, clap her hands like a rifle shot, and shout in command: "*Mes enfants!*" Whereupon three of the loveliest eight- to ten-year-old girls, dressed in sheerest pink and white chiffon, like something out of *Midsummer Night's Dream*, would float, or *seem* to float, so ethereal their aspect, into the room, curtsy to both patron and *Maîtresse*, before she would then command: "*A table!*" Whereupon they would commence their paradisiacal magic . . . of removing the banana oil, inch by inch, from the patron's body, using only their small pink tongues to that end, assiduously avoiding the unanointed genitalia—if only by the fraction of a single, maddening, millimeter—by now a veritable tower (as we used to say in quality porn) of 'pulsating tumescence'! And it was, as the great Plimp observed on more than one occasion, "an extremely taxing affair—though *not*," he was always quick to add, with a twinkle and a raised finger to caution against prejudging, "without its ultimate, and well-deserved, *nirvana!*" His reference here was to that moment when the girl-children would withdraw, and the fantastic *Maîtresse*, eyes like diamonds, would serve you a jigger of hash oil before descending, wet lips agleam, to voraciously engorge the pounding member—*or*, for the more traditionally inclined, she would free the patron of his bonds, and allow him to take his pleasure with his favored *demoiselle(s)* of the evening—not on the table, of course, but on a magnificently ornate veloured and canopied bed which stood only a few feet away. Such were the fabled pleasures of the *Maison de Langue*—the very same to which I was endeavoring to introduce the Von—only to be thwarted by a certain G. Ames Plimpton, he who was now shepherding us along the Boulevard Pigalle and holding forth in grand, albeit somewhat spaced-out, form.

"Yes, there's a rather amusing bistro, just along here, I believe—with fairly decent *caves*, if memory serves," and he ushered us into a typical Pigalle cesspool of harlotry, drugs, and transvestism. I remember the first thing that caught my eye was one of the garish new "peen-bawl" machines the French had just begun to manufacture, featuring the grotesquerie of the Grand Guignol mixed with some kind of insanely twisted Cartesian logic. This one was called *MEFIEZ-VOUS DES RATS DE PARIS*! and was a kind of Pac-Man in reverse, since it portrayed the Player being pursued through the labyrinthine sewers of Paris, by hordes of giant rats. When the rats would overtake the Player, a burst of red light signaled the loss of an appendage. Five losses (the fifth being the head) and the game was over. Unlike Pac-Man, the Player had no retaliatory capability; only by maneuvering two rat hordes into collision (which produced a spectacular burst of flashing crimson) and mutual decimation, could the life of the Player be extended—though not for long, the French being much too maniacally avaricious to allow that. Anyway, it was certainly worth a try. So, lighting up an 'Arab funnel' hash-bomber, and nursing a double Remy (*Cordon Bleu*, if memory serves), I had at it—while Plimp and Vonnegut sat at a table nearby, avidly yakking about God only knows what. (Hardly the *Maison*, I warrant!) In any case, my concentration was scarcely what it should have been for max performance. All that talk about teeny poon—or at least the thought of it—must have rekindled my *ésprit d'amour,* so that after a few games and another Remy, I was ready to head back to the *Maison* and see if young Khan mightn't still be lurking about the premises, ready to spring for more paradisiacal action . . . which I did, leaving Von and the Plimp pretty much to their own devices. Oh, this isn't to say the Von and I didn't have plenty of other *soireés du drogues interessants et litéraires,* and many adventurous evenings, lifting our tankards (*and* our voices) Student Prince fashion, under blue Parisian skies. However, more of that at another time . . . when the price is right, and there aren't all these pesky restrictions concerning length of trib to Von, et cetera, et cetera.

—1984
Evergreen

Origins of the Lampman

Larry Rivers is a well-known American painter whom Terry knew since the 1950s.

During most of 1966, while I was staying at Larry Rivers's studio on 14th Street, we maintained a rather strict vigil on the apartment of a young lady living directly across the street—an attractive blonde whose sexual activity was, even by our own fairly liberal standards, prodigious. The best vantage point for observing her action was in the front room, at the far end of the studio. This was all right for me because I could sit there in a comfortable chair and write, keeping one eye glued, so to speak, to the window under surveillance. Lar, on the other hand, had the disadvantage of working at the opposite end of the studio, practically one (short) block away (big studio).

"She's giving head!" I'd shout, at the appropriate moment.

"*What?*" would be the muted distant reply.

"SHE'S GIVING HEAD!" this time at the top of my voice, hands cupped, aimed carefully in his direction.

A quarter-minute later (often less, for Lar was in top form, and quite agile when properly motivated) he would arrive, usually in time for whatever grand crescendo might be in order.

One late afternoon I was sitting at my post, writing wildly, secure in the belief that our subject had not yet returned from an earlier departure, when I absently raised my eyes from the paper . . . to discover an erotic tableau already unfolding. Blast! So thoughtlessly absorbed was I in my so-called work that I'd missed the all-important prelims—the part where her fretful protests languorously segued into warm response, as each new 'Mr. Good-Dong' methodically fondled and disrobed her.

"*Lar!*" I shouted. "QUICK!"

By now they were already embraced, standing naked in silhouette, features but vaguely discernable in the half light. Lar arrived on the double, and we crouched at the window, peering out.

"I think, it's a black guy," I said, hoping to divert attention from my lax vigil.

"Why do you say that?" asked Lar sharply, ever boss rational—though I noticed he began to peer more intently.

I shrugged. "Just a hunch . . . call it an 'educated guess' if you will," and added knowingly, "I'll tell you one thing, Lar, that Ms. Smart is no stranger to heavy spade dork."

But Lar was not impressed. "So?" In the unlit and deep-shadowed room, it was difficult to see anything at all. "What are they doing?" he demanded, suddenly standing. Then he snatched up his alto sax from the couch nearby, and blew a few riffs.

"He's putting heavy wood to her, Lar," I said tersely, "*from behind.*"

Lar continued to play ("I Surrender, Dear," if memory serves) while keeping an eye on her window opposite. "*C'est faux!*" he snapped, after executing an intricate Bird-riff bridge, "you can't see them anymore." And he hurried away, back to the studio.

It was true, of course, they had gradually sunk to the floor out of sight (and were doubtless now going at it like a pair of maddened warthogs!) but, in any case, that particular image (black hump from behind!) was destined to recur. The occasion was the Janis Gallery 1976 exhibition of "Contemporary Erotic Art," to which Rivers was invited to contribute, along with a dozen or so other painters of stature. In preparing his entry, Lar utilized a 'Plexiglas playmate,' previously commissioned by *Playboy* mag, using a discarded version of the finished piece, to fashion a *floor lamp*. The original construction was the life-size figure of a girl, wearing only a blouse, leaning forward over a table, her upper torso resting there, while her derrière protruded pertly. To serve as the vertical upper part of the structure, where the lights themselves would be, Lar introduced the figure of a man, standing directly behind the girl, arms raised, fingers extended; the ten extended fingers were 25-watt tubular-shaped lightbulbs. An eleventh bulb represented the man's penis, in full penetration, and had the kind of filament that quivers constantly—wattage unknown.

When old Sid Janis visited the studio for a quick look at the finished work, he at once became greatly agitated. "My God, Larry," he said, pointing one clawlike finger at the work, "if the cop on the corner sees this—a black guy having sex with a white girl—he'll close down the show!" He became so stressed out, I thought he might have a heart attack. "Larry," he implored, wringing his hands, "I've got a sixty-thousand-dollar investment in the show! *For the love of Christ, LOSE THAT SCHWARTZE!*"

"Why Sidney," said Lar, in mock distress, "you sound almost like a *racist.*"

"Racist-schmacist," exclaimed old Jan, "I know bad taste when I see it!" And he rushed crazily out of the studio and down the stairs.

In the days that followed, considerable pressure from the gallery was brought upon Lar—phone calls from old Jan, cajoling and threatening by turn—suggestions, hints, and pointed insinuations that if the work was not changed it would not be shown . . . which would amount, in effect, to a reneging on the commission.

In order to ascertain his rights in the matter, Lar asked Janis to come back to the studio again for further discussion, at the same time arranging for his brother-in-law, Norman Becker, a knowledgeable lawyer, to be present.

It was a Monday morning, and the show was scheduled to open in three days. Old Jan arrived promptly at ten as scheduled, flushed and wheezing from the six flights of stairs, but managing to greet us with a bravura smile, confident that "everything will come out in the wash," as he had repeatedly said on the phone since his last visit. Lar introduced him to Norman (disguised for the occasion in sweatshirt and jeans, and needing a shave) as "a poet friend of mine who just happened to fall by."

Declining an offer of coffee, old Jan immediately resumed the protestations where he had left off, but now claiming that a lot of people, "including some top artists" (whom he declined to name), shared his opinion of the work, as he had described it to them. "Let's face it, Larry, the piece is in bad taste," he said, "believe me, I know."

"Racist bullshit," Larry said.

"Sixty thousand I've got in this show, Larry," Old Jan repeated, "you think that's *spit?*" Perspiring now, and gesturing wildly, as in mortal desperation (signaling through the flames, as it were), he started soliciting support from Norman and myself, as well as from a couple of teenies who had dropped by, bopping around the place, stoned out.

Standing next to the work was a rickety stepladder which suddenly caught the eye of Old Jan—whereupon, as if propelled by the sixty thou itself, he leaped to the ladder and scrambled up it, in such an eccentric crippled-monkey manner as to cause Larry to gasp in apprehension: "Watch it, Sid! That ladder's not safe!" But there was no stopping Old Jan; he was atop the ladder in a trice, had seized the head of the figure, and lifted it off, leaving only the bare bulb, exposed and glaring harshly, and down he came.

"Now look at that!" he exclaimed, one arm in a sweeping gesture towards the work, the other cradling its head like a lucky gladiator, "you tell me—isn't that *better?*" His look embraced all of us—including the teenies, who had bopped over to see what was happening—then he focused on Larry, beaming maniacally: "Like this, with the bare lightbulb, it's more *pure*—believe me, I know— as art, it's more pure, more pure."

Lar looked at it, grimacing against the harsh glare of the light. "Are you *kidding?*" he demanded, "it's *horrible.*" He took the head from Old Jan, climbed the ladder, and replaced it.

Old Jan stormed out. "I'm running an *art gallery*, Larry," he cried over his shoulder, "*not a soapbox for your civil-rights crap*! I've got a sixty-thousand-dollar investment in this show! You're . . . you're an *irresponsible* person!"

Larry poured himself a stiff one. "Well," he said to his brother-in-law, "what do you think? Can he actually do it? Refuse to show the piece because it might be controversial? Isn't that 'suppression of artistic freedom' or something?"

"Larry . . ." said Norman Becker, and from his tone, and the way his eyes narrowed to slits of suspicion, you knew it was going to be heavy, "do you have a *signed release* from the girl who posed for . . . that?"

"You mean for the original?" said Lar, "the one I did for *Playboy* mag? Sure, she got paid . . . *and* she signed a *release.*"

"She signed a release for her likeness to be used in the *original pose*, yes— alone, wearing a pajama top, looking . . . provocative, yes. But *did* she sign a release," he leaned forward, fixing Lar with a narrow look, "whereby she agrees to appear in a work that depicts her BEING FUCKED IN THE ASS?!?"

Larry looked quickly, sharply, at the work. "She's *not* 'being fucked in the ass'!" he said in irate accusation, "is *that* what you thought? Jesus! Just because they're not . . . not in your '*basic missionary position*,' doesn't mean she's being fucked in the ass! My God!" He turned away in exasperation.

Norman smiled, tight and rueful. "That's hardly the point, is it? You've portrayed this girl, without her permission, in circumstances she may not find wholly acceptable." He looked at the piece again, and said softly: "That girl can *sue* you, Larry—not just for all the money you have now, but . . . *for all the money you'll ever have.*"

For Lar, this gave rise to a delicate dilemma. His sense of artistic integrity prohibited him from changing the piece under pressure from Old Jan, and along the lines ("For the love of Christ, lose that schwartze!") he had suggested. On the other hand, it was quite clear he must do *something* to the piece to avoid the financial holocaust described by big Norm. In the hours that followed, there was a good deal of ranting and pacing the studio floor, as Lar speculated on how to change the piece without compromising it, and yet not appear that the change was made under gallery pressure.

"I've got it," he said at last, "I'll make the chick *black*—but she'll be *so light* no one else will *know* she's black. We'll tell old Jan she's a 'high yellow'—he'll like that, he probably used to whack off to Lena Horne's picture."

So he shortened the hair, did something to the face and body that gave it a sort of *jaundiced* look—a lot like the girl next door, or in this case, across the street—and the show was ready for the road.

"*She's* a schwartze?" asked Old Jan with rising inflection and arched brows, when he saw the piece.

Lar nodded. "High yellow," he said with genial authority, "pretty erotic, huh?"

Now that he could think of her as black, Old Jan took an interest. "Not bad," he said, with a lascivious twinkle, "looks a little like Lena Horne." With the shortened hair, it also now looked (at least for many who had not seen our fabulous neighbor) a little like a *guy*—but, for some reason, that escaped Old Jan.

So, having satisfied everyone (integrity still intact!) there remained only to name the piece.

"I'll just call it *Lamp*," said Lar.

"But it's not just a lamp, Lar, it's a fabulous *Lampman*!" I said.

Lar considered it. "Yes," he agreed, 'it *is* a kind of *Lampman*—tearing off a piece of poon."

"Yes, and from all appearance, I would say that . . . *Lampman loves it*!"

That grooved Lar. "'*Lampman Loves It*'! Good title!"

The Great Janis Conspiracy

Lampman Loves It was to be the centerpiece of the exhibition. Not only was it the largest and most intricately finished work in the show, but it was also the most erotic. The other artists had taken a more oblique approach to the subject—a crumpled leaf . . . a sandbox . . . a small geyser—in other words, a series of little sexual Rorschach tests. *Lampman Loves It* was destined to dominate the show.

The gallery opened at ten, I dropped in about noon, made my way across the crowded floor to where I knew the Lampman to be, and was surprised to see that his all-important 'genitalia-light' had burned out—or so I assumed, until I gave it a quick twist, and on it went. After a half hour's tour of the rest of the show, I returned to the work—and, again, the bulb in question was mysteriously dark. I dutifully turned it on—this time remaining in wait, though well removed from the work, to see if the mischief would recur—and by whose hand. Scarcely had I assumed my watch before Old Jan himself stealthily approached and, after a furtive glance around, took out his handkerchief and used it to grasp the penis bulb and wrench it from its socket. Although I knew he was using the handkerchief to protect his hand from the heat of the bulb, the image was nevertheless curiously obscene, as though he were using the handkerchief for some freaky hygienic reason of his own. In any case, holding the bulb in the kerchief, well away from his body, precisely (I imagined) as he would have done with a sticky dildo (or worse!), he rushed across the room, and into his private office.

I phoned Lar at the studio. "Mayday, Lar! Mayday! Old Jan has just mutilated the Lampman!"

"What?"

"He took out the cock-bulb!"

"He turned it out?"

"No, he *took* it out of the socket! 'Mutilation City,' Lar! They've de-cocked the Lampman! Mayday! Mayday!"

He hung up and arrived in about fifteen minutes.

At first, Old Jan claimed that the bulb had burned out, but when confronted with the evidence of his lie, he said quite piously: "All right, Larry, you want the truth? I hoped I could spare your feelings, Larry, but we've had complaints . . . about the vulgarity of the piece—because of that cock-bulb. I took it out for your own good, Larry, and for the good of the show."

"Bullshit," said Lar, quite emphatically. "Put it back."

Old Jan sighed, shaking his head, moving slowly, as though under the heavy burden of carrying a sixty-thousand-dollar cross up Calvary Hill.

We watched as he replaced the bulb, then we left, had a drink and came back. The bulb was gone again.

"I *knew* he would do it!" said Lar, "the great asshole! Well, two can play that game—come on!" He led the way across the floor, and into Janis's private office. Old Jan, sitting at his desk (counting his money?), looked up quite startled, as though he'd been caught whacking off (to some kind of weird abstract expressionism, no doubt!).

"Hi Sid," said Larry with exaggerated cheerfulness, "we just want to use the bathroom."

Old Jan looked tremendously relieved. "Oh sure, Larry, sure!" he exclaimed, then added, slightly nonplussed, as the two of us approached the door, "What, the both of you? You use the bathroom together?"

"Yeah, Sid," said Lar jovially, opening the bathroom door, "we're gonna take a lot of drugs in here." And he closed the door.

"Don't kid around, Larry!" Old Jan yelled irately behind us, "it's not funny, believe me."

"Just joking, Sid," yelled Lar, locking the door, "it's a sex thing! We're into heavy sex in here!"

"Don't kid around, Larry!" yelled Jan again.

Inside, Lar took a spare bulb out of one pocket, and two tubes of Du Pont Epoxy ("One Drop Will Lift Two Tons") Glue from another. He applied a dab from each tube on the base of the bulb, and began spreading it over the surface. "What was it Leonardo said?" he chuckled. "'If it won't go in, put a little spit on it'?"

"That was Lenny Bruce," I said.

"I knew it began with an 'L'," said Lar, putting away the glue, and holding the bulb in a concealed manner as we left the bathroom.

"We enjoyed fabulous sex in there, Sidney," Lar said gleefully to old Jan as we passed his desk, "and *puh-leenty* of good drug!"

Old Jan was adding a column of figures, and didn't bother to look up. "Don't kid around," he murmured, "it's not funny, believe me."

Back at the Lampman, Lar replaced the bulb, now permanently bonded in place by Du Pont Two-Ton. "Another blow for artistic freedom and heavy raunch!" said Lar, and we headed downtown.

I looked in on Lampman a couple of days later, and was saddened to see he was *dead*—both as man and lamp—*all* of his lights now dark, its life-giving electric cord having been ripped out of the wall socket.

* * *

The next day I was riding along West 57th in a cab when I looked out the window—and there on the sidewalk in front of the gallery was the Lampman, and his companion, both half shrouded in a faded tarp, being shoved and hustled towards a waiting van. Were they, I wondered, being taken to the East River? In a weighted bag? (All ID torched away!) Just as we came alongside, the tarp slipped to the side a little, exposing for an instant the pert plexi-derrière of Ms. Smart, and, for the discerning, a (presumably) maddening glimpse of the Lampman's dead glass-member—for all the world to see . . . but nobody seemed to be looking. Old Jan quickly adjusted the garment, his eyes darting, like a Pavlovian dog in furtive reflex, towards the traffic cop down the street . . . but he, alas, wasn't looking either.

So this current presentation at the Met of *Lampman Loves It,* in *all* its blazing glory, represents a nifty comeback, for the freedom of art and artists everywhere—and for the Lampman himself a reprieve, a kind of *resurrection,* as it were. And well deserved it is, too, for as anyone can plainly see . . . 'Lampman (Really!) Loves It.'

—1990s

Epilogue: Drugstore Cowboys: a Conversation with Terry Southern and William Burroughs

Terry frequented Burroughs's "bunker" on the Bowery—often armed with a provocative gift or two, ranging from 19th-century walking sticks with retractable sword (or snuff spoon) to a modern homemade aerosol nail-gun. According to Victor Bockris, who took part and recorded the following session, "At one point, their meeting played out almost exactly like the home-shopping pill scene in the movie Drugstore Cowboy, *but then Burroughs—also known as Dr. Benway—and Southern—one of* Dr. Strangelove *fame—were the original Drugstore Cowboys."*

Southern arrived at my flat at about 7 p.m., carrying a shopping bag full of drug samples, given him, he said, by "a gregarious chemist—a social-climbing artist manqué, but a decent enough chap after his own fashion." He plopped the bag down on the table. "I'm afraid you'll not find much of the old hard stuff amongst this lot, Vic," he continued, momentarily assuming a la-di-da British accent he presumably thought matched my own. "I just brought them along for Bill—he enjoys rooting about in these drug samples." After lighting up a couple golden ones, I switched on the tape.

VICTOR BOCKRIS: Let's talk about drugs in Hollywood because that's what people are really interested in.

TERRY SOUTHERN: I thought you wanted to talk about quality lit, subtexts, the sensory perception of sight and sound being more empathetic than prose, that sort of thing.

V.B.: Yes, well, we'll be getting 'round to that in double quick order, but first, let's hear it for dope in the film capital. Do you think it's true that people there spend more money on drugs than anywhere else?

T.S.: Yes, and their generosity regarding certain consciousness-altering drugs —cocaine, in particular—is legend. I won't use names, if you don't mind, because a lot of these people are slightly paranoid, and being publicly linked with dope could only aggravate that condition. One of the most interesting aspects of the drug scene out there is the preoccupation with *weight*. I mean, they *assume* that the stuff is going to be fairly pure, that much is taken for granted, so they just talk about *weight*—"I'm looking to score *weight*, man," they'll say, or maybe, "Hey, I really scored some *weight* last night!" And they're talking in terms of *ounces*, you dig, quarter, half, and, of course, your basic big-boy full OZ.—that being the most common unit of measure in the film capital. You can understand how if someone is making *ten or fifteen thousand dollars a day*, with, ha-ha, the furniture payments all up-to-date, it can affect one's attitude. So *quality* is not such a big deal when you're holding weight. I mean, if it's been stepped on a few times, so what, as long as it's good Peruvian base, you just do six lines instead of two.

V.B.: I heard that part of the budget of each film was now given over to the purchase of drugs, so that a movie has, for example, a coke budget.

T.S.: Of course it isn't spelled out "C-O-C-A-I-N-E" in the contract, but it will be reflected in the budget breakdown under "Miscellaneous Expenses" or, more recently, a heading called "Special Items," which somehow makes it sound sort of weird and vaguely sexual, like it might refer to an assortment of dildos or a case of K.Y. jelly, but which, in fact, everyone knows is *dope* for *the actor*. It's always for the actor because that's how big films are financed, 95 percent of them, on the basis of a name actor. So if the producer or director want a particular actor, and they're out to woo him, waltzing him around a bit, the first thing they'll do is establish a rapport by letting him know they're heavily into toot—whether they are or not—by springing some of their own at the very first meeting. And, actually, when you're holding weight, like they are, already ground up—not chopped, but ground up very fine in a mortar and pestle— you don't do *lines*, but more like out of a *snuff box*, dipping your little finger in, and taking a monstro toot off your nail, which is alright because there are no rocks or anything to burn the old snoze.

V.B.: When I was out in Hollywood, I heard that a big star walked off the set of his latest picture on the first day of shooting because they hadn't included a coke budget. He said, "No blow, no show."

T.S.: Well, that's an apocryphal story on the mere face of it. I mean, a Big Star *would* walk because of that, not because they didn't *supply* the blow, but because of their attitude towards it, and, by implication, towards him. But he could never *say* that was the reason because he would be in breach of contract and would be successfully sued for a tremendous amount of money. I think I know the instance you're talking about, and that "No blow, no show" thing was just *one* of several areas of conflict between the star and the producer-director element. I mean, a lot of coke on the set might have *persuaded* him not to walk, but it was by no means the only difference between them. Script changes had been promised, strong supporting actors, interesting locations, and so on. As I said before, when someone is making ten or fifteen thousand *a day*, he doesn't have any trouble about keeping straight for toot, but what he *does* need is a feeling of toot-camaraderie, peer-group security, that sort of thing.

V.B.: How does the movie industry compare to the rock industry in terms of the money being spent on drugs?

T.S.: Well, movie stars make more money than rock stars, so they spend more on dope. I'm referring specifically to cocaine, of course. I mean, with a little chipping from one or two members of your entourage it is no trouble at all to do a thou a day in good blow. But regarding the industry as a whole, there is certainly more dope in the rock world than anywhere else, including Hollywood. There are people in Hollywood, for example, who are heavily into toot but have never *smoked* anything, and are not interested in doing so.

V.B.: To them, grass is still weird?

T.S.: Yes, there appears to be a generation—or let us say a large segment of the population—out there in movieland who somehow arrived at coke without ever getting high on grass, which is kind of interesting. You'll not be finding that among the rockers, I warrant! But I'll tell you one great thing about the rock industry which is probably unique, and that's the occasional *grand gesture* invariably involving dope. I mean, on a movie star's birthday, the producer might give him something quite expensive—a golf cart with a bar and TV, or a new Ferrari, maybe a speed boat. But *the head of a record company*, his idea of a proper gift for the rock star would be—or at least this did happen on one occasion—a *pint of coke*. A pint ice-cream container choc-a-bloc full of quality toot! Christ, that's over a hundred thousand dollars. A *beau geste* in my view, and something you'd never see in Hollywood.

v.b.: I hear in Hollywood that a screenwriter like yourself is more and more important.

t.s.: You mean, do the writers receive adequate toot? Yes, your basic writer does not have to *score* for toot because it will be converging on him from several sources. The star—or stars!—the producer, the director, and the occasional guest-on-the-set. An ultra-fab confluence of tootski-roo! And *naturally*, you've got to be *sociable*, do a few lines even if you don't feel like it. Surely you can understand that?

v.b.: I can indeed!

t.s.: But I assume you mean the writing aspect of filmmaking is being taken more seriously now than before.

v.b.: I do.

t.s.: No, I don't think so. I mean, *everyone* knows that in making a movie the most important thing is *the story*. The producer, the director, the actor, no matter how idiotic they may behave in other areas, they *all* know and readily admit that much. But you will notice that the writer is still the least paid of the three. Let's say if the star gets ten, the director gets four, and the writer gets two— half as much as the director, one fifth as much as the actor, and I suppose about *one ten-thousandth* as much as the dumbbell producer . . . But of course it's still a lot of money if the actor is getting a million, which is what they get now. That is to say, your basic second-string non-Brando, non-Newman, non-Redford, non-Nicholson, non-McQueen, non–three million a pic actors all get 750 thou to *one mil minimum per pic*. Out-fucking-rageous in my view.

v.b.: You seem to have spent a good deal of time in film work in the last few years.

t.s.: I've done a tremendous amount of script-doctoring for directors and producers, and even more work in dialogue rewrites for actors. I can rewrite and improve dialogue as fast as I can read it, and I mean improve it *vastly*, unless it's by, say, Tennessee Williams or Billy Big Boy himself. And it is amazing how many really fine actors have absolutely no notion of how to improve a line of dialogue themselves. I mean, beyond something like changing "Do not" to "*Don't*."

v.b.: Why do you suppose that is?

T.S.: It's because an actor is like a kind of child genius, a baby Mozart, with this great talent for one special thing which comes out like ultra-empathy, but is probably just an elaborate form of mimicry. And he may be totally immature in every other way. A charming *idiot savant*.

V.B.: Now you're sounding like a director.

T.S.: I *should be* a director, because the screenwriter's only power for conveying his work to the screen, and protecting it en route, is the power of *persuasion*. And that is too time consuming, debilitating, and doesn't always work. You see, in most cases the *director* is simply a pain in the ass, an obstacle between the *creator* of the work—i.e., a certain yours truly—and the director of photography, or cameraman.

V.B.: Well, I believe you did come near to directing a film. Bill Burroughs has mentioned that the two of you were out there. How did that come about?

T.S.: I got a letter from Chuck Barris, the TV producer. He said something like, "I've always admired your work, bla-bla-bla," and he was feeling sort of guilty, I guess, about the success of *his* work, which at that point consisted of really bad-news stuff like *The Dating Game* and *The Newlywed Game*. And he said, "If there's anything you would like to *direct*, I've got $500,000 earmarked for it." Now at just about the same time, Bill showed me this script for *The Last Words of Dutch Schultz*. I said, "That's it!" So I showed the script to Gordon Willis, the now famous cameraman, who was then doing his first movie, *End of the Road*, which I wrote and co-produced, incidentally, directed by the great A. Avakian. I asked Gordon if it could be done for five hundred thou. "No way," he said, "ask for seven fifty." So, like a maniac, instead of taking the five, I asked for seven fifty, and Barris dropped the project. But *before* he dropped it, I got him to spring for Bill to come out for a "story conference," and we had a good time visiting all the heavy perv and loony weirdo bars.

I reminded Terry that we were late in getting over to Bill's for dinner. He lit a big funnel-shaped joint of Columbian gold, we did a bit of the bomber, stashed it for later, dropped in a bottle of whiskey, and headed out. Once at Burroughs's Terry emptied the bag of drug samples on the big parlor table. Bill motioned us to fix drinks, donned his reading glasses, and settled in for good scrutiny of the dope labels, using a magnifying glass like a jeweler examining precious stones.

WILLIAM BURROUGHS: Now then, what is all this shit, Terry?

T.S.: Bill, these are pharmaceutical samples sent by drug companies to Big Ed Fales, the friendly druggist, and to Doc Tom Adams, the writing croak. Anything that won't cook up, we'll eat. Give them good scrutiny, Bill.

W.B.: I shall, indeed.

T.S.: We'll get them into the ol' noggin one way or the other. On double alert for Demerol, Dilaudid, and the great Talwin!

W.B.: "Pain." I'm on the alert for the word "pain." I'll just go through these methodically. Anything of interest I'll put to one side.

T.S.: Now a lot of these may be new synthetics, Bill, names you may not be familiar with because they're disguising the heavy drug within! Now this may warrant some serious research, and a good article for one of the dope mags—on how the pharmaceutical companies connive to beat the FDA.

W.B.: [scrutinizing bottle] I don't really know what this one may be . . .

T.S.: Well then, down the old gullet, Bill! Better safe than sorry.

W.B.: [dryly] I think not.

T.S.: Here's one, Icktazinga. Ring a bell?

W.B.: "Chewable." I'm not much interested in anything chewable.

T.S.: But they're saying, "Chew one at a time," and I'm saying, "Cook up eight!"

V.B.: Here's a diuretic.

T.S.: Good! A diuretic may contain paregoric.

W.B.: No, no . . .

T.S.: I say a diuretic is full of a spasm-relieving nerve-killer. Definitely a coke-based medication.

W.B.: A diuretic . . .

T.S.: It'll cook right up, Bill.

W.B.: . . . is something to induce *urination,* my dear, that's *all* that it is.

v.b.: We can put all the questionable stuff aside.

t.s.: Well, doctor, I suppose we're in for another damnable stint of trial-and-error.

w.b.: Yes, I'm afraid so. Such are the tribulations of the legitimate drug industry.

v.b.: Now here's a "Nicatonic Acid."

w.b.: That's *vitamins,* my dear.

t.s.: Hold on, doctor, it *could* be some sort of synthetic speed!

v.b.: Yes, it says "For Prolonged Action."

w.b.: "Pain," look for the word "pain." That's the key.

t.s.: Listen, Bill, I hope you're not underestimating these synthetic painkillers. Just because they're not labeled "Heroin" or "Morphine."

w.b.: Man, I know every synthetic . . .

t.s.: Don't you understand, legitimate drugs have gone underground. They can't just say, "This will get you high."

w.b.: Man, the FDA has to know before they can even send out samples.

v.b.: Now this one could be speed. It says "Prolonged activity."

t.s.: Good! More activity, more action!

w.b.: Well, what *kind* of activity? I'm not sure I *want* any more activity.

v.b.: "Niacin!"

t.s.: Down the hatch for heavy action, Bill!

w.b.: You know what Niacin is, don't you? It's a Vitamin B Complex!

t.s.: Has a bit of the old Spanish Fly in it, if my guess is any good! Let me ask you this, Dr. Benway, do you acknowledge the existence of an attempt to pass on to a not unsuspecting public—*au contraire,* to an all too eagerly awaiting public—some sort of drug that would occlude pain?

w.b.: I categorically deny this because, you see, in order to consume a drug orally you've got to have the FDA's approval. Believe me, nothing gets by the FDA.

T.S.: But can't they okay something that will get you high without their knowing it? Something *new* which they don't yet know is sense-deranging?

W.B.: No, and I'll tell you why. In the first place, all the big companies are hand-in-fist with the FDA. The FDA are The Company Cops. That's exactly what they are.

T.S.: I'm talking about corruption *within* the company.

W.B.: Yes, but it's more likely that it has something to do with drugs that *kill* people rather than get them high. Very little sneaks through that will get you high. Now this one here contains half a grain of *codeine sulfate*, hardly any, but if you drank one of these bottles you might get a little buzz.

T.S.: Down the gullet, Bill!

W.B.: Here's one: "Confused, forgetful, cranky, unkempt, suspicious personality . . . transient cerebral ischimia . . ."

V.B.: Well, I want to get straightened out. "Unkempt." I'll take one of those.

W.B.: Each to his taste, as the French say, but I advise against it. Now here's something that goes straight in the wastebasket—"Non-narcotic." I don't want anything non-narcotic on these premises!

T.S.: Listen, they can *say* "non-narcotic," but they may have some really weird *definition* of narcotic, like something out of *Dracula* . . .

W.B.: Well, we don't need any inflammatory agents for ancient arthritic conditions.

T.S.: Wait! Arthritis is the word they use now for pain. That's a *painkiller*!

W.B.: This potion is well known to me. It's merely your friendly cough syrup, with all the regular ingredients.

T.S.: But it might cook up into something really sensational! You could cook it up until everything disappears except *the essence,* which would be dynamite in terms of sense derangement. Trial-and-error . . .

W.B.: We'll not go the trial-and-error route on these premises.

V.B.: Bill, was there a lot of cocaine in Paris during Hemingway and Fitzgerald's time?

w.b.: Man, there was *plenty* of cocaine and heroin. In the late 1920s it was all over the place in Europe, if you knew how to go about getting it. And it was 1/100th the price it is now.

t.s.: Hemingway and Fitzgerald never mentioned it. No reference to dope in their entire collective oeuvre, so to speak. They were both heavily into the juice.

v.b.: What I'm asking is, were Picasso and Gertrude Stein and Hemingway snorting coke?

t.s.: No, but in Paris, where you have a large Arab population, they have the strongest hash you can get, so they had that thing in the Gide, Baudelaire tradition.

w.b.: You are confounding your times in this message. You got Gide and Baudelaire at the same fucking table sniffing cocaine. Why don't you throw in Villon for Christ sake? I think you're sniffing something stronger than that. You're sniffing *time-travel*, baby!

t.s.: Doctor! I am referring to the sustained tradition of sense derangement among decadent frogs of the so-called quality lit crowd. Baudelaire, Rimbaud, Verlaine, and the late great Andy Gide!

w.b.: Time-travel!

t.s.: Bill's threshold of tolerance is about the width of a Thai stick.

v.b.: Well, one thing I hate are Quaaludes.

t.s.: The druggist says they're a great favorite with *hookers*. With *students* and *hookers*. They must have something in common.

w.b.: Intense pain.

t.s.: They call them "floaters." I guess they float above the pain.

w.b.: On it, more likely. Floating on a sea of pain!

t.s.: Right again, Doctor!

v.b.: Doesn't it seem obvious that the most salable drug would be the one that would make sex better?

w.b.: NO. I don't think so at all. Because the drug that's always sold the most on any market, and which will eventually replace any drug that makes sex more possible, is the drug that makes sex unnecessary, namely heroin. On an open market heroin would push marijuana, which is a fairly good sex drug, right off the market. See, most people don't like sex. They want to be rid of sex. Their sex life is terrifically unsatisfactory. They have a wife they were attracted to forty years ago, it's terrible. What do they want their sex life stimulated for? Their sex life is horrible. So heroin enables them to get rid of that drive, and that's what they really want.

v.b.: What was the drug you said was sexually stimulating?

w.b.: Well, marijuana usually makes something happen.

v.b.: A good mixture of coke and marijuana can sometimes work, depending on the catalyst, I guess.

w.b.: I don't like coke. Get high on marijuana and then a couple of poppers.

v.b.: Do you keep poppers next to the bed?

w.b.: Well, naturally, you see all the young people do. They say the stink of amyl nitrate fills the halls of the hotels up at Bellows Falls. Apparently the bell-boys come off in their pants.

v.b.: Terry, which drug would you most like to have for yourself?

t.s.: Cocaine is the moat enjoyable drug for me, in moderation, natch, due to its price.

v.b.: Terry was telling me about a record producer who gave a rock star of our acquaintance a pint ice-cream jar full of cocaine.

t.s.: No names, no names!

w.b.: Those are the chic-est presents that may be given or received. You know, a piece of opium as big as a melon. Last you for a while.

t.s.: And a grand legacy for your progeny!

w.b.: You can pass it on to your grandchildren. You don't never have to feel no pain again.

—1978
High Times
Reprinted by permission of Victor Bockris.

Afterword: Now Dig the Archive

Sifting through papers in Terry's archive one day, I came across some stray cardboard, torn from the back of one of his ubiquitous yellow writing tablets. Nearly broken in half due to a severe fold, and written in orange crayon, was a one-sentence declaration:

> *Terry Southern is the most profoundly witty writer of our generation . . .*
> *—Gore Vidal*

I tried to imagine the circumstances under which this was written—at a bar in haste Terry about to deliver the punch line to a story—Gore demanding immediately something to write on to laud his comrade-at-arms. The urgency in Gore's note is not unlike that behind another archival *objet-trouvé*—a four-inch-wide, twenty-inch-long length of wallpaper, which begins, *"Dear Mister Southern, I am tearing the paper off the wall to tell you . . ."*

At Chelsea Mini-Storage in New York City, wading through Terry's archive is like fishing a sea of historical crosscurrents—finding a solid contextual perch is close to impossible. From Cocteau to Caspar Weinberger, Abbie Hoffman to the CIA, every hot-house issue in the public sphere is given ventilation—from the coolest of blowers. Unclassifiable schools of literary invention dart about. To get anything done before closing, one has to resist reading and just try to scoop the thing of vexation into the right holding tank—the one marked *New Journalism, '50s Europe,* or *Kubrick.*

I began working on this book in the 1980s—back when Terry and I had our "filing sessions," which consisted of having the TV on, brews at hand, and going through the "big boy boxes" he had filled during the previous few months with whatever old manuscript draft or mail-order catalog was vying for space around his typewriter. Rarely was a meal taken without his yellow legal pad appearing plateside—some project or outrage under way. I became familiar with an entire body of work which was alive yet languishing: monologues, collage-parodies, letters and screenplays—many of which would never experience the whir of a printing press, no less the light of a projector bulb.

Like Terry's first anthology, *Red Dirt Marijuana and Other Tastes*, this collection captures a dizzying myriad of vocalizings: from Terry's perpetually Dexed-out world-weary narratives, to the philosophical writer of the late '50s and early '60s whose seriousness carried over from his Sartre/Camus days at the Sorbonne. What we have here is the unacknowledged Terry Southern—a man who remains largely *unclassified* by academia, presumably because his work appears more a rhizomatic disturbance than a series of prescient moves in the development of one's literary ouevre. Many scholars are just now picking up on the beat Terry laid down, a bebop line which riffed upon and unbuttoned the postwar American culture: its society, its cinema, and its literature—Terry unified the fields by playing them all—in that brief span of time before money and technology were "cool" and when America's youth saw alternatives to growing up Corporate.

I imagine one of Terry's heroes, Edgar Allan Poe, scoping out this warehouse around the middle of the last century; observing the strange action unfolding beneath the building's massive beams and brick archways; divining the backstories of the fantastic crews and cargoes recently arrived from the world over. This building, the largest and probably oldest storage facility in America, is also one of the least expensive. This is fortunate for The Estate, for Terry died *sans sou*. His incapacity to leave anything solid behind him but his work is strangely consistent with his lifelong existential praxis.

Terry's pages have a tactile feel. His arsenal for writing was like that of a visual artist's—working with glue, scissors, vinyl letters, newspaper clippings and the ever-at-the-ready white tape, which came in single line, double line, and paragraph widths for instantly typed, often crooked, revisions. Dread sets in when I imagine these pasted-together artifacts possibly disintegrating in the quasi-climate-controlled storage facility in New York—I fear I'll open a folder and the strips of his clippings will crumble away, like glued-on filigree falling from a gown.

Many of Terry's literary explorations have not yet been appraised. Who, for instance, would critically assess the art of caption writing—something Terry perfected to such a degree that Perry Richardson, one of his most dedicated latter-year publishers, gave him "book by" credit for *Virgin: A History of Virgin Records*, a tome comprised mostly of photographs. Today, as Terry's executor, I manage a "catalog of content"; I orchestrate a publishing program, and see no shortage of possible film and TV projects. Today, more than ever, Terry's work is attracting Ph.D. students, teachers, university department heads, movie producers, actors and directors who see Terry Southern as validation for a shared mutiny against a tiresome grain.

The alternative title for this collection is *The Quality Lit of Terry Southern*. "Quality Lit"—a phrase Terry facetiously coined around 1962—was his sardonic response to the commercialization of fiction and the consequential artistic limitations such commercialization breeds, a condition which was unique to America at the time. In the live-action replay of The Big Quality Lit Game, Terry is running before the quarterback even calls the play, prancing in open territory—a jack-in-the-box gleaming in the swish-pan where his numbers should be—leaving those responsible for the dissemination of the game's progress to shout "focus . . . FOCUS!" Dig his game. And his moves. He be the *man in motion*!

—Nile Southern
Boulder, Colorado, 2001

Acknowledgments

Some of Terry's best work comes from stories told to him by others. I'd like to offer special thanks to John Calley, the producer and studio head. Terry often recounted "Heavy Put-Away" and "Fixing Up Ert" at dinner parties with the preface, "This is a story John 'Black Jack' Calley told me." And also to Boris Grgurevich, the hipster mercenary who shared his Cuban invasion experiences with Terry.

I'd also like to thank the people who have supported me in my work as executor, particularly my wife, Theodosia, and the family and friends who have continued to support my own talents: Mark Amerika of the Altx Digital Arts Foundation, Andrew Currie, who lent this estate its first computer, Josh Alan Friedman for his razor-sharp editing of this book, estate agent Susan Schulman, Carol Southern for making it all possible, Nelson Lyon for inspring this book's title (with the Terry Southern spoken-word album *Give Me Your Hump, The Unspeakable Terry Southern*, Hal Willner (for co-producing that soon to be released project), Jean Stein, William Claxton, James Grauerholz, Robert Wilonsky, Bill Morgan, Lee Hill for his biography *A Grand Guy: The Art and Life of Terry Southern*, David Tully, Ken Fricklas, Marc Toberoff, Bob Montgomery, Peter Herbst, Ira Lowe, Charles Pike and the Prop Gang, Jimmy Vines who is the agent for this book, Elliot Gould, and Gail Gerber, Terry's longtime companion, for enabling Terry to dream unfettered. I also offer thanks to Terry's spirit. *We'll get the old tub through, Big Mister!*